I0831901

GUY DAVENPORT
and
JAMES LAUGHLIN

ALSO IN THE SERIES

Thomas Merton and James Laughlin: Selected Letters
Edited by David D. Cooper

Henry Miller and James Laughlin: Selected Letters
Edited by George Wickes

Ezra Pound and James Laughlin: Selected Letters
Edited by David M. Gordon

Delmore Schwartz and James Laughlin: Selected Letters
Edited by Robert Phillips

Kenneth Rexroth and James Laughlin: Selected Letters
Edited by Lee Bartlett

William Carlos Williams and James Laughlin: Selected Letters
Edited by Hugh Witemeyer

GUY DAVENPORT
and
JAMES LAUGHLIN

/ • /

SELECTED LETTERS

Edited by W. C. Bamberger

W. W. Norton & Company
New York London

Printed in the United States of America
First Edition

Manufacturing by Courier Westford

Library of Congress Cataloging-in-Publication Data

Davenport, Guy.
Guy Davenport and James Laughlin : selected letters / edited by W. C. Bamberger. — 1st ed.
p. cm.
Includes bibliographical references and index.
ISBN-13: 978-0-393-05950-2 (hardcover)

1. Davenport, Guy—Correspondence. 2. Laughlin, James, 1914—Correspondence. 3. Authors, American—20th century—Correspondence. 4. Publishers and publishing—United States—Correspondence. 5. Authors and publishers—United States—History—20th century. I. Laughlin, James, 1914– II. Bamberger, W. C. III. Title.
PS3554.A86Z48 2006
818'.5403—dc22

2006022102

W. W. Norton & Company, Inc., 500 Fifth Avenue, New York, N.Y. 10110
www.wwnorton.com

W. W. Norton & Company Ltd., Castle House, 75/76 Wells Street, London W1T 3QT

1 2 3 4 5 6 7 8 9 0

CONTENTS

INTRODUCTION

When James Laughlin first wrote Guy Davenport, it was to commend him on an article he had written to honor Thomas Merton, who had recently died in an electrocution accident in Bangkok. Merton, Trappist monk, poet, and author of several books on the spiritual life, had known both men. Laughlin had been a friend, correspondent, and publisher to Merton since the mid-1940s. Davenport, who lived in Lexington, had visited Merton at Gethsemani, the monastery near Bardstown, Kentucky,[1] and Merton had made visits to Lexington. Merton had at least once written Laughlin about Davenport, describing him as "a poet" (he had been reading Davenport's long poem *Flowers and Leaves*). But as of this first exchange in January of 1969, Laughlin knew nothing of Davenport's writings. Davenport, for his part, was well acquainted with Laughlin's work as publisher of New Directions. At one point in this correspondence he describes Laughlin as "a publisher whose books have been the best part of my education (without Pound or W[illiam] C[arlos] W[illiams] I would have been somebody else). . . ."[2]

The first two letters the pair exchanged were complimentary but businesslike. A small flurry of letters followed in 1973 and 1974, when Laughlin sent Davenport a collection of writings by a mutual favorite, Ezra Pound, and Davenport inquired into matters of translations, and about publication rights to some Pound letters he had. These letters are more relaxed and familiar. But it was 1983 before their correspondence and friendship began in earnest. By this time Laughlin had been publishing New Directions books for more than forty-five years—since, as he notes in a letter here, Davenport was nine years old.

Laughlin's story is by now well known: how his well-off parents sent him to Choate prep school, where his teacher Dudley Fitts introduced him to the then largely unknown Modernist writers; how he temporarily slipped away from his life at Harvard and traveled to Europe in the 1930s; how he there met Gertrude Stein and other of his literary heroes; how Ezra Pound scoffed at his efforts to write poetry and told him he should do something useful—become a publisher; and how Laughlin then turned part of his family's steel fortune to the advancement of Modernist literature. With New Directions publications, Laughlin helped determine the course of literature in the twentieth century, its publications inspiring countless writers, Davenport included.

While he never completely let go of the New Directions reins (as we see clearly here when some of the New Directions staff express misgivings about the salability—and even the possible prurience—of some of Davenport's work; in very short order, Laughlin politely but unequivocally marshals and instructs his troops in exactly how they are to proceed), by the 1980s Laughlin had begun turning over much of the day-to-day operation of New Directions to his very capable staff. He did this in part to concentrate on his own long-neglected writing. By the evidence of these letters, and by his own testimony, he would often write several of his colloquial yet classically informed, epigrammatically memorable, almost always short and short-lined poems in a day. If not always pleased with the results of his efforts, Laughlin in these letters seems happy with his sustained engagement in the process of writing, perhaps feeling he had finally found a satisfactory balance between his publisher and author selves. Beginning in the mid-1980s, he would publish at least one book of his poetry, essays, or other prose writings almost every year until his death in 1997.

Davenport in the early 1980s was already recognized, in the circle of those who cared about such matters, as a master of the essay form, as an incomparable classical scholar and translator, as a writer of fiction of startling originality and intellectual breadth, and (less so, but to a circle that was ever widening) as an artist and illustrator of talent and wit.

Davenport seems to have been born to be a writer and artist. He was born on the dot of midnight between the 22nd and 23rd of November 1927 in Anderson, South Carolina, a textile town. Davenport grew up in a decidedly unliterary milieu. Some relatives and friends recognized the importance of books, but mainly for show on their shelves rather than for the thoughts they might contain (young Guy, however, read them all). Still, there was an artistic side to his family. He had an aunt who fancied herself a painter, though no one else could see anything in her daubs, and a grandmother who had been to college and loved telling stories. (He also had an uncle who stayed in his room for forty years.) More than once, Davenport wrote that he was "retarded as a child almost to the point of autism," and lived largely in an imaginary reality. He exhibited artistic talent at a very early age, and his parents sent him to study art with a local teacher (though for his mature work he was self-taught). He also learned the art of hand-printing, and when he was twelve and thirteen produced his own newspaper. Davenport left high school as soon as he could accumulate enough credits—just after Christmas in his tenth-grade year—and attended Duke University, working his way through as a printer and by helping classify the university's folklore collection.

After Duke, Davenport was a Rhodes scholar at Merton College, Oxford, from 1948 to 1950, where he wrote Oxford's first thesis on James Joyce. He returned to the United States and served in the Eighteenth Airborne Corps for two years. He then taught at Washington University in St. Louis, leaving there to attend graduate school at Harvard. From 1961 to 1963 he taught at Haverford College, and then went on to the University of Kentucky, where he taught until his retirement in 1991. He was proud of the fact that for all these years of education—both as a student and as a professor—he always walked to class. Davenport never owned a car and only drove one once—when the wooden leg of the driver who'd given him a ride fell apart and couldn't be reassembled on the roadside. (It has been rumored that when Johns Hopkins tried to tempt him away from the University of Kentucky, he turned them down because he couldn't find a house close enough to be able to walk to classes.) In short, Guy Davenport was very much Guy Davenport from birth.

The present selection has been made, primarily, with an eye toward producing a portrait of the relationship of these two writers. What is unavoidably simplified here is the polyphony of secondary ideas that emerge and recur briefly before vanishing, of small jokes and litanies of ailments, of gossipy humor and ideas that quickly become dead ends. Much but not all of this has been sacrificed in the interest of clarifying what seem to me to be the major points and counterpoint of the literary exchange, and in favor of more straightforward gestures of the evolving personal relationship. Letters detailing trips, weather, etc., have been passed over for those with content bearing on the writing and publication of works, on language and other writers, on matters of personal import, and for those letters which reveal something basic about hearts and minds. This seemed more urgent in the case of Davenport than in that of Laughlin. Laughlin's writings are most often autobiographical, whereas Davenport complains several times in these letters that reviewers and scholars take the opinions of his characters to be his own. We readers can "know" Laughlin in a much more direct way in his published writings than we can "know" Davenport through his. Where Laughlin wrote songs of himself, Davenport was reticent about committing personal matters to print. Some few of his published essays deal with his personal beliefs and history, but they are a small percentage. In one letter here, Davenport describes how a young classics scholar has moved into his house "simply to be in the same house as the writer of my scribbles (who, he has discovered, isn't me)." No more are the James Laughlin and Guy Davenport of these letters the man entire.

We like to believe that reading the letters of writers we admire will not only let us pick up clues as to how they wrote as they did, but also reveal the man or woman hidden behind the printed page. We might, for example, read Laughlin's letter of March 7, 1985, and believe we have gained some psychological insight when we see how almost offhand is his mention of his son Robert's recent suicide. But as novelist and essayist Samuel R. Delany has written, "letters—especially the letters of someone who writes a great deal of them—only play in one section of the personal spectrum (different, of course, for each of us)."[3] We must not expect to learn anything about these two men beyond what part or parts of their personal spectrum they chose to show to one another. For all the openness they exhibit here, they also each stay "in character" to one another. In a letter not included here (dated November 27, 1992), Davenport, in a parenthetical comment, makes it clear that he edits his letters for content: "(here, in the first draft of this letter, was a raging defense of the 2 books I've called 'monsters of the imagination'—breaking my rule not to defend any of my fiction)." Below this is more than two inches of white space, clearly illustrating how, even with Laughlin, he was willing to go only so far and no farther.

The Davenport we most clearly see in his letters here, as in his fiction, is the investigative Thoreauvian, examining the dispersion of cultural seeds from classical Greece to Modernist America. This was the Geography of his Imagination, the turnrows he characteristically tended, even when writing letters. Like most of us, Davenport clearly wrote his replies to Laughlin's letters with the incoming letter laid nearby for reference. Yet the letters that emerged are much like his stories—the matter at hand giving way to personal anecdote, to a philological or botanical image, from there a quick jump to a literary anecdote, then perhaps to a reference to a work of art, before shuttling back to the original thread of the letter.

Among the surprises in Davenport's letters here are his characterizations of his work. When, in letter #70, he writes that he is "simply exploring some areas and moments of human affection, especially the awakening of affection not used up or run in the ground," those of us acquainted with his work might pause thoughtfully, then find ourselves nodding in agreement. But we are genuinely startled when—writing of these same stories—Davenport asserts that he is "essentially a comic-strip artist—everything obvious and boldly colored, with ZAP! And GRR-R! for dramatic *pouf.*" Guy Davenport writes "comic strips"? Everything is "obvious"? "GRR-R!"?

The dynamic in this exchange of letters is somewhat different from those in earlier volumes of this series. When Laughlin and Davenport began corresponding, it was as mutual admirers and scholars of Thomas Merton and Ezra Pound, rather than as author and publisher—a further relationship that would only come about years into their correspondence. Whereas several volumes in this series—the Williams, Miller, and Schwartz, in particular—clearly detail how stormy were Laughlin's relationships with some of those he published, what the Laughlin–Davenport letters most clearly detail is their mutual admiration. For this reason, the relative number of Laughlin letters included here is greater than in the other volumes in this series. This goes against Laughlin's expressed wish that his letters be relatively few in these records of his correspondence, but it seems important to defy him in this particular instance.

It was in his capacity as a Pound enthusiast and, even more so, a classical scholar that Davenport first interested Laughlin. He often wanted to invoke classical allusions in his work, but his Greek was too poor to allow him to include it in the way he wished to. After the death of his longtime friend Robert Fitzgerald, who had been his favored Greek expert, Laughlin began turning to Davenport for similar help. Laughlin was impressed by how quickly and graciously Davenport supplied the needed translations and transcriptions, and soon began asking for critical comment on works in progress as well. Davenport was generally encouraging even while occasionally wincing on the page.

While others certainly must have given Laughlin positive feedback on his writing, Davenport's replies and critiques came with allusions to other poets, to classical studies, with philological asides, literary anecdotes, and other elements from a literary world which for

Laughlin was, with the death of so many of his literary heroes and intimates, fast fading away. As Davenport wrote on February 24, 1988: "I think we've entered the Intellectual Ice Age, and that EP belonged to an older culture of which there are only a few remnants left." This was a culture both men knew well. These letters read much more as a conversation of equals than do Laughlin's with the other writers in this series. Laughlin and Davenport have common roots in their enthusiasm for classical literature and the High Modernism of Ezra Pound, T. S. Eliot, James Joyce, Samuel Beckett, and others—much of which, in fact, Laughlin brought to American readers.

Davenport and Laughlin can also be seen concurring on a more contemporary literary matter here. In what must have been an unusual publishing circumstance for Laughlin, his attempts at securing a book from the brilliant classicist and poet Anne Carson continually met with disinterest on her part. He wrote her after reading some of her poems and asked if he could publish some of her work, but she shrugged him off. This was clearly unexpected, and Laughlin detailed his ongoing exasperation in letters to Davenport. But Laughlin persisted, with Davenport offering insights into her work that made him even more determined to publish her. In the end, Carson relented, and Davenport contributed a foreword to her book.

A further dimension was added to their relationship in late 1990 when North Point Press, Davenport's publisher since 1981, announced it would no longer issue new titles. Laughlin, who had only recently begun reading Davenport's fiction, immediately offered to publish any work he would be willing to offer to New Directions. As a result of this offer, Laughlin was to publish Davenport's last two volumes of stories, *A Table of Green Fields* and *The Cardiff Team,* as well as a reprint of *Da Vinci's Bicycle.* By this time Laughlin had also seen some of Davenport's drawings and paintings, and proposed publishing them in some form. This led to *A Balance of Quinces,* Erik Reece's monograph on Davenport's art. (Laughlin also proposed including his correspondence with Davenport in his series of selected letters with W. W. Norton, and had begun working toward this at the time of his death. The present edition is the legacy of his wish.)

Even after Laughlin became one of Davenport's publishers, few of the exchanges between the two men dealt with business. Davenport was meticulous about the design of his books, and most of his business letters concern this. Of the financial aspects, he was dismissive. Davenport accepted Laughlin as a poet and an equal, not as a business contact, and even in the midst of firming up contractual matters, letters on both sides primarily show a clear mutual delight in the consequent linguistic and intellectual exchange, rather than a scrabbling for advantage, financial and otherwise. I hope I have caught that difference in this selection.

As can be seen in the internal New Directions letters and memos included here, the publication of *A Table of Green Fields* occasioned the only doubtful words Laughlin had for Davenport's work—none of which were conveyed to Davenport, though his own letters show he understood this might well be the case. As Laughlin and Davenport grew more comfortable with one another, their letters became freer, particularly on Laughlin's part. One of the subjects Laughlin introduced was his lifelong fascination with and dogged pursuit of the opposite sex. He was, in fact, well known among writers and others of his acquaintance (including his wives) for his sexual pursuits. Amorous anecdotes, past and present desires, even wondering comments about the grip this pursuit had so long had on him became a common feature of his letters. Davenport would commiserate, reply with a joke, or supply a complementary sexual anecdote—from a literary source, or the life of someone he knew. As a matter of his own personal life, sex was a subject on which Davenport remained mute.

But sex does loom large in much of Davenport's fiction. The sex is a fantasy sex, emotionally utopian sex. Everyone involved is young and fit; there is almost no jealousy between serial partners; mild group sex prompts smiles all around. At times the partners are adult and heterosexual, but for the most part the sex in Davenport's stories centers on young boys, boys whose favorite form of sexual expression is repeated, joyful masturbation, and an open voyeurism (as well as the comradely exchange of underpants). There are many reminders in these stories that they are transpiring in a fantasy world—observers from another world float over meadows in a hot-air balloon; a sailboat is folded and slipped into a pocket; a skateboard carries its rider along at speeds an interstellar spacecraft would envy; the Denmark many of them are set in is not the Denmark we might find in our social studies books, but is of some much more permissive world, where sexual happiness is innocent. And yet the characters Davenport creates seem so real, so plausible, so likely to be encountered the next time we turn a corner in Copenhagen, that all of us who read and admire the stories unavoidably have to decide how to read these passages, have to come to terms with their—in our less-than-innocent time, unavoidable—overtones of pedophilia. Laughlin and the New Directions staff were not exceptions.

When the first manuscript arrived, Laughlin wrote his staff that having a Davenport title for New Directions was a dream come true, and added, "He's odd, of course, and in two pieces perverse—he likes boys—but he does it with a kind of obsessed elegance."[4] Elsewhere he wrote that he finds these scenes "boring." But when staff members voiced doubts, Laughlin expressed confidence in Davenport, and insisted that the book be done just as the author wished. Laughlin, the author of a great number of mildly erotic verses, certainly understood a writer's urge to capture the power of erotic impulses in words.

Davenport, of course, understood that his work could shock people. When he was going over his paintings—which are much at one with his stories despite the difference in medium—he wrote Laughlin in warning: "Some of them can only be shown in Denmark on The Hydraulix of Sex Day (sponsored by the Queen), if they have such a celebration."[5] In the end Laughlin took this aspect of Davenport's work just as Davenport took Laughlin's amorous obsessions: as a rather inexplicable but obviously integral part of the greater whole of someone he admired.

Notes

1. Davenport, who never owned or drove a car, was driven to Gethsemani by Lexington photographer Gene Meatyard. Also along was poet-publisher Jonathan Williams, not Jonathan Greene as reported in *Thomas Merton and James Laughlin: Selected Letters.* (See Davenport's "Tom and Gene," in *The Hunter Gracchus*) Merton's letter is #178, dated January 18, 1967.

2. See letter #67.

3. Samuel R. Delany, "Shadows and Ash," in *Longer Views* (Hanover, N. H. and London: Wesleyan University Press, 1996), 144–173; this quote, 152.

4. See letter #73.

5. See letter #136.

NOTES ON THE TEXT

The extant correspondence between Laughlin and Davenport comprises 480 letters, short notes, and cards. This total is split almost exactly between the two writers: 234 by Laughlin; 246 by Davenport. Also considered were a number of letters and notes from and to New Directions staff, both internal notes and letters to Davenport. There were also a small number of letters between Laughlin's wife Gertrude and Davenport. From this total I have selected 187 items, just under 40 percent of the total, most of which I have edited to some degree. Of these, 127 were written by Davenport and 57 by Laughlin, an approximately 2-to-1 ratio. Also included here are two letters by Griselda Ohannessian, head of the New Directions office at this time, written to Laughlin, and one letter from Gertrude Laughlin to Davenport.

Guy Davenport's letters to James Laughlin are now at Harvard University's Houghton Library, where they make up thirty-five folders. Laughlin's letters will be deposited with the rest of Davenport's papers at the Harry Ransom Humanities Research Center at the University of Texas at Austin. Photocopies from Harvard of Davenport's letters and the originals of Laughlin's letters have been used as sources. Some originals of the Laughlin material are missing, and those copies on deposit at Harvard have been used in those circumstances.

Most of the letters exchanged between the two men were typed (even after Laughlin was given a computer, he preferred to write letters on his typewriter), but a significant number of Laughlin's letters are in his hand, usually written during those times when his arthritic neck made it impossible for him to use his typewriter. The effects of a stroke Laughlin suffered also hindered his writing: at times he would begin typing a letter, then cut it short, unable to make his words come out right, and he would try again another day. As Laughlin's arthritis and other ailments grew more serious, his handwriting also became increasingly difficult to decipher. He tried dictating letters to a secretary who came to his home, but as he found this process unsatisfactory, these letters are few. Those included here can easily be identified, as Laughlin makes self-conscious reference to this process in each of them. Where transcription of Laughlin's handwriting has proven merely difficult, conjectural words are enclosed in brackets; in other places where it was impossible to determine what was intended, "[illegible]" is inserted. Only one of Davenport's letters here is autograph, written while his typewriter was out for repair.

From early on, Laughlin used his personal copying machine to add images to his letters—photos or old woodcuts for the most part—at times commenting on or writing joke captions for them. After Davenport too received a personal copier, he did the same. These images were nearly always irrelevant to the contents of the letters, and none have been included here. Most of the comments relating to them have also been elided. Over the course of their correspondence Davenport also enclosed a few drawings and small watercolors on his letters. Only one of these has been included (see letter #24).

The two earliest surviving letters from Laughlin to Davenport were addressed to Davenport on Walton Avenue in Lexington. All of the others were addressed to Sayre Avenue, where Davenport was to live until his death in January of 2005. All of Laughlin's letters which include an address heading indicate his home in Norfolk, Connecticut. The letters from Griselda Ohannessian originated at the New Directions offices in New York City. Because the points of origin stay so constant, these have not been noted in the headings for the letters.

Not all of the letters have been included in their entirety. Laughlin would at times write very long letters, seven pages or more, single-spaced, including long passages of macaronic humor and self-parody. This was a natural reaction to becoming a literary Lion in Winter, his failing health making travel, reading and writing, even sitting erect progressively more difficult. Writing letters became his primary interaction with the literary world outside his home. Davenport, in correspondence as in person, was unfailingly gracious (which is not to say that a definite tetchiness cannot be read between the lines in places). He would occasionally mock himself as being so "High South Carolina" that he would lose more writing time fretting about not having answered a letter than he would answering it, and so he would unfailingly answer every letter he received, and rarely allowed himself to send just a quick note. So his responses, in addition to addressing whatever matter might be at hand, often include many paragraphs that report on current sparks of his thought—from his reading, researches, his own writing or thinking. However fascinating this material is, some has been cut for length and focus. Edits are indicated by standard ellipses (". . .") inserted into the text. Following the format of earlier volumes in this series, those few ellipses that are the writers' own are given in slanted brackets. Abbreviations used in the notes include JL for Laughlin, GD for Davenport, and ND for New Directions. Abbreviations for books by Davenport are *GoTI* (for *The Geography of the Imagination*), *EF* (for *Every Force Evolves a Form*), *BN* (for *A Balthus Notebook*), *DVB* (for *Da Vinci's Bicycle*), *JVSB* (for *The Jules Verne Steam Balloon*), *HG* (for *The Hunter Gracchus*), *TGF* (for *A Table of Green Fields*), and *CT* (for *The Cardiff Team*). Abbreviations used for Laughlin's books are *SR* (for *The Secret Room*) and *PNS* (for *Poems: New and Selected*). Details of these and other publications are given in the Selected Bibliography at the back of this book.

There are very few silent corrections here. Davenport was so meticulous a writer that when he does use an unfamiliar or "incorrect" form—as his use of "Roumanian" rather than the more familiar "Romanian"—I most often take it as being deliberate, the major exception to this being the form he habitually employs for quotations, placing the period outside the closing quote, in what we might think of as "the British manner." I have changed all these to the more common form, where the period is inside the end quote mark. Laughlin needed a few more corrections, yet even as he struggled to write comprehensible letters, he would go back over them until he was satisfied that he had caught all the typos that could be found. Where there are questionable usages I felt should stand, I have inserted "[*sic*]" to reassure the reader.

Following the form established for this series, each individual item is identified in bold type with a number, a description of its original form, and the number of pages in the original. Abbreviations used are TLS (typed letter signed), ALS (autographed letter signed), TCS (typed card signed; this for either a postcard, a small card slipped into an envelope, or even Christmas cards), TNS (typed note signed; used for small slips of paper). The absence of the letter S in these designations means the item as examined was unsigned, and this is further noted at the end of the item.

Because of Laughlin's failing eyesight, Davenport tried to remember to always double-space his letters, but at times remembered only midway through. At times both of the correspondents utilized eccentric spacing, carriage returns, or used numbers of asterisks or lines or other devices to mark off one area of a letter from another. I have included very few of these, and those exceptions because the change from one subject to another—as with Davenport's reaction to the suicide of one of Laughlin's sons—seemed to warrant special recognition. Davenport had a particular way of addressing his letters, using what he identified as a Danish address form, and when he typed "Mr" he never included a period. These forms, as well as Laughlin's varying forms for dates, have been preserved, and uniformly placed at the upper right. Salutations and closing signatures have been rendered in small caps. The titles of books, plays, magazines, long poems, and paintings are italicized, as are foreign words; quotation marks are used for the titles of poems, essays, and stories.

ACKNOWLEDGMENTS

I would first of all like to thank Erik Reece, who did much of the preliminary work of gathering and sorting the letters before suggesting me as their final editor.

My task here was made much easier by the efforts of those who edited the earlier volumes in this series. Many questions regarding format, as well as information needed for clarifying notes, had already been sorted out through their efforts, and I only had to follow suit. Other concerns were addressed by Brendan Curry, series editor at W. W. Norton, and by Peggy L. Fox, president and publisher of New Directions.

For help with translations of the Greek here and other linguistic puzzles, I would like to thank Samuel R. Delany. Others who helped with languages and various matters great and small were Bill Corbett, Bonnie Cox, Anselm Hollo, Jim Larzelere, Denise Lynn, George Schneeman, Janet Trosino, and Trevor Winkfield. All mistakes and misunderstandings are, of course, solely my responsibility.

Lastly, I would like to dedicate my part in this project to my daughter, Aja.

—W. C. BAMBERGER
Whitmore Lake, Michigan
January 19, 2006.

LETTERS

⁝

***1.* TL—1** [cc]

January 3, 1969

Dear Guy Davenport:

Just a line to tell you what a beautiful piece that was you wrote about Tom Merton in *The National Review.* It moved me very much, you had really "caught him to the life." Your phrase, "boyish happiness," was right on the button. I shall make copies of your piece for a number of other friends who may not have seen it there. It's hard to believe he is gone, and I'm certainly going to miss him.

Sincerely yours,
[unsigned]

/ • /

Tom Merton: Thomas Merton, also known as Friar M. Louis (1915–1968). Merton was a Trappist monk and a poet and essayist who published with ND. The Laughlin–Merton relationship is documented in an earlier volume in this series.
The National Review: GD's piece, "Thomas Merton RIP," was published in the December 31, 1968, issue of the *National Review.*

2. TLS—1

February 25, 1969

Dear Guy Davenport:

Many thanks for your card on January 14th. I was glad indeed to know that Gene Meatyard had taken some good pictures of Tom just before he left for Asia. Tom had shown me some of Meatyard's work and I know how good it is.

I have not heard of any memorial volume, exactly in that form, but several magazines are planning special numbers. But probably Meatyard would like to have something more substantial than that. We here at New Directions will be tied up getting out the books which Tom left with us, but perhaps you or Meatyard could approach some of the other publishers who might be interested in such a memorial volume. . . .

We will doubtless be looking for a good portrait photograph of Tom for the cover, or frontispiece, of his *Collected Poems,* so if Gene has any that might be suitable for that, on which he would like to sell us the rights for that purpose, I would be grateful if you could pass him word that I would like to see them.

Sincerely yours,
James Laughlin
Co-Trustee, Merton Legacy Trust

/ • /

Gene Meatyard: Ralph Eugene Meatyard (1925–1972). Lexington, Kentucky, photographer and friend of GD and Thomas Merton. For details of the relationship between Meatyard and Merton, see GD's "Tom and Gene" in *HG.*

3. TLS—1

10 June 1973

DEAR MR LAUGHLIN:

Thank you for the *EP Prose.* Cookson has done an excellent job. Lots of things there that I haven't seen in years. A thought per sentence, and never a sentence without its thought.

It was an enormous pleasure meeting you; I hope your stay was as pleasant as it seemed to be. We wear most visitors to a frazzle, but you seemed to thrive on it all.

I resist temptations to go a-traveling and work at two books at once; my critical ravings and my *inepta fabuli.*

May I ask what second (and third) thoughts you've had about opening cantos 72 + 73? I have not mentioned the matter to Hugh, as you didn't seem keen to have him in on them, though I can't think who else would be wiser about their significance than he (except yourself, natch). I would love to have a go at an English version of them. If the results are unsatisfactory, they can always be chucked away. I count on at least half of my work going askew, anyway.

My gratitude, again, for the impressive *Prose.*

Sincerely,
GUY DAVENPORT

/ • /

Cookson: William Cookson edited Ezra Pound's *Selected Prose, 1909–1965* for ND.
inepta fabuli: By this, Davenport means his stories. When referring to his own creative efforts, Davenport was in the habit of including some self-deprecating modifier.
cantos 72 + 73: Newly recovered parts of Pound's long poem. These turned up in the Mussolini papers in Italy, and were very pro-Fascist. To preserve copyright for Pound's heirs, Laughlin stayed up all one night typing the text and having it printed offset in an edition of twenty-five copies.
Hugh: Hugh Kenner (1923–2003), prominent literary critic and Pound explicator; author of *The Pound Era* (1971), among many books. Kenner and GD were friends for years until Kenner drifted away, much to GD's disappointment.

4. ANS—2

15 July 73 (Rembrandt's birthday)

Dear Mr Laughlin:

No, I've never seen the texts of LXXII *et* LXXIII. Let's hope that EP made English versions, and that the world will get to see them before the century's out. Glad to hear that you are back in la Principessa's good graces—I've only corresponded with her about things Egyptian.

A strange trick of fate, that finding of copies among Mussolini's papers! And an heroic rising to the occasion on your part!

A world that can stomach Hugh MacDiarmid's "Ode to Stalin" (or is it to Lenin, or both?) can live with Ez's *Imno alle Fascisti* (if that's what these cantos are).

I'm very grateful for your full exposition of the facts in the case. My closest contact there is Omar, though I've been out of touch recently. I really don't think he will care one way or the other, except to take his mother's side.

Excuse my brief reply: I'm trying to finish a longish piece of writing and cannot bear the typewriter any more today. My hope is that Mary will do the translating: she will know all the nuances.

ad interim,
Guy Davenport

/ • /

Rembrandt's birthday: Davenport frequently noted significant birthdays or events associated with the dates of his letters.
la Principessa's good graces: Mary de Rachewiltz, EP's daughter by Olga Rudge.
Hugh MacDiarmid: (1892–1978), British poet.
Omar: Omar Shakespear Pound, EP's son by his wife Dorothy.
ad interim: "meanwhile." This is a common GD closing, but as he and JL grew more comfortable with each other, letters on both sides would include more and more foreign phrases and passages. JL would come in particular to rely on GD to help him with his rusty Greek.

5. TNS—1

18 November 1973

DEAR MR LAUGHLIN:

Greetings, and a question about a matter of policy. One of Carolyn Hammer's printing students, Chris Meatyard (Gene's son), wants to do an edition of EP's letters to me: very limited edition, fine paper, etc. Am I free to print them? There are some 30 only, ranging from 1952 to 58. If I need permission from the estate, how do I go about *that*?

Best wishes to you and Mrs Laughlin for a grand Thanksgiving!

Blessings,
GUY DAVENPORT

/ • /

The Pound Literary Property Trust ("PLPT") declined to give permission for this edition.

6. TNS—1

9 February 1974

DEAR MR LAUGHLIN:

Thank you for your letter reporting the various bleak and most unPoundian decisions of the PLPT. Olga was always crying that us scholars were nothing but an industry, which I felt was unfair; but now by Golly it looks as if she has the real thing to cast an icy eye upon. I don't mean to complain; my interest is solely in literature, and it seems to me a loss for a thing [not] to be done (such as annotation) when one is alive and willing, nothing being certain in this world.

We've had a strange springlike January (crocuses up, and an attempt at sprouting on the part of the hyacinths and daffodils) and as of last week snow and ice aplenty. I hope you get in some good skiing.

Sincerely,
Guy

7. TNS—1

22 IX 74

Dear Mr Laughlin:

All I meant was that my book on the *Cantos* ought to hold fire until Cantos 73 and 74 are published. I'm sorry that Perry made this innocent and thoroughly practical fact sound as if you were Urizen sitting in stony splendor on the Scriptures. I thought I'd explained to him the situation, which you have explained so clearly to me.

Cordially,
Guy

[Added in holograph:] Met Sam Beckett in Paris this summer. We talked a lot about Joyce.

/ • /

Perry: Bernard Perry, at this time the director of the Indiana University Press, had written JL that he understood that GD was holding up a book on the *Cantos* for IUP because of material JL was withholding. Davenport's study of Pound was published as *Cities on Hills: A Reading of I–XXX of the Cantos of Ezra Pound.*
Urizen: Poet-engraver William Blake's figure of cold reason.

8. TL—2 [cc]

October 1, 1974

DEAR GUY:

Many thanks for your very kind recent note explaining that what was holding you back on your Pound book was not the material in the Rachewiltz Trust but the problem of the publication of the two, Italian "missing Cantos." . . . I recently heard something from Donald Gallup, which I hadn't known before, which might expedite your getting copies, if there is no restriction at Yale. It seems that Mary remembered that these Cantos appeared in Italy in some obscure magazine, and that last summer she was able to obtain copies of it, which, I believe, have been added to the Merano Archive at Yale. So perhaps, if there is no restriction, Donald could make you copies from those. That wouldn't, of course, take care of the aspect of the permission to quote, which would have to come from the Trustees, when they make up their minds what they are going to do about the situation, but at least it would put the text in your hands, if you don't already have them, so that you could start working up that part of your book. I do feel certain that the Trustees will not hold back on permission indefinitely. There is to be a meeting of the Trustees on October 10, and I have suggested that this question be put on the agenda for discussion. They are also going to discuss, I believe, what to do about the publication of the Rome Broadcasts.

You may wonder why I never thanked you for your very interesting letter of last May in which you so kindly recommended the manuscript of Ron Johnson. The reason is that only now have I decided what we would do about this very fine work, which, unfortunately, because of the bad economic conditions, must be nothing, greatly to my regret, as I agree with you about his gifts. . . .

With best wishes, as ever,
[unsigned]

/ • /

Rome Broadcasts: During World War II Ezra Pound was living in Italy and he did a number of broadcasts there, attacking American economic and political policies, and individuals such as President Roosevelt. After Italy fell, Pound was charged with treason and kept in St. Elizabeths Hospital ("St. Liz," as it is most often referred to by Poundians) for thirteen years.
Ron Johnson: Ronald Johnson (1935–1998), poet and author of the epic poem *Ark*.

9. TNS—1

9 October 1983

DEAR MR LAUGHLIN:

What a question, what are my favorite light verses. If the epigram counts, all the best of 'em from here to there. Haven't I written quite enough on Jonathan Williams? He deserves another critical voice.

It's not the lightness but the sharpness of "light verse" (WHO coined that phrase?) that cuts the mustard. Why not rename the genre? Hasn't the term become something of a putdown? Minor poets get quotes just as much as major ones. *I'm* a minor writer, a fact that would help pitiful wretches like Hilton Kramer when he says I fail.

Honor the small.
Eros was not big at all.

Cordially,
GUY

/ • /

Jonathan Williams: (1929–), poet, student of Charles Olson at Black Mountain, and founder and editor-publisher of the Jargon Society, a small press that took ND as its inspiration.
Hilton Kramer: Noted art and film critic for the *New York Times*. Cofounder and editor of the neoconservative journal the *New Criterion*.

***10.* TLS—1**

November 2, 1983

Dear Guy:

It was good to have your note.

Yes, it's certainly the sharpness which cuts the mustard in light verse. Since I wrote you, I've been going through several anthologies, and a lot of it is pretty weak. I think for this project we have got to stay with "light verse," because we are rather trapped into it by the Oxford book, and I think that Auden called his collection the same, though I haven't found my copy of it yet. In looking at the Faber "Nonsense Verse," there are a few things which seem right, but a lot of it isn't.

I can understand that you may be tired of writing about Jonathan, but I think you are the best on him. Would it be all right to pick out a few paragraphs of what you have written about him hitherto? Naturally, I would submit back to you what was chosen for your approval.

You say you are a minor writer. That is good modesty. But I'm not at all sure it's true. It seems to me that you are getting better and bigger all the time. Keep it up.

With best wishes,
James Laughlin

P.S. I had a fine time on the Western universities lecture trip. I was able to pick the brains of half a dozen eminent Poundians, and learned a lot.

***11.* TLS—1**

6 June 1984

Dear Mr Laughlin:

Léon L.-Y. Chang, *La Calligraphie chinoise,* Préface de Henri Michaux, Paris 1971.

Printing completed *Janvier* 1971 (the French note these things).

In his *Remerciements,* Chang (some kind of Swiss prof) thanks Monsieur Henri Michaux for his marvelous poem on Chinese calligraphy *écrit spécialement en guise de préface à cet ouvrage.*

Lester Littlefield (whom I assume you know) told me about EP's attempts to translate the Michaux preface to this book. Lester's letter file upstairs is presently buried under all manner of gear and household effects (spring painting and replastering), and it would take hours to find the letter. My memory is that EP gave up trying the Michaux, and the copy I own of Chang's *Calligraphie* is one Lester sent me, possibly the one EP was working from.

So the mystery disappears when we see that Sobin isn't aware of the prose poem as it was used as preface to Chang's book. And either Michaux's memory is at fault, or Chang is stretching matters by saying that Michaux wrote the poem as a preface to his book.

Thanks for the "Alba"—lovely sentiment in pellucid words. You may be the only French poet writing in English.

"The Bowmen" will be one of the stories in *Apples and Pears* (out in November from North Point), considerably cheaper than Leslie Miller's printing. I'm pleased that you have a copy.

I hope I've solved the Michaux Mystery.

Sincerely,
GUY

/ • /

Henri Michaux: (1899–1974), French painter, journalist, and poet. This query was in relation to a special ND publication from 1984: *Ideograms in China,* by Michaux, written (as the French explains) especially as a preface to Chang's book. Michaux's poem was translated by Gustaf Sobin, and the book was designed by Leslie Miller, operator of Grenfell Press. There were only 150 copies, signed by author and translator.

12. TLS—1

9 November 1984

DEAR MR LAUGHLIN:

The Sobin/Michaux—so beautifully done by Leslie Miller and Claudia Cohen—came a while ago, and I am the richer in spirit for it. You bring so much together in it: that densely integritous culture of which Michaux was an exemplar, Pound, Fenollosa, Sobin, Lord knows what all. What pleasure of accomplishment you must feel as New Directions gets better and better with the years. No other American publisher would have thought to do this elegant book, much less with the style you've given it. And Michaux gone now, too.

What a handsome gesture, this gift; I'm very grateful, and proud, to have it.

I'm off to Toronto to give four lectures on painting and poetry, and have a first-class case of stage-fright. The Alexander Lectures, these. I tend to revert, under anxieties, to my native South Carolina dialect, and sound like Edgar Allan Poe reciting Scripture.

Thanks deeply for the handsome generosity of this gift.

Yours sincerely,
GUY

/ • /

Fenollosa: Ernest Fenollosa (1853–1908) was a Harvard graduate who became a professor of philosophy at Tokyo University as well as an expert on Asian art. After his death, his widow gave Fenollosa's unpublished notes on Chinese poetry to Pound, and these formed the basis of EP's view of Chinese writing and poetry.
lectures on painting: These were later collected as *Objects on a Table*.

13. TLS—1

2 XII 1984

Dear James Laughlin:

Have I said how pleased I am by Brad Morrow's Rexroth? I've written him that I wish we had similar volumes for all poets fit to read, where the selection is the best that criticism can do. The museum should be our critical guide. The *best* work of a painter makes the show. *Opera omnia* is for people with strong stomachs, anyway. I, for one, got Rexroth into focus, as I never had before. But then New Directions has always been a *critical* press. Knopf once was, too. North Point could be.

O nobody knows Oscar Mandel. He writes scholarship as well as anybody (except that he writes it humanly, with jokes and brassy opinions); he writes poems that remind me of yours (poetry as a civilized skill rather than a wind from the infinite and the absolute); and he writes some of the best prose in the Republic.

Please do have The Turkey Press send proofs. I'm late answering your letter as we've been to Toronto, where I did the 1984 Alexander Lectures. I had lunch with Barker Fairley (he's 97), we being the only two people in North America who think *The Dawn in Britain* is a great epic. Also Bill Blissett, the David Jones man, and Norrie Frye, and lots of interesting folk. Bonnie Jean discovered that Canadian black squirrels climb your person if you have peanuts, so we spent our time between events with $3.00 worth of peanuts, out in sideways snow and razory winds, for which we've paid with rotten colds.

The Michaux continues to give great pleasure as a beautiful book. I'd like to meet Marjorie Perloff someday; she has said kind things about my ravings.

with every good wish,
Guy

/ • /

Brad Morrow's Rexroth: Morrow, novelist and publisher of the periodical *Conjunctions*, edited Kenneth Rexroth's *Selected Poems* for ND.
Oscar Mandel: Poet and essayist. GD was recommending that ND publish his *Book of Elaborations*, which appeared as an ND book in 1985.
Turkey Press: This small fine press was planning to publish JL's collection *Stolen and Contaminated Poems*, which appeared in 1985.
Dawn in Britain: Charles M. Doughty (1843–1926) wrote this epic poem in six volumes.
Bonnie Jean: Bonnie Jean Cox, Davenport's companion for many years. She figures in a large number of letters here, at times as "BJ."
Marjorie Perloff: Critic, and fan of both GD and JL. When JL went to California he stayed with her in Los Angeles.

14. TLS—1

8 January 1985

DEAR MR LAUGHLIN:

Grand gift, the Patchen! Even if I didn't fancy the poetry or the drawings (which I decidedly do fancy), there's your piece on Patchen which I wouldn't have wanted to miss. And such a fine production the Jap printers have done for the Sierra Club. I got into Patchen at Haverford (having read *The Journal of Albion Moonlight* years before) where a fellow prof had all the works, and where one of my students, Ted Hauri, was a fervent admirer of P. In fact, Ted and I staged a program where I did a minilecture, and Ted read some of P's poems, and we passed the hat to help pay for one of those awful spinal operations.

Patchen and Rexroth (and various others) now look like a school, or movement: social critics, recasters of poetry without turning it into propaganda, vigorous hankerers after Beauty and Justice. Our corresponding members of the Weimar intellectuals. All with guitars on which find inscribed This Machine Kills Fascists. What a pity that it was all gravitating toward Allen Ginsberg, autistic selfishness, and narcotic apathy.

You probably did Patchen a favor by printing "about a third" of his work; he wrote too much too fast, and needed some critical mesh. The dust of our times has yet to settle. Patchen and most of the poets of his generation will emerge as masters of style and form compared to the bilge we've had from everybody, pretty much, since. Or do I betray my age by making such a remark? . . .

Your notepaper becomes more inventive; you're the Max Ernst of stationery.

Thanks heaps for the splendid Patchen: a bit of Klee, a bit of Shahn, but mainly all Patchen. Acrylics, by the way, can be overpainted forever; I think you meant to say gouache, which picks up the under color, and must be got right the first time.

gratefully,
GUY

/ • /

Patchen: Kenneth Patchen (1911–1972) was a poet and painter. The book JL sent was *What Shall We Do Without Us?: The Voice and Vision of Kenneth Patchen,* with an afterword by JL. This was published by the Yolla Bolly Press (Sierra Club Books, 1984).
This Machine Kills Fascists: A reference to a famous inscription on folksinger Woody Guthrie's guitar.
Your notepaper: JL liked to Xerox images onto his typing paper. At times he used copies of old woodcuts, paintings, photographs, even plants. He encouraged GD to get a copier for himself, after which they both incorporated images into their letters.

15. TLS—2

Gertrude Stein 3 Feb 1985

DEAR MR LAUGHLIN:

You could have skied on Sayre Avenue; it has the requisite deep snow, though not Eva Hesse, la Principessa de Rachewiltz, or the delights of Vienna. For the second time now I've watched my kitchen wall being torn out so that the plumber can get at frozen pipes. My house was built in 1925, and is warm and comfortable, but the pipes to upstairs are inside the back wall, next to the brickwork, so that The Wind Shield Factor (*sic loquitor Kentuckiensis*) can freeze them.

Creative Writing courses (I don't touch 'em) seem to subtract that element in the making of a writer where inner necessity sends the creator to a strong model (like Joyce longing to emulate Flaubert, Ibsen, Jacobsen, and D'Annunzio). As Wendell Berry says, "Writers get laid," and the young provide themselves with the trappings (dope, costume as fashion dictates, Bohemian ways), while remaining innocent of grammar, style, and spelling.

Rexroth and Patchen are *American* poets. They had bowels and angry passions and loving passions. Ginsberg (who has just sent me his collected poems) I accept as a prophet from the Old Testament.

I should have remembered those WCW translations in the *ND* annuals. I had a little part in the Sappho translation. That "paler than grass" I showed Williams is "greener than grass," but I don't think he quite believed me. There was a distrust of professors in that house. Flossy said right off on my first visit that English teachers steal books; apparently one indeed had. Glad to hear that Walt Litz is rounding these translations up.

I met Robert Fitzgerald at Yale when I did the lecture at Beinecke, "The House That Jack Built." Mary introduced me, and I only got to say how much I admired his translations. And the Greeks didn't fish with hook and line? Isn't there a wall painting of a fisherman with a pole? *Diktybolos* (casting the net) is another possibility. In the gospels, when Rabbi Yeshua has the fisherman cast again, when they weren't getting anything, the net is a *dikuton* and the verb is *amphiballo* (to throw out amply).

Your Magritte of the ensacked lovers is both Rilke (we make up the people we love) and Wittgenstein (you can't catch the measles over the telephone). Bonnie Jean for years called Ludwig a pitiful idiot, but now she's taking a course in computers and learning all about Wittgenstein and Turing (another p.i.). . . .

The still-life is interesting.

salt: left:: sugar: right (salt and sugar are friends, as salt and pepper are married)
orange + peach
peach + tomato (ketchup)

all but the salt is cooked, that is, mediated by civilization. And all's female: orange (though orange is the husband of lemon in *that* pairing), peach, tomato. All salads (of which ketchup is subspecies, sauce) are female. Butter is also uncooked, though processed by the churn.

That is, displays of food are neat little symbols encoding interesting meaning. Yours in this poem is a kind of Matisse, a tropical flourish (brown sugar from Jamaica, marmalade from Spain by way of England, peaches from Georgia, ketchup from Pennsylvania by way of the South Seas). Even the birds are fed from Peru, whence the sunflower. Super-American, the poem, as we're the country that brought our things from elsewhere. You nest the domesticity and homely between foreign foods and foreign spirits.

Eshleman's disapproval of Oscar Mandel is the highest praise I can imagine.

I've looked everywhere for *"Amari liceat si . . ."* and can't find it. La Waddell knows things other people don't. . . .

What wonderful letters you send! They have as many dimensions as a canto of Ez, for all their surface clarity.

I hope your jaunt has been good.

welcome back,
GUY

/ • /

those WCW translations: In a letter dated January 27, 1985, JL wrote that William Carlos Williams had done a number of translations of Chilean poets Nicanor Parra and Pablo Neruda, of Sappho and others in his epic poem *Paterson,* as well as some Chinese and Mexican poetry in *ND* annuals 9 and 19.

Robert Fitzgerald: Translator and poet whose recent death had greatly affected JL, who had been his friend for more than fifty years. JL had once asked Fitzgerald for a Greek equivalent for "fly-casting."

Magritte: JL had been writing on stationery with Xeroxed art, collages, et al. at the top.

GD is referring to a Xerox of Magritte's *Les Amants* ("The Lovers"). JL enclosed a copy of his poem "Here I Am." This is the "still-life" GD analyzes.

Wittgenstein . . . Turing: Ludwig Wittgenstein (1889–1951), one of the twentieth century's most logically astringent philosophers, and Alan Turing (1912–1954), the English logician who helped outwit the German Enigma code machine in World War II and pioneered theories of computational computing, had a famous series of debates about mathematical logic at Cambridge in 1939.

Eshleman: Clayton Eshleman (1935–), poet, translator, and editor of *Caterpillar* and *Sulfur* magazines. JL wrote on January 12, 1985, that Eshleman had called Mandel a "white worm" for his critical opinions.

"Amari liceat si": JL had asked if GD had a copy of this poem. Helen Waddell had referred to it, but had quoted only the first line.

16. ALS—3

3/7/85

O Maestro di los che sanno—

Please forgive my delay in thanking you for your letter, which gave me both delight and instruction—*[est dialectet, est desce].* The High gods saw fit to deliver a blow which I consider below the belt. Our son (age 26) grew tired of his fate—10 years of six shrinks, 3 visits to the bughouse, and the experiments of the inventors of new medications, and went his way, stabbing himself in 10 places and then expiring, classically, in the bath. In his situation, I think I would have done the same, though perhaps with a less symbolic procedure. Very disturbing—but no condolence is expected. Those roisterers on Olympus deal with us at their pleasure. . . .

One thing that has kept me from brooding has been browsing around in your *Apples and Pears.* I don't yet have the total structure in my head, but I think this is the "Real Thing" in the way of imaginative prose. Would I be wrong in this "progression" of the ideogrammatic method?

1. What EP did in the *Cantos.*
2. How Prof Kenner applied it to lit/crit/hist.
3. What GD is doing with prose construction.

This has been a tough winter. Fitzgerald was a constant support.

We were friends for 52 years. He would tell me when I was paddling up shit creek, and always encouraged me to read the good old books. His own poetry was a bit Eliotine but the prose style of his few essays and his autobiographical chapters, which ND will publish next year, was superb. Do you know the piece on the classical tradition, "Generations of Leaves"? Let me have it copied for you if you don't know it.

I don't remember a Greek fisherman with a pole, nor, I guess, does Fitzgerald as he said there was no casting in Hellas in those days, and he went for the net. . . .

The great Dudley Fitts of Choate, who set both Fitzgerald and myself on the *bon chemin,* urged me to learn some Greek via the New Testament, a grammar and a lexicon. I wish I had. But I was busy starting New Directions. Later I enrolled for Greek in the NYU night school but my brain was too fatigued from office toil to learn much. Now, in old age, I read a bit of both sides of the Loeb *Greek Anthology* and try to puzzle out the words. It seems to me that apart from the "epic sweep" about everything one wants to know about the human condition is in the *Anthology.* I prefer it to Balzac.

You must be the only Beanery Professor who will say anything kind about both Rexroth and Patchen. At least I have not heard it in my travels. Ginsberg is lovable. At the MLA poetry ranting in honor of W.C.W. he produced two poems where Bill talks about breathing to prove that the Bard of Rutherford was really a Buddhist. But he denies my myth that he left his early poems under the milk bottles on the kitchen stoop at 9 Ridge Road. But I'll continue to tell that one because I know it is TRUE. I'm positive. It is what *should* have happened.

E.P. said that Rilke was "soft." And I can't understand Wittgenstein, and feel I am too far gone to try.

Your exegesis of the breakfast poem is beautiful. But I don't deserve it. I did not conceive of any of those concepts. Like the wheelbarrow and those chickens, I just put down what I saw when I was eating my breakfast, plus the little morning prayer to the Olympians—one must never omit that. But perhaps you are leading me down the garden path? Country boys must beware of city explicators. I wrote a simple lyric about how Cynthia's hair fell down over Propertius's face when she kissed him and Prof Perloff said that the poem was about her vulva! . . . And Nabokov said that he had embedded in his *Nikolai Gogol* 3 leg-pulls about me, but that I must find them for myself, and I never have. . . . Nevertheless, whatever it may be, your construction about my stage props is a thing of beauty—and agility, and I love it. . . .

With apologies,
JL

/ • /

O Maestro: Most likely Dante on Virgil: *O Maestro di coloro che sanno*—"O Master of those who know."
Our son: Robert Laughlin. JL's harrowing poem on Robert's death is reprinted in *PNS,* 242.
the bon chemin: the "right path."
under the milk bottles: JL claimed that as a young poet, beat-icon-to-be Allen Ginsberg (1926–1977) used to leave his poems under William Carlos Williams's milk bottles on his porch, hoping for some contact with the older poet.
the wheelbarrow and those chickens: References to WCW's famous short poem "The Red Wheelbarrow."
how Cynthia's hair fell over: See "The Cave," *PNS,* 67.
Nabokov: Vladimir Nabokov (1899–1977), Russian-born novelist and essayist. ND published some of his early work. JL passed on the notorious *Lolita,* suggesting the Olympia Press in Paris, which published it in 1955. *Nikolai Gogol* was published by ND in 1944.

17. TLS—2

24 March 1985

Dear Mr Laughlin—

Of your grief I will say no more than insofar as I can imagine the defeat and hurt of it all I can feel something of the pain.

Blurb enclosed. The book is delightful, both poems and notes. What wonderfully madcap enjambments all over the place.

I can't see what your proof marks mean in the dedication, but the first line should be:

Καὶ σέο, Ἔσρ' ὦναξ, σοφίης ἴδμεν βέλος ὀξύ,

The line as set has a terminal rather than an interior sigma in *Esr',* a zeta instead of a ksi, a rough breathing instead of a smooth on the iota of *idmen.*

An elegant contraction, that *Esr' onax* (for *Esra O anax,* "O Lord Ezra"), where the omega contacts with the alpha ending *Esra* and beginning *anax.*

You realize, of course, that the epigram as you have it says not a "healing balm" but "a sweet need"? (I.e., I don't know what it says: "a healing balm" is no doubt the right guess.) Whoever made the translation (Fitzgerald?) is emending *khrema* to *khrima.* No, that's a kappa. Sorry. Let it stand. The scribe saw something interesting pass the scriptorium window, and we don't now know what he should have been looking at in his copy.

No invasion of privacy on 28: an honor (and a gift to J.W.: who dreamed through the classics).

I consider *Apples and Pears* a failure of the imagination. If you mean "57 Views of Fujiyama" as following Ez, yes, in some sense, and at a much lower power.

In the monstrous big story I was trying to be Fourier himself: using sets of "correspondences." Correspondences have a fascinating history: Jakob Boehme (from Jewish and mediaeval traditions) to Swedenborg to Fourier to Baudelaire to Joyce.

My Alexander lectures (on still life) tried to go at them another way: by asking why apples and pears make a marriage. Language is strangely a separate realm from the reality it supposedly names and describes.

If I've read Fitzgerald's "Generations of Leaves," I've forgotten it.

Ez had (as we all do) wonderful blindnesses. Rilke is a great poet, to my mind. Hugh Kenner says he deals in "bogus emotion." I can't understand Wittgenstein, either, when he's doing logic and mathematics, but there's a poetic side to him and a delightfully batty side ("You can't catch measles over the telephone") and a side that's parallel to Gertrude Stein.

Art knows things *for* the artist. Hugh and I have had words about that. He felt that I overdid my Grant Wood iconography, because Wood wasn't aware of what I was showing. Of course he wasn't. Monet wasn't aware that in zeroing in on haystacks and the lilypond that he was painting the two states of French soil: the marshlands that had to be drained over a thousand years to get the rich fields in which hay grows.

I don't dare commit myself to a session at Brown. I travel badly, and my luck is such that if I plan ahead, the whole damned world blows up. (Not, you understand, that I'm superstitious.) I'm doing a set of lectures at Washington and Lee this fall. I usually do one departure (if any) from Lexington per year. I don't give readings, or attend conferences of any sort. But the idea of a session on the *Cantos* in a class you're teaching is attractive. Have Brown (WHERE is Brown?) spring the idea on me after Xmas.

I'd jabber on, except that it's late, and I have to throw together some notes on Hermann Broch and Joyce, and hit the sack. If the Blurb is the wrong length, I can do it over.

sincerely,
GUY

/ • /

The book: GD read the proofs of Stolen and Contaminated poems and supplied a blurb.
the first line should be: The Greek dedication, *"Kai seo, Ezr'onax, sophies idmen belos oxu,"* can be translated at least two ways, but the most likely is "And Lord Ezra passes, wisdom's own sharp spear."
Boehme, Swedenborg, Fourier: Jakob Boehme (1575–1624), influential German mystic; Emanuel Swedenborg (1688–1772), Swedish scientist, philosopher, and theologian; Charles Fourier (1772–1837), French utopian philosopher.
Grant Wood iconography: See the title essay in GD's *The Geography of the Imagination.*

***18.* TLS—1**

2 April 1985

DEAR MR LAUGHLIN:

The *Cantos CX–CXVII* is here, and there's no way to thank you adequately for so generously handsome a gift. I feel as helpless as last year, when Fred Siegel gave me Louis Zukofsky's chair, the one in which he wrote "A." I will, as with Fred, bide my time. Meanwhile, I can gloat over it, and show it with pride.

7 April Fourier's birthday, and Wordsworth's, and Easter. I've spent the day with Caesar, doing his income tax. I figure that I work eight hours a day for Reagan's satanic weaponry systems. He takes a third of my income; a third of 24 hours is 8, a full workday. Providing cocaine for the poor and death rays for the rich. A Juvenal couldn't *believe* our world. It is no wonder that children go mad. I have no gizzard for shouting at fools and criminals; born an ostrich, which I sadly forget.

I see that Brad Morrow has survived an auto wreck.

I have still not looked at any reviews of *Apples and Pears,* suspecting them of gratuitous meanness. Meanwhile, the good old TLS has devoted two pages to a vicious review of *Geography* and *Eclogues*—written by a cretin or a man terminally stupid. As you know, I don't think a great deal of my amateurish writing, but I can be shocked when a critic ascribes fictional voices to the author. I break my ass trying to understand people different from myself, and here's this sibilant Brit assuming that everything's autobiographical transcription. No point in complaining. There's nobody to complain *to.* . . .

in proud gratitude,
GUY

/ • /

Cantos CX–CXVII: Drafts and Fragments of Cantos CX–CXVII. This was a copy of the 1968 ND–Stonewall Press edition, limited to 310 copies signed by Pound.

Louis Zukofsky's chair: When the poet died, a family member took a load of his belongings to a dump. A Zukofsky fan secretly followed and salvaged the chair and a few other items. GD kept this spindly chair within sight of his worktable.

19. TLS—1

17 June 1985

DEAR MR LAUGHLIN:

The stolen and contaminated are happily here, printed on Urpapyrus from Byblos, surely; the true title should be Allusive and Improved. Bounden thanks.

The Davenport Theory of Biology holds that Man is a metamorphic animal owned and operated by a *daimon.* Infant changed to child to adolescent to mature critter to senex just as a frog egg becomes a tadpole becomes a frog. That is, we are four separate animals once out of the womb. In the metamorphosis from adolescent to maturity, the child's spirit either keeps its daimon, or it loses it. Plutarch puts it another way: that the daimon is made welcome or unwelcome. (Jesus thought this way—his "born again" means backing up to the daimon's welcome and giving it another chance to cooperate, if it has got lost, "becoming as a child again.") My crazy philosopher Fourier designed his Harmony so that maturity could be combined with maximum live-in privileges for the daimon, which he called, using Socrates' term, "the sacred flame."

Which is to say that your daimon, whom you've kept (as witness all the evidence), will write the memoirs for you. Ez kept his daimon, though what part Olga played in sharing it is a speculation only the gods can elucidate. . . .

My daimon badly needs a vacation, which I'm trying to arrange for it. Trouble is, this means working overtime to get enough work done to get away for two weeks. Last summer, we had plans all set up, and Humphrey the tomcat developed epilepsy, as studied by two vets and two RD's (as one of the vets calls them, Real Doctors).

So we cancelled the vac. Humphrey, of course, quit having fits, became healthy as a grig, and got fat and sleek for the winter.

A printer in California is doing my Herakleitos with Greek text. I've solved the problem of diacriticals, iota subscripts, and total confusion of nu's and upsilon's by converting the text into archaic lettering, all caps, no accents (historically right). We're cheating, though, by separating words, which Herakleitos wouldn't have done. Academics will disapprove.

Soon I'll have a whole shelf of bibliographic treasures from your generosity.

avanti
!
GUY

_20._ TLS—2

9/16/85

DEAR GUY—

. . . At a cost of $75 for the exam + 83 for the specs, I got new glasses, and I still can't type properly. I fear the problem is in the top of my head, not the front. . . .

It might save the Lexington burglary squad trouble if you could send me a Polaroid of your likeness of E.P. For the shrine, along with his B.M. Reading Room card that he gave me. . . .

I'm so happy that you'd like to be in *ND* 50. Whatever you like best. I shd. explain why I didn't pursue you long since. About ten years ago I decided to stop reading the magazines and new books, to try, with Fitzgerald's help, to get into the classics. So I just didn't know what you were doing. . . .

Very best,
JAS

/ • /

B.M. Reading Room: Pound's British Museum Reading Room card.

21. ALS—1

10/14/85

DEAR GUY—

Thank you!!! It's a *remarkable* painting, but it makes me so sad because you've caught the misery of those last years. His body so thin, the look of hostility and confusion in his eyes, and the left hand picking at the right as he was constantly doing when listening to a conversation. And the silence, too, is in the whole picture, the pose the eyes. One of the chairs he made? I'm not sure.

Ann, who knows about painting, says that the paint is very well "put on." . . .

Mult Graz Ag!
Js

/ • /

It's a remarkable painting: At JL's request, GD had mailed an eight-by-ten photo of his portrait of Ezra Pound. See Eric Anderson Reece's *A Balance of Quinces: The Paintings and Drawings of Guy Davenport* (ND, 1996), color plate 1.

22. TLS—1

20 October 1985

DEAR MR LAUGHLIN:

In gift for a gift, I always get the better one. Thanks to you, my collection of rare printing is becoming insurable by Lloyd's. As for my painting, I'm old-fashioned and pretty much self-taught. My parents sent me off to art classes when I was a child (Anderson College, this, down in South Carolina) where the Barbizon School was our ideal. (This August, when Bonnie Jean and I were in Fontainebleau and part of the forest roundabout, I felt I had kinships with Rosa Bonheur and Millet which other tourists could not lay claim to.)

Ez had just been around the bay on the Bacigalupo boat, and had had a nap and a bath. The shirt was right out of the laundry; hence the crisp unrumpled ruckles. The chair, as I remember, looked commercial—ordinary deck-chair with canvas back and seat. (Do you know my story "Ithaka" in *Da Vinci's Bicycle*? It's the narrative that goes with the painting.)

. . . God did not mean for me to travel. Last week I was down in Virginia giving the (three) Glasgow lectures for 1985 (+ a reading from my ravings). The actual visit was rather fun (Joan Crane came over from Charlottesville, and Charles Rowell, and a groupie from the Museum of Modern Art), but the usual botch hit the day I left. I was stuck way out in the country at some antique inn, nothing for ten miles in any direction. I was to have been picked up at 5:30 A.M. by a university driver. So I was up at 4:30 (reason enough not to travel, ever), and out in the total dark of a moonless night. When I saw that I would miss my 7 o'clock flight from Roanoke, I felt my way through the dark back to the inn (out of which I'd locked myself by leaving), banged on the back door, and enjoyed waking the chairman of the English Department at W+L, Severn Beauregard Duvall (the William Gilmore Simms scholar, forsooth). So I spent a wasted day at a Marriott Airport Motel, getting back home 23 hours later than scheduled. I made the connecting flight in Washington by a hair, and by sprinting.

So from here on out all people requiring me in the flesh will have to come to my classes at the University of Kentucky. . . .

Now I must get at something for *ND* 50. When's the deadline? Yesterday?

buon viaggo,
GUY

The painting is much darker of color than the photo, which washed out, faded, the color.

/ • /

something for ND 50: Davenport sent the story "Wild Clover," which JL reacted to in the next letter below. This was reprinted in *JVSB* as "The Meadow."

23. TLS—5

December 21, 1985

DEAR GUY—

ZOWIE!! Your botanical *pastourelle* of tumescence is so beautiful. What exquisite logodaedaly. What Danish for the breakfast of our readers. This will be the star turn of *ND* 50 and will hold its own with the immortals of Part I. Your gifts reduce me to stuttering at the keys. But jealousy among friends is so ignoble. God gives & takes away. Maybe I can ski better than you can. . . .

Linguistic quibbles. I can't find "gutulliocae" in my Harvard-days dictionary. Is it so bad they couldn't put it in? All I could find is "gutus," a "small drop."

"Archeotera" looks Greek to me but Liddell & Scott has it not, or my old orbs can't find it in their tiny type. A compound? Maybe it's a sea plant. I think I once read that our cells began in some plant in the watery ooze.

I'm not trying to copy-edit you. I just get curious about new words. . . .

As ever,
JL

/ • /

Linguistic quibbles: "gutulliocae" means small, droplike spots; etymologically parsed, "Archeotera" would mean "ancient monsters."

24. TLS—1

9 February 1986

DEAR MR LAUGHLIN:

We—Bonnie Jean and I—read your "Ez As Was" with great delight. There's no TV here (only a radio, for music and news), and in any case whatever *Dallas* might be (I know what basketball is, the world's dullest sport, right after field hockey), it wouldn't bump a memoir of EP by JL. How could there be "errors" in it? A memoir is a memoir.

The Henghes part is news. The delicious anecdote of the sewing kit sent me to the drawing board, to do a decoration for the ND bulletin board. The Dutch flinch at the phrase "Queen of Holland" and ask politely that one say "Queen of the Netherlands." Holland being to their ears a province at the south of their vast country. Frisians consider it a kind of Morocco, steaming with sin and speaking a foreign language. (They speak Frisk.) . . .

Your letter of 4 Feb: Sure, you can combine Sappho's fragments all sorts of ways. Swinburne and Hardy did. "The Girls of Antiquity!" In my private pin-up Classical Gallery, there's Alkman's Hagesikhera (what a name!) and the nameless younger sister of Archilochos's Neobule (whom he seduces in the Cologne Fragment). And Abishag the Shulamite. Mary Magdalene would be the earliest female saint, wun't she?

I'm up to my kazoo translating Lehouck on Fourier, teaching Cummings and David Jones (that's different courses), helping Juan Carlos Galeano translate WCW (I imagine the permissions wing of ND will be hearing about this soon), keeping my animals in line (Chessy the dog, Humph the cat, and Beeminster and Lucille O. Possum). Also catching up the mail today—40 letters.

I wish I could be at the back of the room hearing you on the Cantos.

χαίρετε!
GUY

/ • /

anecdote of the sewing kit: In the manuscript JL mailed, "Ez As Was," he relates how once in Austria the Queen of Holland had invited him to join her skiing party. On one trip down JL had fallen and split his pants. The Queen took out her sewing kit and sewed them up. Upon hearing this story, EP had insisted that JL mail her his translation of Confucian writings. See accompanying GD drawing.
Cummings: Poet E. E. cummings (1894–1962). For GD on Cummings, see "Transcendental Satyr," *EF,* 29–36.
David Jones: (1895–1974), British poet, prose writer, painter, engraver, and more. For GD on Jones, see "Stanley Spencer and David Jones," *HG,* 112–26.
hearing you on the Cantos: JL was then guest lecturing at Brown University.
χαίρετε!: *"Chairete."* This would translate from the Greek as "Be happy." Both a hail and a farewell, this is the equivalent to the Italian *"Ciao."*

25. TLS—2

2/14/86

Dear Guy—

Your superb drawing of the Dutch Queen reading what my Chinese friends tell me is pronounced the TA-HACHOO (as in a sneeze), the finest thing of its kind I have seen since the picture of Saint Hieronymous in the Alte Pinakothek in Muenchen reading what looked to me like *Tropic of Capricorn,* has lazerated me from a glum pit of despair.

I was enraged because we do not have Social Credit so there would be no more bums in Penn Station, one of whom filched my bag while I was micturating and made off with my copy of Andy D, *oficiana Wechele,* 1533, which I was taking up to Brown to show the kiddies, and a folder with 20 unanswered letters (and I can't remember who they were from), and, most painful, the copy of the *Cantos* in which I have been entering misinformation and semio-deconstructionist thoughts for 30 years. Is this a sign that God wants me to turn away from Ez and start on Wally Stevens? . . .

I was rereading the Kumrad not long ago and I think his best hold up real well. But I never finished *EIMI.* I wish I had had the smarts to publish D[avid] Jones when I first encountered his books. The Ewige Weibchen had one of his paintings once, but I don't know what she has done with it. Do you know his engravings for the *Ancient Mariner*? I'll stat the set from the suite for you, though the copier won't do them justice. The one that has (5) on it is an original pencil sketch which doesn't turn up in the book. The printing part of the book I don't like. The poem is set in an over-ornate swash italic, but the glosses beside it look like the small type in the *Manchester Guardian.*

All learning lost
Because my grip was lifted
And nothing's in my bean
But forward Xtian sojer, up and on.

JL

/ • /

Tropic of Capricorn: A 1939 erotic novel by Henry Miller (1891–1980), published in Paris. ND published a number of works by Miller, but chose not to take on the legal challenges of publishing the erotic works. For the relationship between Miller and JL, see the earlier volume *Henry Miller and James Laughlin: Selected Letters.*

Social Credit: In the aftermath of World War I, British civil engineer Clifford H. Douglas proposed a system of "social credit" whereby goods and services would be sold below cost. Sellers' losses would be made up by government credits. This idea was taken up with intense fervor by EP, who passed it on to JL.

Andy D: Andreas Divus, whose translation of Homer's *Odyssey* into Latin (a copy of which JL had in the bag which was stolen) was one of the inspirations for Pound's *Cantos.*

Kumrad: JL is referring to poet E. E. Cummings. *EIMI* is a travel diary of the Soviet Union.

GREAT MOMENTS IN THE INTELLECTUAL HISTORY OF EUROPE.

HRH KONINGIN WILHELMINA OF THE NETHERLANDS READING EZRA POUND'S TRANSLATION OF CONFUCIUS, THE GIFT OF HEER JAAP LAUGHLIN, WHOSE SPLIT TROUSERS SHE ONCE REPAIRED WITH THE ROYAL SEWING KIT ON A SKI SLOPE OF THE ALPS.

26. TLS—2

23 Feb 1986

Dear Mr Laughlin:

A nightmare. I hope you'll run an ad in the *Times,* (a) offering a reward for the Divus and annotated *Cantos,* and (b) apprising your correspondents that they must try again. The former might alert bookdealers, on the off chance (very off, I should think) that the thief is literate enough to try them for a fence.

Damn. I'm awfully sorry this happened. T.E. Lawrence, Garrison Keillor, and now you. St-John Perse lost four long poems to the Gestapo. Me, I travel with a canvas Danish book satchel, which is over my shoulder. Bonnie Jean gets robbed, poor dear, with a great regularity; two bicycles over the years, all her credit cards many times. I wish I thought Social Credit would prevent this kind of thing.

At Oxford I was a classmate, and close friend, of the anthropologist Rodney Needham, a fluent Chinese speaker, and from him I learned about Confucius. So when I had occasion to pronounce *Ta Hio* at St Liz, Ez looked quizzical and asked what I'd said.

I spelt it.

"Well," said EP, "*I* pronounce it *tah hee-oh*!"

As did I, thereafter. . . .

Thanks heaps for the full set of Jones' "Ancient Mariner" suite. I saw the book at Bill Blissett's in Toronto last year. I agree with you about the type.

And I will frame the Pisan ms. . . .

Metempsychic Roman poet. C. Rufus Ludicrus?

ad interim,
Guy

/ • /

Pisan ms.: JL sent GD a copy of a manuscript piece of the *Cantos* which, he wrote, "looks as if Ez had written it on a paper towel" while being detained in Pisa.

Metempsychic Roman poet: JL had asked GD to suggest a name for a fictional poet.

27. TLS—2

2 March 1986

Dear Mr Laughlin:

I've just sent you a *Laufer*. If it won't do, I'll try another. This one is from Tassili in the Sahara, where LF was one of the first to *erleben.* (I have no German of a useful sort, but assume that *Erlebte Erdteile* means a continent observed.) The conversation in which the *Laufer* came up (St Liz) involved three things desired—a title for the poem, a "*Läufer* from Frobenius" under said title, and a map of China. I've gone through the *Kultur Geschichte Afrikas* (gift from Ez), the *Erlebte,* several prehistoric books, and decided that the *Läufer* must *laufen* + carry a bow (like Odysseus). A symbol, I guess, of *Zweck,* the beginning of civilization, the Hunter.

Frobenius knew more about bowstrings than any man ever. Note detail of how the string is doubly tied to the bow in this rock painting. I had to correct for lumpiness of rockface.

Thanks for sharing Wednesday's class with me. Lucky students. Your "garbage" is better than 98% of the professariat's best efforts.

Sperm is from brain *to* testicles in classical physiology. The mind was the lungs (phrenes) where the voice so obviously originates. The brain was a reservoir of oily gunk which lubricated the joints and made a solution for the seed. Ez's theory is a wonderful mixture of Homeric anatomy and Romantic understanding of a Renaissance supposition about sperm and manliness. Newton attributed his great brain to never having lost a drop of sperm. (The folk belief was, and is, the opposite: that not expending sperm will drive you crazy.) What Gauguin and Vincent had their tearing fight over in Arles was these two theories. Vincent, a Dutch Baptist, believed that his genius depended on his chastity; Gauguin, a pagan, believed that his genius required a visit every day to the whorehouse over that pool-hall.

Taishan, O magister, is in China, as I'm certain you remembered when you got to the bottom of page 6 in class. But these notes are surely headed for archives. Tai is not only a mountain; it is a duke; it was ennobled a thousand years back.

Someone should do a study of Ez's mountains and hills. Like Joyce's rivers, they bring things into a webwork of meaning. They come from the Bible ("cities on hills"), from Mediterranean myths (Olympos), from the East, and from the USA, California to New Hampshire.

Last evening was curious. Bonnie Jean had mentioned to a woman at the newspaper that we run a Café Marsupial out back, to feed two opossums named Beeminster and Lucille. Said woman (quite charming) was fascinated, and came to see the feeding of the possums, as well as to work up possums in general (Wallace Stevens, Eliot, Pogo, folklore, etc). She's a financial and business reporter, which she finds boring, and wants to do more interesting subjects. She's off to interview a woman who raises possums for the table.

One Nancy Blake (who despite her name seems to be French—teaches at Montpelier and is a psychotherapist) has written a study of my ravings, and offers me (in study) a subject for a future story; viz.

Einstein: "When a mouse looks at the world, the world doesn't change."

Niels Bohr: "Yes it does. A little."

(Obviously talking about Heisenberg.)

Bohr's one of my favorite people. He loved westerns, and he and his students wore dimestore holsters with lead pistols and wooden bullets at the *Atomisk Institutet*. When a seminar had gone well, he took everybody to the movies to see Tom Mix or Hoot Gibson, but he could never follow the plot; it took the combined effort of his students to keep him abreast of what was going on.

Another area for deep research: Wittgenstein was a fan of Betty Hutton and Carmen Miranda, and he used to treat *his* students to their films.

And Piet Mondriaan never missed a Mae West flic; he considered her a lady of great spirituality (*geestelijk*).

Vanessa: first time I've had a name for her. Lots of color in the book, I gather from Leslie.

ad interim,
GUY

/ • /

LF: Leo Frobenius (1849–1917), German anthropologist whom EP admired. *Erlebte Erdteile* is the title of Frobenius's multivolume major work.
Läufer: German for "runner" or "messenger." JL asked GD to draw what Pound had wanted, and GD made a drawing for the title page and wrote a short explanatory note for the next ND edition of the *Cantos* that EP had wanted a runner and the Chinese ideogram for *sincerity.* (GD later remembered that EP had specified two runners.)
Vanessa: Vanessa Jackson, artist with whom JL shared both an artistic and a personal relationship. Their collaboration was titled *The House of Light.*

28. TLS—1

29 March 1986

DEAR MR LAUGHLIN:

Well noo [*sic*], the *Collected Poems* are an event. Complete with the Hebridean Viking on the jacket: rocks, ship, pipe, mackintosh.

And good to read, in all sorts of ways. The Texas parade is a wonderful invention—the eye of Saul Steinberg.

(When I'm old enough to join it, you must come down for a guest appearance in the Bell Court Senior Citizens Kitchen Band. It performs in a wagon every 4th of July, which is also Founding Day here, as the frontier fort was named Lexington after the battle. My neighbor across the street won't be in it; he's 96, but plays the drums in a real jazz band.)

The few little boys in with the girls' band is Fourieriste.

Pleased to meet The Bible Lady again.

I hope the critics will recognize that the *Collected Poems* are the centerpiece of the 50th birthday celebrations. . . .

ringraziamente,
GUY

/ • /

Collected Poems: JL's *Collected Poems.*
Saul Steinberg: (1914–1999), artist best known for his satirical cartoonlike drawings.

29. TLS—1

1 XII 1986
Seventy-fifth anniversary of the inception of Tarzan of the Apes, the ms of which is dated 1 Dec 1911, and the hero up to page 5 is Zantar, Lord Bloomstoke. Burroughs was 40.

Dear Mr Laughlin:

Bounden thanks for the graciousness of "Ez as Wuz" (which you'd sent me in typescript). What you had to put up with as a publisher! Ez is wonderful on the Greek font, "fly specks." Beguiling photos. Fine study of you on page 25; a Scots philosopher at Cambridge or Oxford pondering an abstrusity.

Just this afternoon I was informing John T. Irwin (English chair, Johns Hopkins) of your flat-out goodness as a poet. . . . Strange how alienated academics are. The office next to John's is Hugh Kenner's.

North Point has just accepted *The Jules Verne Steam Balloon,* for next fall. Nine stories, dedicated to Humph's memory, nine being a cat number.

And everybody's forgetting English. A colleague in Florida writes to know what I mean by "the get of the radicals of the 60s"—turns out he'd never heard *get* (it's been in the language since the 14th century, at least) meaning progeny.

I've just read Hugh's *The Mechanic Muse,* brilliant and full of things good to know.

Reading your account of Ez at St. Liz, I'm reminded of a complaint he made to me once, about sleeping badly. "I can't get flat in the bed." Insomnia, from tension, I suppose, but I like the Americanness of the phrasing. . . .

ad interim,
Guy

30. TLS—1

27 XII 1986

DEAR MR LAUGHLIN:

Perhaps we'll be lucky enough to have some Deconstructionist debate whether Tasilo Ribischka's "Acumen and Decible" or my scribble in *ND* 50 was generated by the dirtier mind. Neither can keep up with Hiram Handspring. I've enjoyed and learned much from the headnotes you've provided: little masterpieces of civilized criticism. It's a fine book.

I hate to agree with C.S. Lewis about anything (he was the Devil's Representative on earth in his day and tried his damnedest to flunk me at Oxford) but he's right about the health of a literature showing in its R. Austin Freemans. Ez explained that before Jack Lewis thought of it: a high style can be used by lesser fish (Swinburne makes Kipling possible; Kipling, Service; Service, Eddie Guest). As a minor writer myself, I know what Molesworth means. Good review. I still haven't seen the offensive *Times BR*, and I wonder if they printed Jonathan's rebuttal. *Major* and *minor* are snob terms, anyway. A poem is a poem.

Antigua. That's where Archie MacLeish used to winter. I have the between-semesters free time (now that Xmas is over) to roll in. We had the novelist Percival Everett, his wife Shere, and 11-yr-old son Ben for a good cozy Xmas Day. Jacket proof for *Every Force* (the second book of essays) came on Xmas Eve, from North Point. The design is a Celtic coin, with a horse on it that evolved from a head of Hermes through a century of transformations. Jack Shoemaker says it looks like a chicken.

It's a grand state of affairs to be in ND at last—an ambition of many decades. I have one fan letter already, from a Methodist minister in Ohio, who says that my spicy scenes are Christian visions of a redeemed world. And then *Granta* sent back, by way of rejection, a ms I sent them *two* years ago.

Back to Perry Mason (book, not TV) by the fire.

A Prosperous New Year!
GUY

/ • /

my scribble: GD's "scribble" in *ND* 50 was "Wild Clover," reprinted in *The Jules Verne Steam Balloon* as "The Meadow."
C.S. Lewis: C. S. Lewis (1898–1963), critic and novelist (most famously of the *Narnia* fantasy books, and *The Screwtape Letters*). In a review of JL's *CP* in the *American Book Review*, one Charles Molesworth had quoted Lewis's famous comment that a nation's literary health could be measured by the vigor of its minor writers.
Antigua: JL had written GD from a family vacation on Antigua—where he was holed up working on *Byways.*

31. ALS—1

4/10/87

O He Who Knows All—

That after reading the book you so kindly gave me. It bars belief that anyone should have so much in his head and it burst not. And the style is so lovely. It flows.

Page 69 about "answering." That's what I try to do but usually fail.

Thank you for receiving such a horde so graciously. When the Voluble One had broadcast to his colleagues at Bellarmine that he was coming to see you it would have required a bus to bring all your admirers.

For me the visit was a Sacred Event. Neither the oracle nor the shrine disappointed me.

Ann is going to have the local carpenter make a table like yours from the picture in Kenner.

If you sketch the design E.P. did for theirs and mark the colors I can paint it in my childish way. I have a box of show-card colors and a small brush to do the edges and a larger one to do the fill-ins. "Thank you very much," as all the black saints keep saying in one of my favorite operas.

The Voluble One means very well. He gave me the top lines for the enclosed versicle. Like Henry J. I try to keep my ears open. Ron Seitz was a pal of Merton's. He has a great eagerness to be a famous poet. He is hypoglycemic, but maybe he'll make it anyway: I like him.

The only trouble was we didn't meet Bonnie Jean. I hope you explained about catching the plane. And especially I hope there is nothing badly wrong with her eye. She looked pretty in the picture—and intelligent.

I'm trying this month to write tersely like my other master Bob Hutchins, for whom I worked at the Ford Foundation. Some of his best letters read only—"No. Sincerely." But he let me spend those millions on cultural Boy Scout works, until Henry found out. Henry found out because a Ford dealer in Alabama read cummings poems in my magazine *Perspectives*.

Very best,
THE NEW JAS

/ • /

Laughlin, his wife Ann, and Wade Hall had visited Davenport the afternoon of April 10th. The book GD gave JL was *Every Force Evolves a Form*. The passage on "answering" that JL refers to is in the essay "The Artist as Critic." GD observes that what an artist does is answer other creators.

the Voluble One was Wade Hall, who taught at Bellarmine. (See next letter.)

a table like yours refers to a table GD built after one constructed by Ezra Pound. The picture referred to is in Kenner's *The Pound Era,* 392. The table can also be seen on the back of the jacket of *EF.*

the enclosed versicle: JL enclosed a poem manuscript, "Homecoming," about his father.

my magazine Perspectives: Beginning in 1952. JL edited *Perspectives,* a journal that was backed by the Ford Foundation. For the five years of its existence, *Perspectives* was published in four languages, with the goal being to inform Europeans about American cultural accomplishments.

32. TLS—1

Easter 1987

DEAR MR LAUGHLIN:

I only wish the visit had been longer. It was wonderful to talk with you again, and to meet Ann. And the honor of the visit is doubled by your so kindly reading my ravings. A Feminist Terrorist in San Francisco (who, incidentally, thinks that Balthus is a writer) has denounced it as chauvinist claptrap, and Donald Hall says the book is obnoxious.

As for Ann's reconstruction of the Gerrit Rietveld table, the best model I can point to is the Guy Mendes photo on the back of the *Every Force* jacket: how it fits together is there on display. I built mine from a verbal description from Hugh, and the outlay was $16.

Lord knows what will come up when visitors' eyes see one's workshop of a house. Bucky Fuller went straight to Mallarmé's oeuvre and talked about him for an hour. There are two original Picassos in the living-room, and two original Rouaults.

For all the modesty of the nifty poem precipitated by the voluble Wade Hall, the footnote is not your fate—you will decidedly be among the poets, justly belaureled.

Bonnie Jean, in turn, was disappointed that she couldn't get back in time from the eye doctor. When she did get here, she was wearing bifocals and had a bottle of Artificial Tears, both of which seem to have alleviated her burning eyes. I was anxious to have this seen to, before we traipse off on vacation as soon as school's out. She has the brains in our alliance.

Will the Henry Ford–Alabama car dealer–Hutchins anecdote (a little more folded out) be in your autobiography? I have a hunch that American history is one long farce of good intentions thwarted by busy-bodies sticking their noses in other people's affairs.

The story I'm working on has now passed 200 pages, with no end in sight. Amateurs must settle for what happens: design is beyond them.

ad interim,
GUY

/ • /

Gerrit Rietveld: Rietveld (1888–1964) was a Dutch architect and furniture designer associated with the De Stijl movement.

story I'm working on now: This was almost certainly "Wo es war, soll ich werden," which was 101 pages in length as published in *The Drummer of the Eleventh North Devonshire Fusiliers.* A longer, "original" version was later published as a limited edition.

33. TLS—2

8 June 1987

DEAR MR LAUGHLIN:

We're just back from Denmark, Bonnie Jean and I, and some 60 pieces of mail had backed up here, and I apologize for saving your good letter with all its enclosures for last, among the last, as dessert and reward, after all the recommendations for NEHs and Guggenheims and blurbs and other damned nuisances. . . .

Having set five stories in Denmark, I thought I ought to go look at the place. Lordy, how I've underestimated it! BJ and I always travel as anthropological spies, and even managed to become a little bit Danish—I in a blue denim student cap (as worn by Nietzsche in Turin after Brandes began lecturing on him) and BJ in a fetching Lutheran housewife's dress which she bought in Dragør.

The first naked sunbathers we encountered (in the park at Friedriksborg) were female and eighteenish. I didn't realize that I'd see hundreds more. I think I'll join the Lutheran church, which all the Danes belong to.

One day on the very crowded pedestrian street (one of six) we lucked on a young Dane being wheeled along on a platform by his buddies. His membrum virile was all the way out through his jeans fly, applauded by young and old. A placard carried behind him said, *"Ork jo! Jeg skal gifte!"* which I translate as "You bet! I'm going to be married!"

Back to your enclosures. Henry James, you know, thought he was Napoleon in his last weeks.

Walter Abish was here reading toward the end of the semester, though I didn't presume to introduce myself.

I haven't read anything, or written anything, in a month—a true vacation, and must now refind my routine. Red Ozier thinks it can publish my new book (which I don't want done commercially—and they're willing to promise NO review copies, NO ads, and NO announcement of publication, as they did before with "The Bicycle Rider").

ad interim,
GUY

/ • /

His membrum virile: This incident obviously made an impression. It is included in "Journal I," in *The Hunter Gracchus* (219), where the card reads, *"Ja, jeg skal gifte!"* and the translation is given as, "Oh boy, do I ever need a wife!"
Walter Abish: Author of numerous volumes of short stories and novels including *Alphabetical Africa,* published by ND.

34. ALS—2

10/27/87

DEAR GUY—

No, I have not gone under earth, or become forgetful of your many kindnesses. I have been these several months in a burrow of abuleia (Ezra's term), a phase in the cyclothymic rhythm. Very annoying and very rude-appearing to friends. The pills are quite ineffectual. But, with patience, these things pass.

What is troubling is that the regular flow of spontaneous verse dries up. It has been necessary to fabricate verse by an effort of will, of which I disapprove. This method—I call them "synthetics"—produces very turgid stuff, as you will see from the samples. My consolations have been reading your elegant pieces in *Antaeus* and *Parnassus,* and some minor works of Stendahl and some correspondence of Flaubert (surely L. Colet was the most obnoxious female on record) and a heavy book of art criticism from the new museum in L.A. *The Spiritual in Art,* which proves that the great abstract painters were alchemists, anthroposophists, admirers of Böhme, Cabalists, Neo-Platonists, Rosicrucians and devotees of Paracelsus. A loony book but it has to be true because it costs $65. I don't usually look at such things but Vanessa asked me to get it for her. I hope these dark truths will not affect her work. Things are bad enough over there with Charles and Diana now residing in "separate palaces." (TV)

The young lady at Graywolf Press tells me that you have been most helpful about my Ezbook. I hope you have not compromised yourself. The first notices have been indulgent, but I'm sure I'll be kicking myself when the Poundian 75's are unlimbered. And, of course, I worry about what Mary de Rachewiltz may think of it. In her view Ez is still spotless.

Despite lapses it is ever my hope to give friends a helping hand on life's slippery ladder. . . .

Yrs friendly in xt,
JL

/ • /

abuleia: See the etymological notes in GD's following letter. JL was bipolar.
L. Colet: Louise Colet (1810–1876), whom Flaubert called his muse. They had a passionate, stormy relationship from 1846 to 1854. His letters to her are considered by some to be some of his finest writing.

35. TLS—1

8 November 1987

DEAR MR LAUGHLIN:

The distinction, of course, is appearing in *Antaeus* with you. I'd seen the essay—you kindly sent it to me in manuscript—and it's even better in print.

Silence is also part of a correspondence, as of a conversation. Your abuleia is probably the price you pay for being able to write, and speak, so well, when you *bouletai* on all cylinders. Ez's "abuleia" is a characteristic Latin-Greek bastard word. Greek is *abouleia,* the Latin *abulia.* Behind both words is the fact of being a senator, the essence of which was decisiveness. *Bouleia,* a seat in the Senate; so *abouleia* = indecisiveness. Think of it as being on vacation, owing to the Senate's not being in session.

Glorious list!—yours of the spiritual exercises of abstract painters. I know that Mondriaan was some kind of Theosophist, like Yeats; and Kandinsky went in for Ethical Society bilge. The private lives of geniuses are full of damned peculiar things. Joseph Cornell was a Christian Scientist. . . .

The energy of the new poems is in the monosyllabic words. So that when a polysyllable comes along it makes a crescendo. I like "The Limper." It has existential wit.

A pedestrian, I encounter things motorists don't. Viz., Louie Holwerk, aged 4, who frequently waylays me on my way home. Friday, he said he couldn't talk to me, but his Bird could, his Bird being two fingers, for which he provided the words.

"What have you been doing?" said the bird.

"Teaching school."

"You're a *school teacher*!!"

"Oh yes. I taught your mama and daddy when they were in college."

"You DID?"

"Yes, I'm one hundred years old, you know."

"O wow! I'll bet you can do anything you want to!"

Very Calvin, Louie, as in the comic-strip Calvin and Hobbes—best one since Krazy Kat, or maybe the Toonerville Trolley.

I'm behind with everything (it's Rhodes Scholar selection time, and I'm the State Secretary).

In unseemly haste,
GUY

/ • /

the essay: JL had enclosed a copy of his "Inhale and Exhale: A Letter to Henry Miller."

36. TL—1

[ca. November 1987]

Verne Balloon Attacked
By Aerial Goons
Lives of local boys endangered

RAIDERS THOUGHT TO BE
IN EMPLOY OF MARXIST-FEMINISTS

Pilot Faustroll vows he'll fight to
The last drop of helium. Appeals to
Governor for assistance. Boys defiant.
Just let them try to push *us* around,
Say youngsters.

[unsigned]

/ • /

Toward the end of 1987, JL sent GD several comic "boys' adventure"-style notes, with collage illustrations, in response to publication of GD's *The Jules Verne Steam Balloon.* GD replied in kind. See next letter.

37. TLS—2

13 XII 87

Wireless contact with balloon lost somewhere between Grønland and Island owing to severe aurora borealis and an unusual angle in the cosmic winds. Last message, logged at Rejkjavik signed Faustroll asked College Pataphysics locate M Jarry or M Proust with request that one or the other or both deposit funds in sloty at branch office Bank of Poland Norfolk Connecticut or Prince Edward Island also request best cure for hiccups.

DEAR MR LAUGHLIN:

I've just bought from your estimable publishing house HE Bates's *A Month by the Lake,* Guigonnat's *Dæmon in Lithuania,* Borges's *Seven Nights,* Weinberger's *Works on Paper,* and Queneau's *The Blue Flowers.* Loyal customer, moi. I'm reading them all at once, except the Weinberger, which I've finished. . . .

The semester is almost over. Classes ended Friday. Exams and termpapers this week.

I'm almost through vol 4 of Parkman's history of Canada and New England—5 to go. The Church had its own ideas about geography, so the first bishop of Montreal (or was it Quebec?) was designated Bishop of Arabia Petrea, of which Canada must be the other side. Not quite as whonky as Columbus' suspecting that Peking was somewhere around Atlanta.

Speaking of Columbus, I've explained the colon that begins *Paterson* all sorts of ways (Europe: America) until it dawned on my feeble mind that Cristóbal Colón is that gentleman's real name. Keeping to the formula *pater:* son.

have a fine Christmas!
GUY

/ • /

Paterson: WCW's epic poem about Paterson, New Jersey. *Pater,* of course, means father, so "father: son," which is poetically equivalent to "Europe: America." GD could be said to have been right either way.

M Proust: GD wrote in *A Balthus Notebook* that "Proust's 'little band' of adolescent girls at Balbec derives from Fourier, and . . . Saint-Loup and his circle constitute a Little Horde, the complement of 'Spartans' to the Athenian Little Bands."

38. TLS—2

6 January 1988

Dear Mr Laughlin:

A Great Snow is said to be on the way. Flix the Tomcat is out in the bitter cold, as the two extremes of temperature mark the partying season for the Felidæ. I have an oak fencepost of great age in the fireplace—my neighbor took down an old fence this summer, and I got the posts, by right of estovers (Coke upon Littleton), namely that any subject may gather firewood from any property, so long as said wood is lying ungathered on the ground. Sir Walter Scott, however, made his crofters *pay* for theirs. Good for their character, he said.

Is Faustroll in *Le Surmâle*? When ND brought out its translation, I was halfway through one. My usual luck. Anyway, no messages from the balloon. I should imagine they're all in Lhasa, chasing lamas, and being chased by lamas, and that the world's largest Jewel is involved in the chases. Bandits on yaks arrived to cause yet more trouble. But a French archaeologist who has been chained up with scorpions and spiders in a lightless and airless dungeon for years makes himself heard. Biff and Jim throttle a lama and make him say the magic words that release the archaeologist. Faustroll recognizes the F. a. as an old schoolmate at Leipzic. The F. a., it turns out, arrived in Tibet through a tunnel which he entered at Rejkjavik.

Speaking of which, one reads in this month's *Smithsonian* (I think) about a woman who regularly pesters the State Department about her little problem. She has known for some time that she is the hereditary empress of Atlantis and Lemuria. She ran across the fact that one loses one's American citizenship by becoming head of a foreign state. Congress, however, can pass a special bill allowing one to be both a citizen of the USA and of a foreign country. This she asks them to do. The boffin who gets stuck with her letters always sends them to the subdepartment of Geography and Boundaries once he has given up trying to find Atlantis and Lemuria.

"Our Bicycles" is a little masterpiece. Was it generated (it would be interesting to know) by St-Simon, or was the queen's pompons added for historical rhyme?

My most outrageous Xmas present (in a good year for loot) was a Danish scoutmaster's uniform (nametag, TVEMUNDIG and with NFS GRUNDTVIG on the left shoulder patch), made in Copenhagen by Spejdersport SV, provisioners of scouting equipment to the Queen and the Archbishop. They were thoroughly cooperative, and thought it Quite Jolly that someone wanted a complete outfit for a fictional scoutmaster at a fictional Danish school. Norwegian blue, indestructible. The plaid forager scarf is particularly spiffy. A fan of my ravings in Arkansas sent it to me.

In Italian you spell Copenhagen Copenaghen. Makes sense.

For my Pound seminar this semester I'm not doing the Cantos, as usual, but the critical writing + selected poems (both ND texts), as I think I need to take students back to the basic values. I keep seeing a great blank ignorance in modern literary discourse (e.g. Updike on La Oates in the last *New Yorker*).

with best wishes for a grand New Year,
GUY

/ • /

estovers: This legal principle is just as GD describes it.

Le Surmâle: Alfred Jarry's 1902 novel about a reclusive aristocrat who has conditioned himself into having superstrength. A five-man cycling team Jarry includes here figures in GD and JL's parodic exchange about boys lost in the balloon. Faustroll is not in this novel.

"Our Bicycles": See *PNS,* 248.

Danish scoutmaster's uniform: The name tag refers to a character in GD's imaginary Danish scout troop.

Updike on La Oates: The work of Joyce Carol Oates was of particular annoyance to GD. He would often use her name when decrying the poor state of American literature.

39. TCS—1

4 Feb 1988

A triumph, the *Ez Az Wuz*! I'm very proud of the inscription and of the compliment on page 25. It's a book that will be a permanent part of American Literature. I've admired it all: that's the response it elicits, admiration, for the firmness of its learning and of its courtesies to the reader. My seminar will have it recommended tomorrow. As for "the color of the stars," doesn't that refer to the fact that each of the circular walls represents a planet (these classically included the sun—gold—and moon—silver—then Mars, Venus, Mercury, etc). This from Mircea Eliade. All designs are from Up—the redeemed Jerusalem, Wagadu, Ecbatana. "As it is in heaven, so shall it be on earth." . . .

And earth's lid over Duncan. He was far too mystical and cerebral for my taste, but I recognized that he was a poet of a high order.

A letter, later. I wanted to get off thanks before the outgoing mail.

I think you may well have written the BEST book on Pound for the civilized, educated reader.

χαίρετε!
GUY

/ • /

Ez Az Wuz: JL's *Pound as Wuz.*
Mircea Eliade: (1907–1986), Romanian-born philosopher and historian of religion. He lived and taught in the United States from 1956 until his death.

40. ALS—3

2/15/88

DEAR GUY—

They heard the bombs popping as far away as Torrington the day your extollatory letter came. Wow!! I was nearly an hour in the P.O.

reading that great paragraph to the *concittadini.* Some even wanted to read for themselves. "Gosh, Jim," said old Vogelfahrt, wiping the rheum from his eyes with a kerchief last washed in 1957, "an I allus thot you wuzze haifwit like me. . . ." Some letter. I was floating. But when I had read it about 20 times I thought to supply the acrostic test of the Contortionists. That gave me some pause. By that reading you may be setting me up to write a book about your secret favorite, Ella Wheeler Wilcox. If this is true, I'd hate to disappoint you but there are so many deep lines in Ella I just don't understand.

I think you and Eliade are right about the planets and the circles of [illegible]. I'll write that in my "corrections copy." God knows if there'll ever be a second printing, but I can fix things in the foreign editions. Good old Peter Owen who did *Spirits of Romance* years ago when Faber wouldn't be bothered will do me if a 2% royalty is OK. Fine. I want to get mine out to counteract Humphrey Carpenter's negativism. (I read his first draft.) Humphrey just doesn't *like* Ez. Little ridiculing jabs at him all the time. Faber is stuck with HC because they gave him such a big advance.

In Paris the agent reports that Flammarion and Bourgois are at each other to do the true pitch. Hauser has rejected in Münich but there are good small firms. No action yet in Ichaly or Spain.

Duncan's death was "for the best"—to coin a phrase. The last year has been hell for him and he could no longer write or enjoy anything. One complication piling on another. (Did Laurie send you volume II of *Groundwork*? Please let me know.) I think I only understand about 15% of Robert but I get a great feeling of "mind music" and beautiful sounds from him. And I venerate him for what he stood for. When I heard, I replayed the tapes of his monologue I made once when he was visiting here. Marvelous! Rich and strange surmises flying in all directions.

I'm chagrined that you laid out good Kentucky money for a batch of ND books. Anything you'd like, new or old, you must ask for, without limitation. Laurie's last name is Callahan. Really.

I've given up Our Brave Lads for lost. But, in a small way, they'll live on. *Yale Review* is going to print "Our Bikes" and it will also be in the next "anomalous" edition, ΚΟΛΛΗΜΑΤΑ, and the next regular book *The Bird of Endless Time.* (Is that too corny a title? It's right from the poem which is a real sweet love-stuff poem, I think.)

I'll spare you the dithyrambs of the present infatuation. Suffice it to speak of an onion [*sic*] made in heaven, two neuraesthetes in schmaltz time. She knows some of my verses *by heart,* so lovely in her soft, deep, slow voice, ones she learned before we ever met. Like that.

"The Inn at Kuchsteten" is her momentary favorite. If you believe, as I do, that the irreal can become the real, then that poem did happen, just like it says, though Trakl in the Stefansplatz is decoration. . . .

Next week to chat about Those Classix for Gary S. at Davis and Marjorie P. at Stanford. I hate the travel.

As ever,
JAZ.

/ • /

Ella Wheeler Wilcox: (1850–1919), sentimental poet and mystic Rosicrucian.
Humphrey Carpenter's negativism: Carpenter's biography of Pound, *A Serious Character,* was published in 1988.
ΚΟΛΛΗΜΑΤΑ*:* See also GD's letter following.
"The Inn at Kuchsteten": See *PNS,* 120–22. To this poem, JL appends a note claiming that it comprised short love sentiments found written in the margins of a volume of the German poet Georg Trakl.
Gary S. . . . Marjorie P.: Gary Snyder (1930–), American poet, essayist, and ecological activist, and Marjorie Perloff.

41. TLS—1

24 February 1988

DEAR MR LAUGHLIN:

You seem to read your mail standing up in the village post office, and to recount the event as if it were a Norman Rockwell painting.

Please don't write a book about Ella Wheeler Wilcox.

I'm discouraged to hear that Carpenter has not done well by Ez. I think we've entered the Intellectual Ice Age, and that EP belonged to an older culture of which there are only a few remnants left. Hugh tried to indicate this when he began *The Pound Era* with James. We have to put up with jackals who come down with the cold, new Flat Earthers who have no way of *feeling* the world Pound lived in.

In fact, nobody under 50 knows anything any more. I gave a lecture at Transylvania yesterday, on Revolutions and Evolution (the set topic) and talked about *Erewhon* and the history of Denmark. I could tell they were not getting it, at all, at all.

Didn't know there *was* a second volume to *Groundwork.*

Good title, "The Birds of Endless Time." And a good poem. *kollēmata,* "collages"? Or "glued together" as by Eros? Lordy, but you're as incurably susceptible to a well-turned ankle as my protégé John Allen, the lifeguard at the Y (and student of French). He outdid himself the other day by raving about an 18-year-old he'd just met, the raving being over the phone, but between then and his coming over for supper, about an hour later, he announced that he'd met a total stranger, "really neat," on the way here, and with whom he's moving in. We asked her name. He'd forgotten to ask.

Middle age is a second adolescence.

. . . I'm still with Parkman, where Versailles is in the reckoning. Louis XIV thought that if the Jesuits could get the Algonquins into knee-britches, civilization would follow.

Did any of the snapshots you took come out well? I remember one where I was sitting at your knees. I'd love to see that one.

ad interim,
GUY

/ • /

Hugh: Hugh Kenner's *The Pound Era* begins with an evocation of Henry James and his niece Margaret (William James's daughter) encountering Ezra and Dorothy Pound on a London sidewalk.

Transylvania: A university in Lexington not far from GD's home.

Erewhon: A utopian novel by novelist, painter, and scholar Samuel Butler (1835–1902). GD referred directly to Butler's novel in a number of places, including the long story "The Dawn in Erewhon" in his first collection, *Tatlin!* "Erewhon" is, of course, "nowhere" reversed.

42. ALS—2

4/12/89

DEAR GUY—

. . . [You] can see from the newspaper report that things were a bit scary here at one point. Much praise is due to the heroic volunteer firemen who contained the blaze to the living room. Ann lost the Magritte *Mental Calculus* she inherited from her mother's collection, and I lost my whole classical library. But the south wing with its underground vaults was untouched so the archive is safe. And Penny Fitzgerald wants to give us Robert's classical books, many of which have his marginalia. Now the house is swarming with (Brazilian) cleaners who sing Portuguese songs as they clean away the smoke streaks, and the painters. The carpenters will come when the cleaning work is finished. We are living across the road in my aunt's old house, where I lived for 15 years. (We sold it to a swish interior designer.)

The fire has been very hard on Ann, who is holding her own against myeloma with magic pills from the U. Conn. Doctors. But it has not thrown me into more gloom. To the contrary, having something important to attend to, has rather invigorated me from my melancholia. This phenomenon is recorded in the poor verse on the subject. I feel the stirrings of composition coming back though not yet much visible product of the rising mood. (The poem from *Poetry* was written nearly a year ago.) I'm pulling things out of the drawer and these are to be a collection of *Random Essays,* a book of early stories, and a selection of the WCW/JL correspondence later this year. I hope the old zips for collage and coy humor will return in due time.

Very best,
JAS

/ • /

a bit scary here: JL's careless smoking caused a fire in his home which destroyed many of his books.
myeloma: small, malignant tumors which begin in the blood-producing cells of the bone marrow and spread throughout the body.
poor verse on the subject: This has not been identified.

43. TLS—2

15 April 1989
Leonardo da Vinci
Henry James Jr
Robert Walser

DEAR MR LAUGHLIN:

Great God! And at the mercy of a volunteer fire brigade, at that. Naturally, you write a poem about it. I grieve for your books and the Magritte, but I rejoice that you and Ann came through unscathed. I hope you accept the Fitzgerald library: you deserve it, and it deserves you.

And none of this has even slowed you down.

I'm not going to fill the page with commiserations. I've had the firetrucks here, too: for an overloaded wire that burned in two (I needed to know if the house were on fire). And the plumber: for an ancient pipe which began to leak, ruining a ceiling (repaired, the ceiling, by the last plasterer in Fayette County).

Back in January, a boy (23) who went bonkers reading my ravings turned up in Lexington and said he had to live with me. I said he didn't. He persisted, signing up for Greek and Latin at the university. After a dozen eloquent pleas, Bonnie Jean said, "Oh, what the heck: let him." So he's installed in the guest room. Runs errands, scrubs the bathroom, cooks, types. He's from a well-to-do family up your way, and has a BA in physics and math. He speaks German fluently, and French, Danish, & Dutch. He has taken to the classics like a duck to water, and makes 100 on all quizzes. He'll go to Harvard (PhD in linguistics when and if he tears himself away from here). This sounds awful, but is innocent. . . . Tonto (as BJ calls him) moved in simply to be in the same house as the writer of my scribbles (who, he has discovered, isn't me).

I've asked Jack to put a clause in my contracts saying that readers may not move in with the author.

Otherwise, I've finished my book on Balthus (Ecco) and another on Paul Cadmus (Rizzoli) and am revising the still-life book (Toronto). I've done an intro to Cornell's new edition of Joyce's critical writing, and an essay on St. Paul (for Penguin), and am way behind with reviewing chores. . . .

BJ and I are heading for the *rue Chateaubriand* as soon as school's out; we haven't seen the Picasso Museum, or the annex to the *Louvre*. Our Danish hotelier was expecting us back again, and will be put out that we're patronizing the French. "The French, you know," hr. Hovedman told us, "have their trains down in the sewers."

Robert Bringhurst—Canada's best poet, by my reckoning—announces his marriage to one Charlotte, in Nepal, by some ineffably holy medicine man; and, for good measure, again in Vancouver, by a shaman of the Tlinkit. Poets.

Marc Chénetier has just sent me his *Au-delà du soupçon: la nouvelle fiction américaine de 1960 à nos jours* (Seuil), in which my ravings are discussed, and in which I find, and pass on: *"S'il ya toujours existé éditeurs comme James Laughlin, Ted Solotaroff ou Jonathan Williams pour faire confiance à des jeunes écrivains d'accès difficile, l'évolution de la politique des grandes maisons d'édition ne leur a en rien été favorable."* What grammar!

Who's Solotaroff?

I hope Ann fares well, and that you'll soon be back in your house. John Quinn, I remember, *sold* his library, for the fun of beginning over.

Last week I was sent a technical manuscript to referee for a geographical journal. I kept my mouth shut about not being a geographer, corrected some howlers ("Ortega Y. Gasset" being the best), suggested that the author read Ullman on verticalities, and made other suggestions for improvement. But I recommended publication, so there's no harm done.

How brave you're being about the fire. I wish it hadn't happened.

Bonnie Jean says to give you and Ann her best wishes.

mazel tov,
GUY

/ • /

I've asked Jack: Jack Shoemaker was GD's friend and publisher at North Point, Counterpoint, and Shoemaker & Hoard.

Who's Solotaroff?: Ted Solotaroff (1928–), essayist and editor. The French critic was most likely commending his work as editor of the *New American Review* (later the *American Review*), a mass-market paperback format magazine that published twenty-six issues between 1967 and 1977, and included dozens of important writers, mainstream and experimental.

John Quinn: an important American collector of the early Modernists. GD included his portrait in a painting he did of Ford, Joyce, and Pound. See Erik Anderson Reece's *A Balance of Quinces,* color plate 9.

44. TLS—2

7/30/89

DEAR GUY—

I've just read a book that is really NEAT. You'd like it. It's about some oddball painter named Balthus and a lot of other things. This painter sounds sort of sordid but the ideas the author of the book got from looking at the pictures are really TERRIFIC, all sorts of egghead things I never thought about before. I know you like cats. There's quite a bit about this painter's cats which is very sharp. You'd otta trot over to the library and get the book.

THANK you for having Ecco send me the book. It really lifted my spirits, watching the dance of the intellect. (I'm entitled to use that phrase because it was I who gave it to Marjorie Perloff for her book, not, to be sure, that she gave me a credit line, but a friend is a friend especially when in need.)

Ecco asked for comment and I sent them some wordage, but I'm afraid it was just that, too many large words of imprecise meaning.

I used to own a Balthus. I was in Skira's office in Paris one day and he had it on the wall. It pushed all the other paintings into a corner. I talked him into selling it to me. I had it in my office for some years but it caused too much fuss. Many people got upset over looking at it and some even moved their chairs so they wouldn't have to look at it. So finally I put it to auction and got a *nice* painting to replace it, one of my cousin Marjorie Phillips's landscapes. It was a picture of a young girl with no clothes on lying on a couch with her legs apart. "Virginity and Desire." This girl, whose skin was greenish (and the couch and wall were in tones of grey) was daydreaming. She had a petulant, fatigued, indolent expression which left little doubt what she had been doing or was about to do. I miss her. I had gotten very fond of her and she didn't upset me at all.

I have pulled *Mitsou* out of my set of Colette (beautifully bound by a gloomy old man in the rue St Dominique). I've never read that one. It sounds good and will be good for my fading French.

I haven't yet started replacing my classical books that burned up because the carpenters haven't yet finished the new shelves in the living room, but when I do I'll look up Peitho and find out about the "inflaming" red ball of Eros. Fitts never told me about that. Perhaps not suitable even for sixth formers. It's the kind of tidbit that always excites me and there may well be a poem in it for me if I can get at the facts.

It's curious what stimulates a poem. Ann points out that I have never written much about nature, though shadows are useful in love poems, and snow in its various forms (including avalanches and glaciers) have come in handy. What startles me today is what came out of three words at the bottom of your page 72. How did that happen? I guess it can be explained by the great melancholy here in the home. Ann's myeloma has become active again and she can hardly walk or be comfortable in any position in bed. When it was first diagnosed a year ago she was very optimistic. Some people can get it into remission with "chemo." But we fear she is not one of them. She is still very brave and uncomplaining, but not optimistic. I am the gloomy one as you can see from both poems.

But not much is coming out of Donderbeck's machine these days. My muse sends me postcards of dead birds from Valdez where she is making fistfuls of green helping Exxon clean up their mess. She says there is a lot of drinking.

It's hard to find one's niche. Uncle Charlie Simic, whose work I revere, says that I have a "devastating simplicity," but Carey Perloff, Marjorie's daughter, whom I also revere for her wonderful production of Ez's *Elektra,* says that she laughed all the way home from DC reading *The Endless Bird.* So it goes. I think there's also something for me in Balthus's liking to paint people's backs, but it hasn't quite come to me yet.

You're so right about Nabokov. He had beautiful manners but his blood was icy. One day that summer when he was staying with me in the mountains of Utah he came in for dinner and told me that he had heard what sounded like groaning in Grizzly Gulch. What was it? He hadn't gone to investigate because he was chasing a lepidopteroid he had never seen before. Next day some hikers found the body of an old prospector who had fallen in the steep gulch and cracked open his head and bled to death.

I hope you and BJ had a fine time in Paris. I can't see myself going anywhere for a while and I hope the while will be considerable as long as it doesn't mean bad pain for her.

Does Robert Bringhurst write the kind of poetry "our editors" would like? I've been so distracted I haven't paid much attention to what they are doing down there. It's always embarrassing to invite someone for the *Annual* and then have him not liked. But do let me know his address and I'll risk it. I've annoyed so many people, a few more won't hurt me, though I do in principle hate to hurt them, which is why over the years I haven't written most of them that they would do better selling real estate.

While I was still circulating in New Babylon I used to cross paths with Ted Solotaroff now and then. He seemed to be bright and in favor of literature. I'm pretty sure it was he who edited the paper *New American Writing* and is now an editor at Harper & Row. I believe he is a fairly big wheel in the P.E.N.

Very best as ever,
JL

/ • /

I've just read a book: GD's *A Balthus Notebook* was sent to JL in galleys. He contributed a blurb which was printed on the back of the jacket. Balthus (1908–2001), whose real name was Balthazar Klossowski de Rola, was a French painter who painted a number of subjects, but is best known for his controversial paintings of adolescent or prepubescent girls in sexually suggestive situations.
I have pulled Mitsou: GD quotes from this work on page 11 of *BN.* Colette was the pen name of Sidonie Gabrielle Claudine Colette (1873–1954). Colette was a French journalist and critic, but primarily a novelist. A number of her works detail the sensuality and relationships of young girls, often with underlying tones of sexual domination. She was a great celebrity in France, and virtually the entire nation mourned her death.
Peitho and find out: See *BN,* 42.
Uncle Charlie Simic: Poet Charles Simic.

45. TLS—2

5 August 1989

DEAR MR LAUGHLIN:

When the essay "Balthus" came out in *Antaeus* (it's also in *Every Force*), Count Balthazar Klossowski de Rola (as he fancies himself, unless he's now Kronprinz of Polska) sent word that the writer of it was to be congratulated. *"Encouragez cet jeune homme."*

You're kindness itself to have gone to the trouble of writing a blurb. I wish I'd known you once owned a Balthus. I would have put that in.

Your adventures with it sound like the Earl of Rokeby and Velázquez's nude Venus, which he hung up near the ceiling, to spare ladies and the clergy. Sir Walter Scott said he always got a crick in his neck at the Earl's. (It was Rokeby who, when Sir Walter was showing off the waterfall in his rock garden at Abbotsford, said, "Begging the ladies' pardon, but I can make a more respectable waterfall than that from my own person.")

Part of the reason I did the Balthus was the rotten reception his work got at the latest showing in NYC. Hilton Kramer and his pack of puritans all sniffed, seeing kiddy porn, and lots their pea brains couldn't understand. Some jerk in *Vanity Fair* found scumbling, and made it sound like low mumpery.

Peitho is in Sappho and Anakreon. Eros's sister. . . .

I forget what I said about Nabokov. I think the old prospector was lucky to be desamaritanized by him.

Whether your editors would like Bringhurst I don't know. He's a first rate poet, and like none other. (He can recite Greek with the pitches in place—sounds like an Amazonian bird.) His address is. . . .

13 Aug This letter got bumped from the typewriter by some nuisance. Fatal to continuity. . . .

Did I thank you for the hardback *Bird of Endless Time*? Inscribed. Surely. I keep a stack of books to be acknowledged, and somehow it's still in it, even though I'm pretty certain I had manners enough to thank you.

What a spate of deaths. First there was David Orr, my philosopher friend (and rich—rare combination); and then Donald Barthelme; Jacques Marsal; and now Bob Kaske.

Bob (Cornell) was *the* medievalist among us. He was old-fashioned in his scholarship, breath-takingly meticulous, and a man for whom the footnote was an art form. I knew him in St Louis (those remote days when I could have WCW read poems to a sophomore class).

Marsal (about whom my story "Robot") discovered Lascaux in 1940. I had a long conversation with him in 64, just when they closed the cave because of micro-organisms between the sinder [*sic*] and the paint. I met Barthelme but once, too.

The dean of the College of Architecture read in a book that I paint, and has commanded me to have a show in September. So at 62 I have my only show. I've been repainting, and brightening colors, and framing. I could be the world's greatest painter and Kentucky wouldn't know it. My colleagues are mystified by reports that I am a writer, and once, years ago, the mathematician Kac grossed out the vice-chancellor by asking on a visit here if he could be brought over to my house. Vice-chancellors you understand do *not* even know where members of the English department live. But Kac was a Somebody, and there was nothing for it but to bring him over.

My hot-pepper garden thrives, but the tomatoes are shy.

be well,
GUY

/ • /

"Encouragez cet jeune homme": "This young man should be encouraged." What amused GD about this was that he was nearly sixty when he wrote it.

Hilton Kramer: New York Times art critic, who, as Calvin Tomkins once put it, "managed to take most advanced art as a personal affront."

Donald Barthelme: (1931–1989), author of several enormously influential story collections, including *Unspeakable Practices, Unnatural Acts,* and several novels, including *The Dead Father.* GD credited Barthelme's collagelike style (which he likened to Max Ernst's collage novels) with inspiring some of his own fictional techniques.

46. TCS—1

[ca. December 1989]

Dear Mr Laughlin:

I have thought about you a lot this year's end, and about Ann. I wish I were a closer friend, so that my sympathy would not be an intrusion from outside. Perhaps it isn't.

Random Essays arrived today, and I've been reading them by the fire (this is Kentucky's coldest winter since 1901). These pieces are as bright and warm as the fire (afghan over knees included + Flix the cat). I learn from every page. For candor, sincerity, graciousness, and wit there's nobody else who can write like this. You are our uncorrupted and incorruptible witness to an age. I still have the Saroyan to read, and the Romain Gary—one mustn't read up so good a book all at once.

The end of the Cold War (if that's what it is) has me looking at TV, something I otherwise don't do. And how do we Americans get some *glasnost* and *perestroika*?

with best wishes for the New Year,
Guy

/ • /

about Ann: JL's wife had recently died.
glasnost and perestroika: Russian for "openness" and "economic reform." In November of 1989 the Berlin Wall was torn down, and the Cold War effectively ended in 1991 when the Soviet Union dissolved itself.

47. ALS—1

1/5/90

Dear Guy—

Your liking the essays has raised me from the floor of despair. Ann's death, though we saw it coming, was a blow, nearly a knockout, certainly a knock down, as you can see from the verses enclosed.

I suppose I'll regain equanimity but I don't think it will be very soon. I've not been able to concentrate on anything [word illegible] not like what I was.

Bless you!
JL

/ • /

the verses enclosed: See "The Empty Room," *PNS,* 231.

***48.* TLS—1**

18 March 1990
The birthday of Stéphane Mallarmé, cynologist
+ Lawrence Sterne, digressor

DEAR MR LAUGHLIN:

I thought for sure I'd answered yours of January, but here it is in a logjam of letters, and I stand disgraced and guilty of mumpery, dilatoriness, and irresponsibility. Then again, I probably put the letter at the back out of a feeling that a friendly silence was the only answer. Bonnie Jean says that there are people who "try to steal grief," and I don't want to figure in their number.

Your poem is eloquent. That it got written is an awesome measure of courage and faith.

I've spent spring break (the past week) working on a 9 × 5 ft painting, the largest I've ever attempted. The illusion of being a painter is exhilarating. I don't mind that I can't actually paint, any more than as a child I didn't mind that my red wagon wasn't a real locomotive, or that a cardboard box fitted out with dials and levers wasn't an interplanetary radio.

I've been reading a manuscript for Yale, by Jennifer Bloomer, who deconstructs Piranesi and Finnegans Wake, all in the service of architecture from the postmodern feminist point of view. Surprisingly, it makes good sense in a crazy poetical sort of way. It turns out (this from another book I've been reading) that Mies van der Rohe was under the impression that he was the keen disciple of T. Aquinas and Spengler in all his buildings. So you never know what people think they're doing.

Yesterday I decided to quit reading the newspaper—the Lexington one, and all the others. What, ultimately, has all that nastiness and small-mindedness to do with me? Everything, of course; but why start every day with the sins and accidents of the world with one's breakfast? I'll miss Calvin and Hobbes.

I am, along with all your friends, anxious about you, while feeling perfectly helpless to make the kindness and love we feel of any use to you.

with every best wish,
GUY

/ • /

manuscript for Yale: Jennifer Bloomer's *Architecture and the Text: The (S)crypts of Joyce and Piranesi* was published by Yale University Press in 1993.
Mies van der Rohe: (1886–1969), German-American architect. He originated the idea of "less is more" for architecture. He led the way into the glass and steel architecture known as the "International style." The influence of Oswald Spengler, author of *The Decline of the West (1918–23),* on Mies was most likely by way of his idea that cultures possess unique souls, and that they all go through a cycle of growth and decline.

49. TLS—1

3 October 1990
Thomas Wolfe
Henri Alain-Fournier
(Wolfe's brother was manager of Dixon's
Blue Bird Ice Cream in Anderson SC
when I was a child, and his sister lived
on the corner of Franklin and Main,
two blocks from our house, at a nice
place called Seven Oaks, now replaced
by Bubba Shiflett's Used Car lot)

DEAR MR LAUGHLIN:

Do you really share a birthday with EP, between Boswell (29 Oct) and Keats (the 31st)? Calvinist and rationalist that I am, I still feel there's something to synchronicities. October 15, for instance, gives us Nietzsche, Wilde, and Virgil, each of whom was blurred as to gender, each out of his time—Nietzsche would be a success now on the boulevard St-Germain; Wilde was a displaced wit from the court of Charles I, and Virgil should have been a contemporary of Sophokles.

When depression has a cause, it is not depression but reaction.

Oh yes, this million-dollar-a-day ball-rattling in Saudi Arabia is for gas in Michelle's and Tanya's new car Daddy bought them to drive from the sorority house to the liquor store.

I'm trying to decide whether to retire early, or keep plodding in the traces. Teaching is my stabilizer. I am essentially, I think, a person who loves routine and purpose; but I also like subverting duty by sneaking in my own work. Macaulay wrote his history while holding down a seat in parliament, with all its committee work. "And yes," says Bonnie Jean, "they had servants." She's probably right.

with every best wish,
GUY

[added in holograph:] Hugh Kenner has moved to the University of Georgia, did you know?

/ • /

for gas in Michelle's: This was the approach of the "first Gulf War." GD felt that the "automobile is an insect that eats cities," and he never owned one. He only drove one once: see letter #111.

Macaulay wrote his history: Thomas Macaulay (1800–1859) wrote a five-volume *History of England.*

50. ALS—1

11/30/90

Dear Guy—

Yes, Ezra and I share a birthday. Is that why I share his old age abulia and [anhedonia]? It's been somewhat diminished of late, but it's still a problem. Along about midnight I begin to feel positively human and a lot of inferior poems have been coming through. Better than none.

Seriously, since I'm not one of your students I hope that you find a way to be a full-time writer. The *Drummer* is *so* good. I'll spare you my trite adjectives and just say that you are unique and a cultural monument.

As to your future, I was saddened to see this clip about North Point in the *Times*. They've done such wonderful and important books. I'm sure you realize that there would be great jubilation if you decided to sign on with New Directions. I think we are a fine little operation, and Norton's distribution is excellent.

I'll be sending you my story-book, very flat stuff compared to yours, all written actually some fifty years ago before I abandoned fiction. I couldn't think up plots.

Georgia has made Kenner silent. I hope he's all right.

Best as ever,
JL

/ • /

anhedonia: This word is nearly illegible. If "anhedonia," it would mean finding nothing to be pleasurable.
clip about North Point: This was an article noting that GD's longtime publisher North Point would cease issuing new titles—in effect, going out of business.
Drummer: GD's *The Drummer of the Eleventh North Devonshire Fuisiliers,* his final book from North Point.
my story-book: Random Stories.

51. TLS—1

4 December 1990
Samuel Butler II

DEAR MR LAUGHLIN:

My instinct, of course, is to drop everything and work on a book that New Directions might accept. You are kindness itself to open the door and invite me in. I've been in the dumps since Jack called last week and said that North Point is folding. Eight books I have there, and whether I'll ever see another royalty from them is a pretty question. I imagine Bill Turnbull will dump all the stock on the remainder counters.

Thanks heaps for reading *The Drummer;* it's honor enough to have you for a reader. I don't read reviews, so I don't know what kind of reception it has. None, probably.

And you have a book of stories coming out? Wow.

I haven't heard from Hugh, either. He disapproves (I think) of my fiction. . . .

I remember Olga saying that Ez came out of his silent snit at nights, and read to her. Sartre, *Les mots,* at the time. I remarked that its prose was very flaubertian, and got glared at.

Did I say I've done a preface for a book of Gene Meatyard's photographs of Thomas Merton? And I've just reviewed the third volume of the letters. Lord, what crap Tom had to put up with from ecclesiastical red tape!

I teach my last class this Friday. The university wants to keep me on, as Scholar in Residence. The Chancellor took Bonnie Jean to lunch today, to try to get at me through her, but she took the occasion to get money out of him for Woman's Studies (of which she's the head).

φιλως,
GUY

/ • /

Bill Turnbull: Jack Shoemaker's partner in North Point.
φιλως*:* Approximately, "With kisses to you."

52. ALS—1

14 XII 1990

DEAR MR LAUGHLIN:

I've so far read "Melody with Fugue," "What the Butler Heard," and most of "The River" (interrupted by a student). These are masterful stories. If I were a real scholar, I would have known them before. I envy the technique of the first story: its ability to keep so many things moving. Written in 1934! And so damned contemporary. I began with the Cambridge butler's story, as that's where the book fell open, and I was anxious to see how you write fiction. It is a Henry James story by Gertrude Stein.

What I admire is the authority of your art. No fumble, no dither, but clean transparent moving narrative and all in language as fresh as lettuce and radishes.

I would have read it all by now except that I've been grading exams and reading long termpapers from the seminar, *and* going through all the red tape of retiring, the finances and whichwhat.

Your two letters—the one offering to take me on as a New Directions author and the one offering to buy all my unsold stuff from North Point—have had me walking on air since they arrived.

I called Jack Shoemaker about the latter. Alas, he says that the books belong to Bill Turnbull, who proposes to distribute them via Farrar Straus. In any case, it is a matter between you and Turnbull in which I have no say. (And apparently Bill's health, an undiagnosed illness, was a big factor in closing down North Point.)

From Hugh I've heard nothing. We used to be the best of friends.

I have the evening open for reading all your stories. Meanwhile, I want to get this off to thank you for the most generous offers of the century.

in unseemly haste, and with more to come,
GUY

53. TLS—1

12/18/90

DEAR GUY—

Uncle Henry and Gertrude were secretly married. Edith Wharton put up a terrible row about it. I thought I was the only one who knew about it. So smart of you to figure it out.

I think you are heautontimorumenonic if you can wade through those juvenile stories. I wrote them at Harvard or slightly later. I gave up stories because I could never think of any plots. I bought a book called *100 Masterplots* but none of them seemed to fit. . . .

Very best,
JL

/ • /

heautontimorumenonic: "Masochistic." *Heautontimorumenos* ("The Masochist") was the title of a lost play by Meander. GD may have misremembered it as being by Aristophanes.

54. TLS—2

22 XII 1990

Dear Mr Laughlin:

Izzat your coinage, or Aristophanes', heautontimorumenonic? Golly. The stories are interesting for many reasons: they're good, they're yours, they are soaked in their period. It's their *feeling* (not like anybody else's) that gives them great readability. What you have over E. Hemingway is a sense of humor. He had none at all.

Jack Shoemaker says he doesn't think Bill will part with the books; we'll see. Meanwhile, your gesture beats all other generosities of the century hands down.

Cathy Henderson has just sent me a pebble from Kafka's grave. Joan Crane once sent me a sweetgum leaf that Walt Whitman had pressed in his bible. Secular *pigges bones.*

Xmas cards are indexes to the past. For 35 years I've had no communication from one Mary Ellen Beatty, and now she turns up with a card (saw my name in the paper). Nice girl, but my vividest memory is of dining with her family one evening. Suddenly a sheriff, with star on his shirt, was in the room. He removed Mary Ellen's younger brother by the ear, out to a police car. This incident was not remarked on by anybody, though the mother did shrug her shoulders and sigh. A William Saroyan story, I should think.

I will think twice about writing again for the Museum of Modern Art. I was at first pleased that they gave my intro to their *Art of the 1940s* book such scrupulous copy-editing. When a second, and third, and fourth, copy-editor went through it, nit-picking and double checking, I began to get tired of it all. Then Saturday all alarms went off when William Rubin, Curator Emeritus, looked at it for the first time (in blues). He demanded to know how I dared say that Klee is a narrative painter, and that Matisse is not.

Also, my anecdote about Brancusi, where did I copy it from? (I didn't: it comes from a friend of B's, who told it to me.) And why hadn't I mentioned Masson? And who am I to be writing about art at all?

New York is the most provincial place I've ever heard of.

The real trouble was that they didn't ask Rubin before they commissioned my introduction.

His main concern seems to be that Hilton Kramer will be displeased and give them a bad review. I said that I rarely, if ever, thought about Hilton Kramer at all.

All these people are probably your dearest friends; if so, I beg indulgence.

My prose is vastly improved in its French translation.

Masson, above. I suggested that my essay be made to end with, "And, in addition, I'd like to mention Masson."

In imitation of the little Niels Bohr's grammar-school homework so ending. He had asked his daddy (Prof, Univ Copenhagen) to look over his report on the chemical elements. His father said he'd left out hydrogen. Whereupon little Niels added, "And, in addition, I'd like to mention hydrogen."

greetings of the season,
GUY

/ • /

E. Hemingway: Ernest Hemingway. Not a Davenport favorite.

a sweetgum leaf: Coincidentally, after GD's death the tree that was dedicated to him at the University of Kentucky Arboretum was a sweet gum tree.

pigges bones: Chaucer's name for questionable holy relics.

Art of the 1940s book: Art of the Forties (1991).

(in blues): blues are the final proofs of a book that is being printed by photo offset. At this point the book is supposed to be completely ready to be printed.

Masson: André Masson (1896–1987), French Surrealist painter, some of whose work is in the MoMA collection.

Niels Bohr: (1885–1962), Danish physicist who helped develop the atomic bomb after fleeing the German occupation of Denmark in 1940. After the bomb was dropped Bohr was one of the most insistent voices for international control of atomic weapons.

55. ALS—2

3/27/91

Dear Guy—

I'm sorry not to have written for so long. I have been in the slough of abulia. But the spring should pick me up a bit. I hope so.

I was *very* disappointed that the North Point weren't interested in my proposal. But I understand. You are the jewel in their crown and they wouldn't want to part with you. And not knowing how ill he was, I had written in a rather light tone.

I hope you will write something you will want to send to ND, whatever it may be. The door is wide open for you. And I can reassure you that whatever happens to me, ND is in good shape to have a future. The business makes money, it has an excellent staff, and my will sets up a trust to carry things on as long as it does a good job and maintains high standards.

The war is still depressing. All that starvation and slaughter in Iraq. And George is planning to set up a branch of the Pentagon in Bahrein. (This was in the *Times.*)

Best as ever,
JL

56. TLS—1

14 April 1991

Dear Mr Laughlin—

We're back. I got your last letter just as we were setting out for Paris, and dashed off a reply. Your poems (except the Catullus) are on the philosophical and thoughty side. As for our Arabian caper, it's a war we lost. Saddam trashed Kuwait (a nasty little tyranny in any case). There were no battles. We merely harassed the rearguard of a retreating army. And look what hideous misery we caused.

Christian Bourgois would seem to be the French New Directions *cum* the old Grove Press. We were scarcely off the plane before he took us to the *Restaurant de Paris* for a three-hour meal. There was a reception at the US Embassy, and a day-long symposium and speeches at the Museum of Modern Art on the avenue Wilson. Some species of actor read from my stuff. The *Prix Coindreau* went to Pierre Gault for his translation of Annie Dillard's *The Pilgrim from Tinker Creek.*

Nice person, Gault. He's directing Laurence Zachar's thesis on my ravings (at Tours, or as Bonnie Jean likes to say, Rabelais U.). Laurence came up; we had two dinners with her.

We got away enough for some favorite walks and to see the Camille Claudel show and a reconstruction of Colette's rooms.

I met scads of people: Ivan Nabokov (nephew, or cousin), Grasset, my translators (a nice bunch), Alex Theroux (who instructed us that his elder brother is merely a journalist). I had on the only ironed shirt at the symposium. Brice Mathieussent seemed to be properly dressed, though on inspection his shirt read *Buvez Pepsi-Cola* on the pocket. I was interested in this shindig's being French/American—not a Brit in sight.

Especially brilliant spring here (but wet). If you take the *T*[*imes*] *L*[*iterary*] *S*[*upplement*], cast an eye over the lead review this week (about Alexandre Kojève), who seems to be the evil genius that gave us the French Left and its literary Frankensteinen.

χαίρετε!
GUY

/ • /

Your poems: JL had enclosed four unpublished poems: "Catullus XLVIII," "Creatures of Prometheus," "Knowledge," and "The Prisoner."

the French New Directions: This publisher was issuing French translations of *Tatlin!* and *Da Vinci's Bicycle.*

Camille Claudel: (1864–1943), French sculptor and protégée of Rodin. Psychiatric problems marred the last thirty years of her life.

Alex Theroux: Author of such brilliant, word-drunk fictions as *Three Wogs* and *Darconville's Cat.* His elder brother is Paul Theroux.

Alexandre Kojève: Born Alexandr Vladimirovitch Kojenikov in Moscow in 1902, he immigrated to Paris in 1928 and changed his name. His reading of Hegel's *Phenomenology of Spirit* influenced a great number of philosophers, including Georges Bataille, Roger Caillois, and Maurice Merleau-Ponty.

57. TLS—1

9/28/91

DEAR GUY—

I'm sorry not to have written for so long. I've fallen back into the Slough of Despond—abulia and anhedonia, as Ezra in the sad last years. My shrink has been trying Prozac but it might as well be marshmallows for all the good it does me.

One thing I have been keeping at is to select the poems for a *Collected* that Moyer Bell wants to do. Much must be cut from the accumulation. There are too many facile and redundant poems, especially among the love poems. And too many snobbish "language & literary" poems.

But, since you have been so indulgent about my verse, I thought you might like a copy of this letter to Hayden Carruth whom MB thinks they would like to have do the introduction.

As ever,
JL

/ • /

Hayden Carruth: Poet and editor who had known JL since his *Perspectives* days.

58. TLS—1

3 October 91
Thomas Clayton Wolfe

DEAR MR LAUGHLIN:

. . . [The] Prozac don't cut the mustard anymore? Damn. Depression is the No. 1 ailment in the USA. My mother always said "being blue." One blithering hitch is that we think we're going to feel blue the rest of our lives. Depression feigns normality, whatever normality might be.

I wonder if your poems need an introduction?

I like to think that if I were the founder of New Directions I could not with any fairness think otherwise than I *have* raised the level of literature. *Mon Dieu!* Look at North Point—12 years and ker-flop! Simply to have published *Nightwood,* the *Cantos,* and *Paterson,* never mind all the rest *[. . .]*

I'm up early, waiting for the house-painters, who probably won't come at all. The tattoo'd Bryan (a purple and red dragon around his torso) and the vague Wayne, no last name ever forthcoming. They seem to share a wife, who's the sister of one of them; the anthropology of Kentucky is something the professors of the science know nothing about. They lecture on the Trobriand Islanders while imagining that Kentucky can be accounted for with a Marxist phrase or two.

(Belinda the cat has come to help me type.)

We were going to dinner tonight with Carlos Fuentes, but that *hidalgo* sends word that he's cancelled his jaunt to Lexington. Monday I had the Minister of Culture of Uruguay here. He is touring North America to interview writers about their working habits. He passed over a photo of himself, much younger, leading the blind Borges. Borges once changed an adjective in one of his stories. His Spanish was sibilant and mushy. He had just been with Jone Barr at Zhon Opkeenz, *un hombre muy simpático.* He had not read a word of my ravings, and the mystery is, why was he here? We got along fine, however. He insisted on being photographed with me, taken by Ed Stanton (Eduardo Estanton), who also got us out of linguistic quagmires from time to time.

I'm in the midst of repainting all the woodwork in the house. Talk about tedious! Washing the brush in turps after each go is one of the world's great bores. There is a mean little devil whose sole duty is to make paint drip.

every best wish,
GUY

/ • /

Carlos Fuentes: (1928–), Mexican novelist, author of *Christopher Unborn*, among many other books.
Borges: Jorge Luis Borges (1899–1986), Argentinean master of the labyrinthine short story.
Jone Barr at Zhon Opkeenz: Most likely novelist John Barth, at Johns Hopkins.

59. TLS—1 [GD to Griselda Ohannessian]

19 January 1992

DEAR MS. OHANNESSIAN:

What about *Da Vinci's Bicycle* instead? I know that it is used in classes, and has been for some years, and a fair number of articles have been published about it. Johns Hopkins has it, but they have let it go out of print (I'm pretty certain). The rights revert to me, as I remember the contract. It was part of an ambitious publishing program that has fallen to pieces. It is the best known of my books. It came out in French last year, and stories from it have been translated into Japanese, Spanish, and Roumanian.

I don't say no to *The Drummer*, but I've taken a fierce dislike to *Apples + Pears*—the book I worked hardest on and which was universally misunderstood.

I'll find out what the status of *Da V's Bike* is at Hopkins and let you know.

I very much appreciate your offer. You're right about the North Point stock.

Sincerely,
GUY DAVENPORT

/ • /

Dear Ms. Ohannessian: Griselda Ohannessian of New Directions wrote JL on December 1, 1991, that Farrar, Straus was offering to sell the remaining stocks of GD's North Point books. She strongly advised against taking them on. When JL responded that her decision put him in an awkward position, she wrote GD herself. In a letter dated January 13, 1992, she explained to GD how the ISBN numbers of the North Point books would not meld with those of New Directions, and even suggested that he might gain more readers through the remainder bookstores than if ND should warehouse them. She then inquired after the possibility of issuing paperback editions of *Apples and Pears* and *The Drummer of the North Eleventh Devonshire Fusiliers,* neither of which had yet been available in that format. ND did reissue *DVB.*

60. TLS—1

7/12/92

DEAR GUY—

Last night I saw you in one of my Delphic dreams. You were on the *terrasse* of the *Deux Magots* with a plausible young lady. I haven't met her so I'll not vouch that it was *Ewige* Bonnie. She looked scholarly but very pretty. You were drinking Pernods. I must warn you about absinthe. It's what Swiss peasants gave their young to make them stop hollering.

Tomorrow we are going to Oireland. My ancestor was born near Portsferry, County Down, in 1804. The annals describe him as an "intelligent and thrifty farmer." I think this means he lived in a hovel and had a potato(e) patch. If I can find his tomb I'll lustrate it with Guinness. Then a few days in London. There is to be a reading with that randy fellow Gavin Ewart. Two dirty-minded boys chaunting together.

I trust my packet of effluvia reached you. I hope it didn't turn over your stomach. *Mylanta* helps when sickening poems must be read. There is no hurry about your piece. I hope you can compare me to Cuchucklain (or however he spelled it) or the Bard of Oisin.

The enclosed are not for your book. They are for the book after that. All epigrams and all about sex. Very Greek.

Best,
JL

/ • /

Ewige: German for "eternal," "or constant."
potato(e): JL is alluding to then Vice President Dan Quayle's famous spelling bee error.
Gavin Ewart: (1916–1995), British poet.
my packet of effluvia: JL sent GD a collection of poems written since the gathering to be used for his forthcoming *Collected Poems,* requesting that GD write an introductory note. GD did write a foreword to *The Man in the Wall.*
Cuchucklain: Properly spelled Cuchulain. He was a legendary ancient Celtic hero who defended Ireland's Gap of the North.

61. TLS—1

6 August 1992

Dear Mr Laughlin:

That was a quick trip to Ireland. The intro's begun and will be up soon. I've been struggling to get my second Penguin O. Henry book finished. And then my very High South Carolina sister and two nieces came up to visit, stopping all work except proofs for the *Yale Review.* The nieces are quite lively, and even literate. My sister doesn't know B from a bull's foot (a phrase of my grandmother Davenport, *geb.* 1862, and I think it must refer to a hornbook: A is for Apple, B for Bull, *kai ta loipa,* and it must mean an incapacity to distinguish the letter of the alphabet from the woodcut). One day the South Carolinas and I had lunch in Versailles (VURR-sales) in a kind of time warp (1935, perhaps), a Chatterbox Café where all the diners were out of Eudora Welty, local gentry I assume. . . .

I've been interested in Antiphilos, whose poems are distributed through the *Anthology,* and reference books (*pontes asinorum*) can't tell me if Antiphilos of Byzantium is the same bloke. He has a remarkable poem about a tree, how leafy and shady it is, not quite as if he were Wordsworth, but an infant step toward.

But I should be writing your intro, and my O. Henry,

in unseemly haste,
GUY

/ • /

my second Penguin O. Henry: GD wrote the introductions to two selections of this author's stories; see *HG,* 192–204.
kai ta loipa: Greek meaning "and so forth."
Antiphilos . . . the Anthology: A poet in the standard *Greek Anthology.*

62. TLS—1

20 August 1992

DEAR MR LAUGHLIN:

I'd forgotten about the emolument, which is very generous for so few words. I took your "it needn't be long" to mean "keep it short." In any case, I'm glad it passes muster, and who reads introductions except the idle and the nosey?

So:

" *[. . .]* didn't publish, until now, is James Laughlin."
("didn't until now publish" sounds Bavarian.)

And: " *[. . .]* Austrian snow *[. . .]*"

The Man in the Wall is to come *after* the Big Collected? You're writing us all under the table. What I admire in your work is the hard-edged, sharp-focus clarity: the classic virtues. A Greek coin; whereas Ashbery is a dust ball from under the bed of a sluttish housekeeper. No, to speak a better truth, what I admire is the *sense.* My mother used to say that somebody had "said a mouthful," meaning the right thing in the right words. . . .

I want to put this in the mail, to acknowledge your approval and the generous check, and the phone just rang: a grad student coming over (I'm retired, but still have to see my doctoral candidates through their theses and defenses). I learned the other day that Søren Kierkegaard's defense-of-thesis (Univ of Copenhagen, on "The Concept of Irony with Continual Reference to Socrates," 600 quill-pen pages) lasted 7½ hours, the most excitement they'd seen since the British bombardment, when the hens wouldn't lay for a week.

ad interim, and gratefully,
GUY

/ • /

Ashbery: John Ashbery (1928–), Pulitzer Prize- and National Book Award-winning poet, fiction writer, and critic; author of the long poem *Flow Chart* and many other books.

63. TLS—2

23 September 1992
Augustus Caesar

DEAR MR LAUGHLIN:

Under separate cover, as they say, the manuscript of the book I'm submitting to New Directions is being mailed along with this. *A Table of Green Fields,* 10 stories, variously inventive. Only two have been published before, and yours will be the first eyes to see the others. I gave up showing people—even Bonnie Jean—my stuff years ago. I hope I am not repeating previous work, though I know I am in many ways. I sometimes think of the critic (since eaten by bears) who said that my stories are "perfectly pointless."

Yours of the 13th. (My excuse for falling behind with the mail is not as per above but having to read John Irwin's 809 pp ms about Borges and Poe + a doctoral thesis (700 pp) on Zukofsky and Spinoza.)

As William James explained it, we cannot know the good without the bad (the word white being meaningless without black), so evil exists so that we can know the good. I've always found this fishy.

I like your easy allusion to "the poets" (and their dealing with alcoholic gods. Oof! No).

What your 16 June text proves is that nothing changes. I used to get papers like that after spring break and the kids had been to Florida. Except that your account is grammatical.

Afrodite was born on Cyprus (homophonic misspelling).

It might be daring to use the Greek names of the gods, unfiltered through Latin.

Phoibos Apollon.

I've always chafed at the formula "Delian Apollo" / it means that Apollo cult on the island of Delos.

Apollon of Delos?

A phrase like "Eros the child of Venus" is a macaroni of cultures. Cupid the child of Venus / Eros the child of Aphrodita.

Are you taking love-madness to be a kind of drunkenness? If so, you've got lots of breadth for equating *mania* (anger, love, poison) with wine.

I worry about your diction. E.g. puissance. Also the thees and thous of archaic English. This *is* 1992. Dart no longer means arrow. The spoils of beasts.

(I used to have a student named Diane Hunter.)

I believe all feminine forms (poetess, huntress) have been interdicted by Political Correctness, and you will be zapped by their Police.

What you've done, O Poet, is mesmerized yourself with an Antique Diction, out of some kind of reverence.

These two poems suffer from automatic (formulaic) phrasing.

"Without warning she became hostile," and so on.
I can see Ez closing his eyes in despair.

Tennyrate
GUY

/ • /

we cannot know the good: In his letter of September 13th JL had written how at Sunday school he had asked why bad things happen if God is good.
What your 16 June text proves: JL had sent the text of the then opening of *Byways,* what he called the "Daphne/Dawn Texas" sequence. This was printed as the opening pages of the selection in the Gale Autobiography Series. It was drastically edited for the published edition. This sort of close critical analysis is what JL sought when he sent manuscripts to GD.

64. TN—1 [JL to ND staff]

10/6/92

GJO & PG—

Davenport's stories have come in and they are lovely. Vintage Davenport. What ravishing invention and fantasy. Of course, he's odd, as he always is, and a bit obsessed in certain areas, but he's unique, the kind of thing ND should do now and then.

To be sure he won't sell much, but I can subvene that, and we'll at last have his name on the list.

J

/ • /

but I can subvene that: In the end, this was not done. The contract was with ND itself rather than with JL as underwriter.

65. TLS—2

10 October 1992

Dear Mr Laughlin—

Two cards from you today. You got at least as far as my riff on Lucian's "Zeus and Ganymede," and seem to query "*[. . .]* the palace that rules the world, save for some infringements by fate and necessity, love and time, which are tyrants over us all." Is the wording whonky? *Moira* and *anangke* constrain even the gods: I've added love and time. I can Xerox the dialogue for you.

I'm not used to publishers reading my ravings. I think Jack Shoemaker glanced over every manuscript, without actually reading anything, before sending it to a diabolic Bennington girl to query my every spelling and proper name.

What's going on in the "ideograms" is that the story goes right on, transposed for the moment into different imagery. Zeus and Ganumedes is a classical overture to the next section. The boat at the beginning (of "Gunnar and Nikolai") is lifted from a fragment by TL Peacock (the folded and pocketed sailboat).

Janusc Korczak, and his orphans (Treblinka, gas, 6 Aug 1942) is the moral ground against which the story is set, though the reviewers won't notice.

Nikolai should of course be spelled Nikolaj. I decided to make it an orthographic *i*. (The Danes spell one of their English loan words *fvck,* and have made their own verb of it, *to fvcker.*)

One learns about the Friendly Trees by reading John Harshberger's *The Vegetation of the New Jersey Pine-Barrens.*

Who is the writer in your "Partial Eclipse"? Cendrars with two arms? I wish I could write that kind of story—a dense web of nuances, written with the authority of *knowing*. It's a Balsac [*sic*] story. The great French self-delusion and Roumanian genuineness.

I'm essentially a comic-strip artist—everything obvious and boldly colored, with ZAP! And GRR-R! for dramatic *pouf.*

How wonderful to have known Brancusi. Gaudier was a god, but Brancusi was God.

A few years back Bonnie Jean, who can do anything, figured out how one actually gets into B's studio now outside the Beaubourg. (Buy a ticket to the top floor, get it stamped, come back down, all on the right day, as the studio is open on alternate Tuesdays except in Lent, from noon to 1 pm.) We had the place to ourselves, sat in all the furniture, handled his tools (his folding rule was in inches, so much for the metric system). No evidence of the trapeze, and I've never heard anyone else who knows about it.

Apparently he was wholly sexless, or have the mistresses been kept a secret?

ad interim,
GUY

/ • /

Moira and anangke: Refers to a sentence in the story "Gunnar and Nikolai" where Zeus tells Ganymede, "We walk over that knoll yonder and into the palace that rules the world, save for some infringements by fate and necessity, love and time, which are tyrants over us all" (*TGF,* 59).

What's going on in the "ideograms": Davenport here refers to his technique of switching from one scene or epoch to another, at times from paragraph to paragraph, as a story proceeds. This can be one of the most "difficult" aspects of reading the stories, as well as one of most fascinating.

TL Peacock: Thomas Love Peacock (1785–1866) was an English novelist and poet as well as Shelley's literary executor.

Gaudier was a god, but Brancusi: Henri Gaudier (1892–1915), French sculptor of the famous "hieratic head" of Ezra Pound. GD made drawings of some of Gaudier's work. Romanian-born Constantin Brancusi (1876–1957) also inspired drawings by GD—see his rendering of Brancusi's *The Kiss* in *Apples and Pears* (74). The trapeze mentioned here is in JL's "The Sculptor" (*SR,* 144):

> *Brancusi didn't have much to say but he*
> *Cooked a great Romanian stew and liked*
> *After eating to swing upside down by his*
> *Knees on a monkey's trapeze while his*
> *Phonograph blared out Ravel's* Bolero.

This appears in a section of *SR* titled "Thirty-nine Pentastichs," a form JL favored at this time. He defined it as "a poem of five lines, without regard to metrics." GD supplied the term, and pointed out to JL the five-line epigraphs in the *Greek Anthology*. See *SR*, [131].

66. ALS—4

10/11/92

Dear Guy—

The (bad word) arthritis in my neck too strong today to sit up and type. Them deities punishing me for early evil. Present saintliness don't count with them.

Thanks for filling me in on the Danish background. That's the kind of lit-crit-hist I like. May the Deconstructionists choke on their own jargon.

I guessed Aircraftsman Ross pretty quick. An odd duck. I couldn't finish his *Seven Pillars* but I rather liked his *Odyssey.* The [word illegible] of "August Blue" is nice. What would you think of putting that piece first in the book? An easy entry to the big story, which might baffle timid readers. But as you wish. . . .

There is a beautiful young lady poet in England named Julia who writes me the most spiritual letters I've ever received. She is very concerned about my verses because there are things in them which aren't *true.* Truth is the essential quality of poetry, she says. I guess I'd better not send her your book.

Wordsworth's sister Dorothy is a knockout. In case you didn't know it, it's a superb prose poem. Then there is the second level of the weavings of language. *Very* fine. You can make a story out of anything.

Fitts never talked about Thoreau. So I never read him. But now I will. Somebody in school told me he was an old nut who ate rabbits. I'll look for the fine effluence, and the sentiments of the heart. Of Mencius I know a little from Ezra the benevolent. The poem is beautiful. The right measure.

The movement from theme to theme is excellent. Ideogrammatic? A wonderful piece. . . .

You may wonder why I'm such a slow reader. I'm an every-word reader. And if I come on a good sentence I may say it aloud several times, hoping the noise will stick in my head. It seldom does. The most noises in my head are bits from childhood's Bible. . . .

This has been long. I'm sorry.
JL

/ • /

Aircraftsman Ross: T. E. Lawrence (1888–1935)—"Lawrence of Arabia"—appears in the story "August Blue" under this pseudonym.
Wordsworth's sister Dorothy: Refers to the story "The Kitchen Chair," in *TGF.*
Of Mencius I know a little: The Book of Mencius was one of four books of Confucian knowledge published during the second Han dynasty (A.D. 25–220). It was in Mencius, according to GD, that Thoreau encountered the passage that inspired his statement about having lost a hound, et al. See also next letter.

67. TLS—2

16 October 1992

Dear Mr Laughlin—

I am inordinately proud to be accepted by a publisher whose books have been the best part of my education (without Pound or WCW I would have been somebody else), and to whose list I never dared hope to be added. So it's a triumph for me. And is the sweeter for coming on a rainy blowy day when I had to get dressed in a suit and tie and walk a mile through the rain to the Convention of American Editorial Writers to be on a panel with a Baptist preacher and a writer of bodice-ripper "romances."

An arthritic neck sounds perfectly horrible. I like a less abstract source for my pains than Yaweh, and blame the XVIII Airborne for my whonky left foot and (off and on) bad right knee.

Writing doesn't become real until I see it in print, or have to anticipate that reality in copy-editing or upon someone's actually taking my ravings seriously. I'm glad you fancy the Dorothy Wordsworth story; it would *go* better as a poem, but I'm not a poet.

I'll ponder reversing the order of "August Blue" and "Gunnar and Nikolai." I'd thought the quartet-form of AB would be more confusing to the first-time reader than the *collagiste* G + N. Right now I'm too excited about your acceptance to start fiddling with the order.

Thoreau was our Diogenes. I tracked down the Mencius source (only you and I and Bonnie Jean know it as of the moment) and tried making an ideogram of it. MAKE IT NEW first appears in American writing in *Walden;* Henry was a great Confucian. He was a crack classicist also: translated Anakreon. He was a vegetarian, by the way: no rabbits.

Apta Julia is the Roman name for the modern Apt. The story grew out of a photograph by Bernard Faucon, who was born there. I like his peculiar work, and realized one day that his photo of a startling blue lavender field (the local industry since Roman times) shot across the family wash on the line was a pun: our word "laundry" and the French *lavanderie* derive from *lavender.* (Romans washed their togae in piss, and then sweetened them up after sun-drying with lavender.)

I have Aristotelian truth: arbitrary dress for human possibilities. Remind your English Julia that dreams aren't true.

I'm an every-word reader, too. And slow. . . .

After Political Correctness has bored everybody to death, and Deconstruction has been flushed into the Seine, Ez is going to emerge as the brilliant critic and master poet that he was.

A drawing, a spot. I'll get at 'em. Also ideas about type, page design and whichwhat. I suffered under the *lines* (rules, as printers call 'em) Dave Bullen put everywhere.

"Belinda's World Tour" is being done in French (by the girlfriend of Bernard Hœpffner). In *La Main de singe,* a magazine that may or may not have some lastingness to it.

Tennyrate, I couldn't be more pleased. In a world where mss disappear for months and years at publishers, I bask in the glory of the founder and head of the firm's reading and deciding on my scribbles in so courteous and encouraging a way. I normally, by the way, pass up advances.

Details about design and type later.

in bounden gratitude,
GUY

/ • /

A drawing, a spot: JL had asked if GD wanted to do a drawing for the cover or for the title page. In the end, GD decided against doing so.
Dave Bullen: Designer for North Point Press.

68. TLS—1

21 October 92
Samuel Taylor Coleridge
Trafalgar

The gorgeous peacock struts and flirts
And drags his tail, but when his mind
On peahen dwells, he lifts his skirts
And shows all Persia his behind

DEAR MR LAUGHLIN:

That's Apollinaire, the Orpheus suite. In a story I'm working on, I needed some verses for two lively French kids to recite, and am giving them sections of the *cortège.* I've done the Owl and the Rabbit as well. I used the arctic fly in the story in *ND* 50; I remember your asking about the adjective *ganique.*

In the matter of design for *A Table of Green Fields.* As for type, in these days one has to hope for body and substance when every other book (especially university presses) have anemic, blinding computer-set pages that are gray to look at and trying to the eyes.

I'll leave the actual typeface to you and your designer, as long as it's normal and traditional. (Red Ozier originally set *The Bicycle Rider* in telephone-book sans-serif, which fortunately mashed into dough in the hand-press.)

A collage drawing for the cover? Various things—a lavender plant from an herbal, or whichwhat. I'll come up with something. Chisel and maul. A kitchen chair.

Students coming for the afternoon—I'll put this out for the postman and his mule.

more later,
GUY

/ • /

the Orpheus suite: The story GD refers to here is "The Cardiff Team."

69. TLS—3

24 October 1992

DEAR MR LAUGHLIN:

My sister and I tore the hands off a banjo clock, and got our butts beat for it. I will not enjoy the recitation of my destructions at the heavenly bar. The throwing of grandpa's false teeth into the fire (I think I included that) was the work of my nephew Jim, who is now a respected forester, conservationist, and teacher of trout fishing at an idyllic spot in the Georgia mountains. Japanese capitalists turn up, get dressed in red plaid shirts and waders, and learn zen of fly casting. They tip with hundred-dollar bills. The grandfather was a saintly minister.

Was Wm Buffalo, the #2 chauffeur, an Injun?

Yep, Kierkegaard means cemetary in Dansk; literally, church yard. Pronounced kyerk-uh-gore. I made the curator of his archives

(City Museum, Copenhagen) teach me how to say him, though I never got the Søren right.

As the fantasy's all fiction, I thought I'd translate his name. All the elements are real, however; that is, I've made a casserole rather than a soup with the same ingredients that might go into either. The same Troll Wood (that's its name) is at the beginning of "Gunnar and Nikolai," to introduce Zeus as eagle and the Friendly Trees.

SK wrote "the god" where other theologians wrote "God."

Whoever, whatever, the god is, in this collection of *récits* he is constantly present as the god Eros, born of Chaos, and older than all the others. I take it that the Greeks, shapers of *our* civilization (the Romans merely added sobriety and high seriousness) were neither idiots nor sentimental fools when they believed in Eros. His games were in Arkadia.

He, and his sister Peitho (too much for the Romans!), and his pal Anteros (Love Returned) along with their Mama Aphrodita, born directly from the sperm (*aphros*) of Time (Khronos) could neither be supplicated nor placated. They had no sacrifices.

Meleager the erotic poet. You had enjoined me to be inventive. This piece is Eros and Anteros playing a game with each other, making it up as they go along. The other side of Greek genius was geometry (that's Euclid, from the *Britannica,* first edition, 1771). Two nudities: the hidden structure beneath all shapes, and the body.

Meleager wrote a fascinating poem about standing at the other Meleager's tomb, interpreting the torch as Eros's.

I hadn't expected to have your past exposed by my stories. *I* made A's in geometry (and was once the state algebra champion). I once squared the circle in a dream. Supervielle has a poem about a kid bored in geometry class, who makes wolves' mouths of angles and a trapeze out of a parallelogram. "Math class."

Tennyrate, after Greek kids had wrestled and tumbled in the fine dust at the palestra, the dust was smoothed flat, and used to do geometry on. It is recorded that Arkhimedes did geometry on his dusty body while everyone else was being strigilled down by their tutors before their bath.

(They were oiled with a dill-flavored slick'em before wrestling.)

Good God! You lie in bed on your Elvis-Presley heating pad and read the *fragmenta disjecta* of Ezra Pound and Tennessee Williams, never mind the integral ravings of Simic and Davenport. They should bring candidates around to gaze at all this.

BUSH: "Well, I mean, I guess Culture is all right in its place, but I'd be ashamed, I really would, to do it on foreign soil."

BILL: "I heard some people talking about Culture at Oxford."

DAN: "I'll bet he's a whiz at spelling."

ROSS: "I approve of books. They make a man smart. We have a row of books in our den in Dallas. It makes people think more of you, I'm here to tell you."

"O Gadgo Niglo." The gentile hedgehog. You've read a third revision. Rhymes with "Nikolai and Gunnar"—one is streetwise, nydansk, polyfaceted; the other dark, chthonic, Bergmanisk.

That Montana air makes nature jump.

It is my wholly unscientific belief (also E. Pound's) that a lively sexual nature is also a creative one, though this can easily be argued against. Isaac Newton says he never lost a drop of sperm, and van Gogh attributed his genius to quelling Priapos (he rubbed camphor on his dick).

Dr. Kinsey reports a spirited boy who could jack off 24 times *per diem*. Prepubescent, however, with only a droplet of Bartholin's juice for issue.

The duke of what's-it, James I's favorite, used to *mastrupate* while poor old Thomas Hobbes taught him geometry (in Aubrey's *Brief Lives*).

I'm simply exploring some areas and moments of human affection, especially the awakening of affection not used up or run in the ground.

Thoreau's masterpieces are *Walden* and *A Week on the Concord and Merrimac Rivers*. His Anakreon was the pseudoanakreon (the omicron of pseudo eliding into the alpha). I've done the real Anakreon, as best scholars can restore him. The pseudo was never meant to fool anybody: it was a Byzantine Festschrift that muzzy-minded Renaissance boffins thought was the author himself. . . .

I can't "see" my scribbles until someone else has. So I've read (as it were, for the first time) the "Meleager" and "Mr. Churchyard," trying to see them with your eyes. They are, I think, underivative, in "a new direction" (name of the publisher), and damned strange.

I was reading Flannery O'Connor's letters last night. Her every page was sniffed over by fifteen friends and six editors, through revision after revision. The end product was masterly, but the messiness of it all makes me squirm.

I "took creative writing" at Duke, under Bill Blackburn, in a class with Bill Stryon and Mac Hyman (*No Time for Sergeants*). The result was that I was paralyzed for years, until I saw that if I wanted to write I would have to do it the way I wanted to, without thinking of myself as "a writer" (I still don't).

The breakthrough came when I realized that I mustn't write about anything from my own experience, or anybody I've known, but to work with pure imagination, and to work with that hiatus between the mind and the world in which the pragmatic always fails and the imagination has to take over.

So the first book (*Tatlin!*) was about people (Vladimir Tatlin, Poe, the discoverers of Lascaux, Herakleitos, Kafka, Charles Fourier) who saw the world through very different eyes.

It's as simple as that. I'm trying to make the most I can out of a minor talent.

But I'd better put this out for the postman on his mule. I wish I could convey how appreciative I am of the attention you're giving my stuff. As I've said, at North Point, they opened the package and handed it over to the typesetter.

ad feliciter interim,
GUY

/ • /

tore the hands off a banjo clock: This refers to a passage in "Mr. Churchyard and the Troll," *TGF,* 98. In a letter dated October 21, 1992, JL wrote that he had torn the hands off his grandfather's clock, and "the #2 chauffeur" had glued them back on. He also mentions that he got E's in geometry.
the fantasy's all fiction: These comments are again in relation to GD's story "Mr. Churchyard and the Troll." Other explanations in the letter pertain to other stories in the collection.
Supervielle: Jules Supervielle (1884–1960), Uruguayan-French poet. ND published a selection of his work in 1967.
Arkhimedes: More often spelled Archimedes. Ancient Greek physicist who famously discovered the principles of water displacement while taking a bath ("Eureka!"). A strigil was a scraper used by the ancient Greeks to scrape their skin clean.
fragmenta disjecta: One of JL's duties as ND publisher and scholar was to look over unpublished fragments by authors whose work he had published. He also admired the poetry of Charles Simic.
That Montana air makes nature jump: JL's reading of "O Gadgo Niglo," which like many of GD's stories includes boys delighting in self-gratification, prompted him to write (in a letter begun on October 21, 1992, but which continued on for days) about an experience of his own: "I have been a votary of this cult since August 22, 1928. (I had marked the date in my diary.) I was at summer camp in Montana. . . ."
Bill Styron and Mac Hyman: William Styron won the Pulitzer Prize for *The Confessions of Nat Turner* and also wrote *Sophie's Choice,* among others. Hyman's comic novel of two draftees, *No Time for Sergeants,* was also made into a film.

70. TLS—2

10/28/92

Dear Guy—

. . . Since you don't speak of an earlier book you would like to copy for the typography, I'll ask Gertrude to knock out a couple of sample pages for you to see. She did book and jacket design for ND for many years. She has a nice, light touch and a good sense of *mise-en-page.* She doesn't work much now because that miserable bald-headed surgeon touched her optic nerve when he was removing from her head the "spaghetti" (as he humorously called it) which he said would sooner or later give her a stroke. He touched the part of the nerve which governs peripheral vision. But last month she did a beautiful title page for my *CP*. She is so clever she can copy from a type specimen book with her pencil so that it looks like type. Now she does wonderful watercolors of floating flowers: roses floating in the sky over St. Mark's Square, anemones over the Pont Royale, that sort of thing. Lovely fantasy.

She will want at some point to see a stat of what you draw for the title page and the jacket to make it all harmonize. A collage for the cover could be interesting. And a drawing of lavender from a herbal might work in well with the type on the title page. But I leave it to your "invention."

I share your dislike of computer-set composition. They did my CP that way and I groan. Most ND books are computer composed to save expense, but yours is not a book on which I wish to economize. I'll see if we can't find a compositor who still does linotype. Monotype, I'm afraid, entirely exstorped [*sic*] some years back, at least in this country. I wish we could use Bixler—wait till you see the limited edition of my little novella *Angelica*—but he is sky high, it's really hand-setting. They say he'll reset a whole page to avoid one bad spacing. Mardersteig, who was the greatest, did that. He did four books for me—Gide's *Theseus,* Ez's *Diptych* and *Cavalcanti,* and a Dylan Thomas. Utter beauty. . . .

Yours for mighty grace,
JL

/ • /

Gertrude: JL had recently remarried, and his wife Gertrude had been a designer for ND for years.

71. TLS—2

4 Nov 1992
Caporetto

Dear Mr Laughlin!

You're inventing a new poetic form: the sculpting of prose into poetry. Herakleitos got it right: character is fate. I had a discussion of this with Tom Merton once, in which I tried to tie fate to money (the accidents of the rich are not those of the poor) but he only smiled.

Greek *moira* turns up as Calvinist (and Augustinian) predestination. But, as I have a lively theologian say in *The JV Steam Balloon,* knowledge of the future is impossible as it hasn't happened yet. So the god is as surprised as the rest of us by the outcome of anything.

For days (and all through the election returns last night) I've been working on the problem of a cover. Yesterday's idea was to find an image to quote photographically—a perfect meadow (Pissarro, Monet) or Eros in statuary. There's a terrific Eros riding a splendid lion by Thorvaldsen, one of his bas reliefs illustrating Anakreon, but the photograph I have of this is my own camera work. Thorvaldsen (pronounced something like *torrels'n*) is, like Hammershøj, a master kept secret by the Danes.

I've edited two vols of O. Henry for Penguin, and we've been choosing paintings for the covers. If we were to think of that route, there's Tuke's *August Blue* that gives one of the stories its title; it's in the Tate, and is a marinescape, row-boat with nekkid boys, or the painting Tuke's working on in the story, shore, boat, more nekkid boys: this one belongs to Major General Sir Robert Stephenson Smyth Baden-Powell, 1st Baron Baden-Powell of Mafeking, and hangs in Baden-Powell House, London, world HQ of the Boy Scouts.

Or: several of Pissarro's fields around Pontoise / e.g. *Banks of the Marne* (Art Inst. of Chicago).

If you would like to know what a quixotic idealist you are, O Publisher, consider that I have just had a royalty statement from Farrar Straus (distributing for the defunct North Point) for *Every Force Evolves a Form, The Drummer of the 11th North Devonshire Fusiliers, Apples & Pears, The Geog of the Imag, The Jules Verne Steam Balloon, Eclogues,* and *Thasos & Ohio,* (that's 7 books), all of which earned a grand total of $2.00 in the last six months. In the previous six months, nothing. Not that they've sent along a check for $2.00. . . .

awaiting instructions,
GUY

/ • /

Dear Mr Laughlin!: GD wrote that this was the way the Danes punctuated their letters.
Tuke's August Blue: This is the image used on the cover.

72. TLS—3

7 Nov 1992
Marie Curie
Albert Camus

DEAR MR LAUGHLIN:

Congratulations and whole-hearted concurrence in the National Book Medal. What took them so long?

. . . I see that I must talk business. True, I've never had an agent. I've been translated, one thing or another, into French, Spanish, Jap, and Roumanian. I'll reserve translation rights for Germany only, as I refuse to have anything to do with them.

Notes! I can see how "And" might be identified (M. R. James, *The Apocryphal NT*). The Kierkegaard story is made of so many disparate texts by the gloomy Dane that it would take me a month to track them down. The kind of reader who has never heard of Thorvaldsen, Brandes, Bourdelle, *et alia,* is precisely the kind of person who is unenlightened by notes. There's also the mean spirited critic who will only read the notes. Though they could be done in a fresh manner. E. g.

YESHUA. Migrant rabbi, of peasant origin, follower of Iakonaan, a reformist Jew who revived the ancient rite of washing away transgressions in running water. Advocating self-discipline based on mutual respect while acknowledging the supremacy of spirit, imagination, and lovingkindness over a code of laws, he angered and threatened both the legal and ritualistic conservatives in the rabbinate, who charged him with heresy and turned him over to the Roman consul as a dangerous revolutionary. He was crucified on the day before Passover in the nominal reign of Tiberias Caesar. His life is recorded in four pseudonymous biographies. *[. . .]* in the last year of the nominal reign *[. . .]*

THOREAU, Henry David. Pseudonym of David Henry Thoreau, inventor of the lead pencil and raisin bread. He was by profession a surveyor *[. . .] kai ta loipa.*

KAFKA, Franz Josef. Lawyer and insurance adjustor specializing in industrial-accident compensation.

Blurbs. I suppose Milton's and Ben Jonson's poems up front in the First Folio are technically blurbs. What BJ calls my being "too High South Carolina" rebels against asking for 'em. But they're a business convention. . . .

I don't remember what I said in the letter you take as some species of my Theory. I think I was trying to assure you that I do not write off the top of my head while foaming at the mouth, but with some care and deliberation. I don't think I have an ego. That is, I have nothing to say for myself, or as from myself. It annoys the hell out of me when reviewers say I like or dislike whatever: they're always looking at what a *character* likes or dislikes. In a confessional age I keep my mouth shut (in fiction; not as a critic, natch). . . .

hello to the sheep & the bear
GUY

***73.* TLS—2** [JL to ND staff]

11/15/92

JL TO GJO/PG/PEGGY—

A dream come true. I've always wanted to have a Guy Davenport on the ND list, and his *Table of Green Fields*—10 stories—if you can call them that—they're linguistic and imaginative constructions—about 160 pages in type, though maybe only 128. I've always considered him perhaps the last of the great experimental writers—nobody at all like him. He's odd, of course, and in two pieces perverse—he likes boys—but he does it with a kind of obsessed elegance. However our new president says he's going to make that sort of thing popular in the Navy, if it wasn't already. . . .

Peggy. For the contract, he says he doesn't care about an advance, but I think we should put in $1000 on principle. I explained to him how we can handle foreign rights—he has no agent—and he likes that. I explained that the foreign agent takes a commission, and then we take 10% on top of that. But he wants to "reserve German rights" because he hates the Krauts and wants to be sure it doesn't get done there by mistake. Contract should be with ND, not the Prop.

He is a marvelous drawer and he is drawing something for the jacket and also one for the title page. As I wrote Dan, he detests computer comp so we shd try to find someone who still does linotype. I've queried Bixler who does monotype, but that will probably be too high.

Peter: I have never seen such a perfect manuscript—I think it would be a waste of time to get in a copy editor at first. He uses words I've never seen before though I'm sure he has them right. He likes now and then to drop in a bit of transliterated Greek, Danish—he has a fix on Denmark—and even some Romany, which gypsies talk. Of course the compositor could foul up his words so that should be checked.

There are good blurbs on his North Point books, but we could do with some new ones. He has given me a list of critic fans, so we should figure on some bound galleys.

The way her eyes are now Gertrude can't do comps, but I think she'd like to do some sketches for jacket and title page. She has her old typebooks here.

I asked GD if he wanted a section of notes at the back to explain some of his sources. He's thinking about that, and I'll let you know.

Three of the pieces have been in magazines. I've asked him for the copyright lines on those, and does he want us to get assignments for him.

GD's letters are the most learned-funny that I've received since Dudley Fitts left this earth. Peggy, you should put him on your list among future possibilities for the Norton series if Don doesn't get tired of it.

J

/ • /

GJO/PG/Peggy: Griselda Ohannessian, Peter Glassgold, and Peggy Fox, all of ND.

74. ANS—1 [GJO to JL]

11/18

JL—

Great re the Davenport—I could live without boy love stories—let him just not dream up a lascivious drawing for the jacket. . . .

G[RISELDA]

75. ANS—1 [GJO to JL]

11/20

JL—

Re Davenport. PG raises a point I touched on and says "Davenport's drawings are often unpleasantly pedophilic." We really do not want this category on a book cover. Also, as the book is going to need interior design, with all due respect to Gertrude, it makes things difficult with our designers to give them only part of a design-job, so if she isn't doing the whole job it would be best not to have her do cover & title page.

G[RISELDA]

76. AL—3 [JL to GJO]

11/26

DEAR GJO—

Re Davenport. I certainly wouldn't like a lurid cover. Let's see what he comes up with and worry about it then. He has spoken of several possibilities, and they sound OK. For the title page drawing he is looking for a print of the lavender plant, which appears in one story, an old etching from a horticulture book.

I have a reason for wanting to involve Gertrude. Only my relations bought paintings from the show she had here in the library. She fears she isn't good and has stopped painting. . . . I'd like to raise her spirits a bit—not a complete job but one of sample pages which Dan could follow. The book calls for visual lightness and plenty of space between lines. There has been a visual heaviness in *some* of the recent books that I would like to avoid. . . .

Love from A Tedious Old Man

77. TLS—3

4 XII 1992
Sam Butler II

Dear Mr Laughlin:

Your exercise-book Greek would seem to be poetry, to account for the literary word order, and the lack of *men, de,* or *gar.* The shape of the letters you use are those of Porson, whose Greek *Handschrift* was taken by typecutters for a model. Oxford has since given up the two stigmata, as Byzantine intrusions, and use the Soviet one, *c,* for both internal and final *s*'s.

I'm fascinated by your versions of the *Anthology* erotix. You have your own voice (and a bright schoolboy's spirited liberty with the texts). I stay confused as to tone: whether the poet is smiling, grinning, or playing dumb. You make me realize that I read these poems as an anthropologist. Looking for information about ancient and different emotions. You *know* what these poets mean.

The "Melissa" is a damned good poem. It's in your, and nobody else's, style and has radical reality. Were I an editor, I'd delete the apologetic quotes (knickers, mum). It would fit splendidly in an anthology of love poems to English girls; I'd put yours next to Apollinaire's *La Chanson du mal-aimé.*

Thomas Hardy would approve of it. Curiously, I think EZ wouldn't—he was a Romantic. I'm depraved by the handkerchief, though I recognize it as deep European custom. (Scandinavian girls put their dancing partners' hankies in their armpits.) "No smell is a virgin."

You can't spell *fetishist.* Jacques Lacan was, as far as I can tell, quite mad, but he has the only true theory about fetishes. They are *"le petit autre,"* true signifiers of the beloved. Freud, who had no compassion, saw them as Perverse, seeing that the *petit* could replace the *grand autre.* That knights rode into battle with their girlfriends' kerchiefs in their helmets, and were the braver for it, meant nothing to Freud. He would have taken candy from a child.

I've signed contracts. Thanks for humoring me in the matter of forbidding German translation. People who stuffed 182 Polish orphans into the gas chambers at Treblinka (age 4 to 15)—Janusc Korczak's orphanage—could not possibly understand any of my stories. Rabbi Yeshua was an admirable fellow, and died a hideous death, but he did not die *with* 182 innocent children. At the loading into the cattle cars, the shit-brained SS explained to Korczak that as an officer and doctor he did not have to accompany the children. "I will go with my children," he said simply.

Gat-toothed Denise, yes. The charming thing is that they put a bit of whistle into her words.

I must look up your *Grand Street* Hiram Handspring poem.

"The acorn of the tail." *Glans penis. Glans* is an acorn; *penis* is a tail. The Greeks had the same image, the head of the *posthos* being the *balanos,* acorn.

I don't keep copies of letters, so I don't remember either context or my muddle.

One of the 100 bawdy Greek terms for cunt was *pig;* the polite one was *meadow.*

In SC when I was a child the prevalent word was *christmas.* For penis, *blue-jay.*

Urso is carved of wood? . . .

I noticed in the contract that I swear upon my honor that I wrote every word of *A Table of Green Fields,* which fudges in the matter of my *collage* quotes.

E.g. sentences of Kierkegaard dropped into the text. Thoreau, Santayana. The only copyright material, I think, is a paragraph of Stanley Cavell in the Thoreau, acknowledged as such.

There's never been any trouble with this sort of thing before. Though Hell keeps spawning nastier and nastier breeds of lawyers.

My only theory about writing is that words have to *mean* something.

My one typesetting anxiety is that my quotation dashes occupy just enough space that the paragraphs all begin at the same distance from the left margin, both exposition and dialogue. I've typed the ms this way (North Point didn't always oblige).

Urso Ursonius Ursus growled that he was hungry.
—I want a bowl of honey, he said, and a spoon to eat it with, and a napkin to wipe my nose afterwards.
These were brought to him forthwith, by the butler.
—Thank you, said Urso, even though you were rather slow in getting here.
(Joyce wanted this invisible secondary margin, but never got it.)

Do I gather from your stoic and brave remarks that you are abandoning the Reformation for Rome?

Both the Waldrops are accomplished folk, and one of 'em (which?) has lifted my collage-paragraphs (which I took, modified, from Barthelme, who had it from Joyce, who had it from Sterne).

I choose not to believe you when you forswear poesy. I've forsworn writing with every book. My second book, *Da Vinci's Bike,* was an abandonment, complete with statement that it was. I wanted to be the author of two books in which I had said everything I had to say.

So now I've written 5 more.

5 XII Apologies for not double-spacing all of this letter. Meanwhile, your letter has arrived that invites me to draw pictures for a Turkey Press. The prospect is attractive, the actuality daunting, as my drawing (symbolic, pedantic, allusive, flat-footed) is the opposite of your poetry (erotic, candid, witty, and winged).

Perhaps if I talk with the Reeses I can get a better idea of what they see in the NP drawings. And, nope, I can't do etchings.

(Was it you who passed on the great anecdote about Turkey Press? Berea College, for an arts fair, ordered a shipment of the Merton journal. UPS delivered it. Nobody could find it, though somebody had signed for it on arrival. Some inspired person had the bright idea of looking in the college kitchen, and there the parcel was, in the freezer, clearly marked TURKEY PRESS.)

I have the limited signed edition of *Stolen & Contaminated*—a gift from the generous author.

Of course I'd like the new edition of *Paterson.* I've read Denise's "essays" (more like lectures and chats). Does she have *any* sense of humor? My friend Tony Stoneburner is writing something about her da, who was some species of religious virtuoso, in Wales, I think.

(Once, crossing the Atlantic by ship, the PA system announced that some of our passengers, namely a Welsh Baptist delegation, wished to sing a selection of sacred music, which they did.)

Enough.

A technical letter about the drawings, later.

Greetings to Urso,
GUY

/ • /

exercise-book Greek: In a seven-page letter of November 26, 1992 (not included here), JL had sent GD "the last line in my exercise book for Greek I" when he was briefly a NYU night school student years before.
The "Melissa": an excerpt from JL's *Byways* memoir, which he had only recently begun, to fill hours of insomnia. "Melissa" was the British artist Vanessa Jackson, referred to in several letters earlier. The published version is on pages 271–75.
the handkerchief: This handkerchief comment will be used by JL for his short poem "In Scandinavia."
Jacques Lacan: (1901–1981), controversial French psychologist and theorist, he did much to move psychology away from a Freudian basis.
Gat-toothed Denise: Commenting on an ND photograph of British-born poet Denise Levertov (1923–1997). JL had remarked on how attractive her smile was. Levertov's father was an Anglican priest, a convert from Judaism, with an enduring interest in Hasidic mysticism.
Hiram Handspring: JL had published the poem "How to Write about Sex" in the magazine *Grand Street,* crediting it to "Hiram Handspring"—"Have to think of the morals of the grandkidlets."
"The acorn of the tail": GD had mentioned this definition, and JL requested more information.
Urso: On his birthday, JL's wife Gertrude had presented him with a large wooden bear which JL named Urso.
My one typesetting anxiety: GD was not to have this secondary margin in *A Table.* His second book of stories published by ND, *The Cardiff Team,* did have it.
Both the Waldrops: Rosmarie and Keith, writers and publishers of Burning Deck Press.

ND would later publish Rosmarie's *A Key into the Language of America,* which has a collagelike structure.

78. TLS—5

December 7, 1992

Dear Guy—

. . . The dinner table at Woodland Road.

My detestable brother: Mother, James is babbling again, and he's pushing with his fingers.

I intend to go on pushing with my fingers until they cinder me, but the babbling has got to stop. It is unproductive and will lead only to Chestnut Ward of St. Liz—though there they wouldn't mind if I improved the language by inventing words. I admit that "logophobia" is not in some dictionaries, but it will be. I was ascribed four new words in the last printing of the big Merriam-Webster. Unfortunately, I've misfiled the editor's letter, but I remember one of them: *puffery.* That was when Delmore made a pact with Blackmur that he would say in his review of *The Double Agent* that RPB was the greatest critic since Aristotle, and Blackmur would say that *Genesis* was the greatest poem since Dante. I do remember that all four of my new words had been found in the introductions to the *ND* annuals.*

You may not hear from me for a month—lucky you—because the page proofs of the *C*[*ollected*] *P*[*oems*] have arrived and I'll have to look at every page because the idiotic printer, who does it all by computer in Deatsville, Alabama—has done such strange things with the placement on the pages of notes, glosses and epigraphs. If this task drains the last force from my frailing embodiment I hope you will put out a press release explaining that all references to the opposite sex in my work are purely allegorical, and that you and Humphrey II will have a little Rosicrucian service in your garden. I hope BJ will be there, too. . . .

I am so ENCOURAGED that you think the Melissa segment of *Byways* works. I think there are several tones in the *G[reek] A[nthology]* thefts, but the general intention is that the poet wants to get laid.

The *Times* says that Smiley reads not only Marcus Aurelius but Plato. There's our boy.** But how to get him to look at Ezra's ABC of EC? The problem for getting people to take that seriously is all the anti-semitic and *Fascist Schmarren.*

Ad astra,
Or if you prefer what the Abbot***
at Gethsemani used to say:
All for Jesus through Mary with a smile.
JAS

* Two other candidates: *femulist*—Susan B. Anthony with a mentula *[. . .] sedulate*—extended, langorous seduction. And I think a lot of Ez should go in, such as *beanery.*
** but he has picked two Wall St. investment bankers to his team, that's not so good.
*** who was a graduate of Harvard Business School.

/ • /

Chestnut Ward of St. Liz: Ezra Pound was confined in the Chestnut Ward of St. Elizabeths hospital in Washington, D.C., from December 1945 to May 1958.
the GA thefts: the *Greek Anthology.* See the notes to "Melissa" in *Byways.*
Smiley: Bill Clinton.
ABC of EC: Pound's *ABC of Economics.*
Ad astra: "To the stars."
Gethsemani: The Kentucky monastery where Thomas Merton lived.
beanery: A university.

79. TLS—2

29 XII 1992

Dear Mr Laughlin:

Santa Claus took to heart your recommendation of a Canon personal copier and brought me one. I enclose two pages which it has copied from an old notebook of mine of the kind I jot down ideas in, copy passages, and draft stories. These two pages caught the eye of Ezra at St. Liz where I was making notes on his conversation. Further on, he wrote in it an introduction to Achilles Fang and Archie MacLeish.

Merci 1000 fois for the *Paterson.* I have to pinch myself to realize that as late as 1953 I could have WCW read poems to me sophomore class at Washington University. About 3 other faculty had ever heard of him.

So all critters named Belinda are. I wish mine didn't nip onto the roof and have to be got in through an upstairs window at great peril to my neck.

And BJ's advice to the lovelorn has become a poem. I have in the notebooks many Bonnie-jean-isms. Of some American tourists, "Travel is so narrowing."

These may have been the people who were told by one of their group that Elsinore was where Shakespeare wrote *Hamlet* and that Denmark is the capital of Scandinavia.

The Foundation for Thought in the Mind could only be in Denver. I once had a long letter from some psychiatric boffin out there whose goal is to stamp out sex. He runs a clinic that cures people of love, affection, hugging, kissing, and all such. I put a flea in his ear.

I had to sign a book, too: my *Drummer of the XIth North etc.* For a father who, I discovered once I'd signed it, was going to give it to his son for Xmas. I quickly gave him *Every Force* (a book of jolly essays) and tried to explain that I didn't think *The Drummer* was appropriate for his teenage son. WHY do people assume that all books are pretty much the same? Likelihood is that his brat can't read *any* book. I also resent the assumption that a book written by a neighbor, Prof. D. over to the university, is sure to be an uplifting book about Kentucky.

The *Collected Poems* sounds like a great production, but aren't there book-design people to do all this pasting and type-placement for you? My God! next I'll hear that you're in the bindery sewing signatures and slapping glue on cloth.

Vincent only sliced off the top of his ear with his razor. It was Gauguin he was going to carve on, but G. prudently took the next train out of town.

Bonnie Jean got a pair of roller skates for Christmas. We had a lovely snowy day, and spent it by the fire except for a slippery errand across town to feed a friend's cat. I also got 20 detective novels. Far too much candy and cake and cookies came from too many directions. South Carolina sent up cases of blackberry jam and wild fox grape jelly.

Felix the cat is on a vet's diet: he lives off *Hill's Feline Formula* and crunchies called *I AM's*. But for Xmas he got a big helping of roast hen, so he's out singing to the ladies, like Popeye when he's eaten his can of Spinach. And naturally he won't even look at his diet food.

Barkless Mexican dogs makes me remember Cocteau's tale of a kindly French couple who took in a mangy stray and gave it a home. They were out walking it one evening when a car pulled up. In it, a vet. "None of my business," he said, "but you really ought to keep your jackal on a leash."

In the "Mr. Churchyard" story there's the sentence "And nobody laughed." (After an account of a sermon to rich folks.) Do you agree that it would be terser and better as "Nobody laughed"? I'm sending the NY office a page, so revised.

A Happy New Year!
GUY

/ • /

Achilles Fang: Chinese scholar at Harvard who visited Pound at St. Elizabeths. Archibald MacLeish (1892–1982) was a poet and two-time Pulitzer Prize winner who taught at Harvard and Amherst and was Librarian of Congress for five years. GD was for a time MacLeish's student-assistant.

All critters named Belinda: GD had a cat named Belinda. JL remembered having "a fling" with a cute girl named Belinda, but to his chagrin he couldn't recall her last name.

BJ's advice to the lovelorn: GD had earlier passed on a comment of Bonnie Jean Cox and JL had made the poem "Better Than Potions" of it. See *SR,* 128.

80. TLS—6

January 3, 1993

New Year's Resolutions

Short, terse letters
Use only words that are in the dictionary
No peripheral eroticism
No sideways broadjumping

Dear Guy—

Please keep tabs and debit me 50¢ for each infraction of the above rules. Time is money. . . .

Let me run through various letters for biz matters.

Thank you for doing the notes. Just what the doctor ordered. Very solid. They'll help serious readers to know what's going on in your method. May even lead a few to read some books that will be good for them. A case where a computer did something useful. I remember now that you did tell me when I was there that Bonnie Jean worked in the "Liberry," as Henry called it when he was eight. Henry is now awash in computers. He was doing computer graphics last year when he was in Oregon. Now he's doing some kind of programming, so abstruse that I can't understand what it is. He describes it in the jargon of the trade. All Swahili to me. Wot *forma mentis* izzet? And that dawg, a pretty lab, but so lazy she'd rather you stepped on her than move six inches to let you by.

Thanks also for the enlarged acknowledgements. No problems that I can see.

Thank you for abdicating your advance. Conserves working cash. There is no legal compulsion for advances. They are just Mammonism enabling rich publishers to compete with each other, which has become a monstrosity. As dear old Alfred Knopf once told me: "If I hire a mason to build a wall I don't pay him till he has built it."

What are your thoughts on a publication date? Griselda was asking. It takes quite a while for them to put a book together, so it would be either Fall 1993 or Spring 1994. If you aren't in a rush to parturiate (penalty for that one) I'd favor the latter. The depression is still very much with the book trade; the Norton sales manager tells me the stores still have inventory constipation and are not buying much highbrow lterschoor; playing it safe with Sidney Sheldon and Judy Krantz. What do you think? Should we give Smiley time to get the system flowing? . . .

Going back to your collage quotes. As I read along I didn't spot anything which looked like a permissions problem. It's all, I think, what the copyright rules call fair use. The law does not define the allowable length of fair use, but I believe Peggy figures it at 10 sequential lines of poetry, and 150 words of sequential prose. We have never had any problem with claiming that short bits—what you are using—are fair use. In England they are much more liberal, for quoters, on fair use, whole pages can be incorporated. Actually, nobody sues on things of this kind because it is just too expensive to litigate. Of course, if some Hollywood shark lifted one of my poetical narratives to make a mini-series that might be different. . . .

JL

/ • /

New Year's Resolutions: GD's response on January 12, 1993 was, "You must break them all. If kept, they would cancel the chief delight of your letters. Peripheral eroticism may be out of place in your correspondence with William Jefferson Clinton and Denise Levertov, but is welcome here."
Thank you for doing the notes: Explanatory notes printed at the back of *A Table of Green Fields.* Comparing this comment with the opening of the next letter may suggest these are out of sequence, but GD went through several drafts of these notes.
Henry: JL's son.
birds on the towers of silence: JL is alluding to the Parsi practice of leaving the dead exposed on towers for vultures.

81. TLS—1

5 *janvier* 1993

DEAR MR LAUGHLIN—

Here's the revised Acknowledgements (for up front) + 3 pages of Notes, to go at the end. The question being, What do you think? Literate readers just might be interested, and re-assured. They are not as learned as the notes you've done for some of your books of poems. It was an awful process back-tracking, and Bonnie Jean and her computer at the library had to be called into service to re-locate sources. Some graduate student may be grateful.

Speaking of students, one of my brighter ones published a book of poems last year (I finagled a small publisher into doing it). Yesterday he called to say that The Fund for Poetry (of which I'd never heard) had sent him a check for $2,000, out of the blue, and very welcome. Erik's smart and charming wife is finishing her doctoral thesis, and Erik is teaching jug-eared Kentuckians and sex-mad sorority queens the rudiments of punctuation, spelling, and sentence structure.

The sun has not shown His face for over a week down here. Yesterday was hot; today, cold. These are the 12 days when the daimons who live in the roots of the World Tree are loose on the earth. They go back tomorrow. The *kakadaimones* the Greeks called 'em.

ad interim,
GUY

/ • /

one of my brighter ones: Erik Anderson Reece's *My Muse Was Supposed to Meet Me Here* (Bamberger Books, 1992). The publisher was not in fact finagled, but enthusiastic.

82. TLS—1

1/21/93

DEAR PETER [GLASSGOLD]—

Here is a copy of Guy's *A Table of Green Fields,* but don't let this pass into the design phase. I've arranged with Griselda to have the layouts and mark-ups done by Gertrude. I know what I want and she'll do it under my supervision. I want it to tone in with the cover art and title page drawing he is doing, but these haven't turned up yet. I've promised Griselda that we'll keep Guy's obsession with pedophilia off the cover. I find it boring, but I guess genius is entitled to its quirks. . . .

Best, and thanks,
JL

83. TLS—5

1/28/93

REVERED BOTANIST [GD]—

. . . The penibility of an arthritic day was eased by the arrival of your blurb, which is JIM-DANDY. It explains exactly what needs to be explained about the process, and with what elegance and ease. No sweat, no strain. I was up shit creek with that ponderous business about the cubist painter. A dozen phrases that hit right on the noggin. A "kind of music to which the characters dance." I feel dumb that I hadn't spotted where the title came from. Good to get that in.

I called the office at once and adjured Declan Spring, who will be working there on the book, not to change a word, except to add as a short lead one of the blurbs picked up from past books to signal, since you haven't been on the ND list before, that you are a very important author. . . .

Please make my apologies to Mme. Angelou the next time she calls. I don't understand much about a poem from *hearing* it read. For which reason I never go to poetry readings. I have to *see* a text and have time to study and ponder it. If I didn't catch the echoes of Whitman it is because Fitts didn't like him and didn't have us read him, and I never got around to him since, being busy with other poets, except perhaps in anthologies something about "O Captain" and lilacs in a dooryard, and "Out of the Cradle Endlessly Rocking," which Bunting told me at Hexham Ezra knew by heart. BB said that poem was the basic rhythm of the *Proprietus,* and Ezra says somewhere, "I find myself using his rhythms."

You'll be surprised to learn where I got my slight education in Whitman. It was from Edith Sitwell once when I was visiting her at Renishaw. It turned out that Walt was one of her favorite poets. She read him to me for several hours. The mix of her accent with his tone was rather bizarre. Except for the gorgeous gardens Renishaw must be the ugliest great house in England, and the most dilapidated. Edith's father, potty old Sir George, had wasted his inheritance fixing up a 200-room 13th century *palazzo* in Italy. Only a third of the rooms at Renishaw were open. Once I heard a frightening subterranean rumbling. It was the coalminers working in their tunnels under the place, the source of the family's wealth. There was as yet no hot-water system. My bath was a large tin "hip-personge," with circular seat, which arrived in my bedroom at eight, brought in by the footman with two tiny cans of hot water. I owe more to Dame Edith than just Whitman. She told me of an astounding young poet whom I would find in a certain pub near Red Lion Square. It was Dylan Thomas. *Was für eine tragische Leben!.* . . .

["signed" with a tiny figure drawing]

/ • /

Revered Botanist: JL would at times ask GD to "prune"—i.e., edit—his poems in progress.
about the cubist painter: To begin the process of arriving at jacket copy JL had drafted a blurb comparing GD's technique to a Cubist painter's. The flap copy on the published book is what JL received here from GD, with a descriptive sentence added at the top.
where the title came from: GD's text reads, "Falstaff's dying vision of 'a table of green fields,' probably a mishearing of his recitation of the Twenty-third Psalm."
apologies to Mme. Angelou: JL had been disappointed in Maya Angelou's poem at Clinton's inauguration. GD defended it, suggesting it evoked Whitman.
Bunting: Basil Bunting (1900–1985), English poet.
Edith Sitwell: (1887–1964), English poet and critic.
Was für eine tragische Leben!: "What a tragic life!"

84. TLS—3

3 *février* 1993
Gertrude Stein

Dear Mr Laughlin:

. . . In case you're curious about my prejudices, I'll go on record as saying that the most interesting human being I've ever heard of is Charles Marie François Fourier, followed by Herakleitos, W. Shakespeare, and Plutarch. Several hundred more, of course; these bob to the surface of my disorganized mind.

Well, the wonder of Dr. Angelou's poem was that it *could* be heard, and I'm glad I listened, as the poem in print isn't as great as the recitation. I agree that read poetry goes by too fast.

Fancy hearing Whitman at Renishaw. "Read him to me for several hours"! It's a Max Beerbohm cartoon: Dame Edith Sitwell, *châtelaine* of Renishaw, reads Mr. James Laughlin, Democrat, his national poet Walter Whitman, for several days on end. With the rumbling of coal-mining beneath.

In some sense the *Cantos* are *A Passage to India* rewritten in particular detail, much as *Guernica* is a repainting of Goya. I'm thrilled to know that Ez could recite "Out of the Cradle Endlessly Rocking."

"O Captain My Captain" was written for school children to say; the grown-up version is "When Lilacs Last in the Dooryard Bloom'd." . . .

In your blurb you were not wrong about cubism. The whole business of the cubists has always been wrongheaded in the public (and critical) mind. It is actually close to Ez's ideograms: Braque trusts us to recognize a violin by a few details of its parts, just as Ez can work in a poem with a single Anglo-saxon phrase, or suggest a landscape with the wind through an olive tree. Braque was painting a particular culture (French middle class, that reads newspapers, drinks *apéritifs,* plays a musical instrument, and has well-ordered houses with furniture).

Note (just thought of this): in your stories your characters move in streaming motions (walking, crossing Paris, driving, shifting from room to room in a house) whereas my characters make small decisive movements, and usually stand, or sit, still.

The skier and the pedestrian.

I don't dare look up Holinshed's Disease (which you've twice mentioned) as I catch everything I know the symptoms of. The only Holinshead I know is the Elizabethan historian, pronounced Hollin's Head.

I'd better put this out for the postman. Yellow and mauve crocuses are up, and there are tips of daffodils in the back yard. I keep finding new things for my copier to copy. I've even broken my rule of not showing people unpublished work (except publishers, of course) and my correspondents will soon deplore my easy ability to make copies. My friend Tony Stoneburner (the last Methodist circuit rider) has been sent "And," as he's an ardent theologian, as well as a fan of my ravings.

ad feliciter interim,
GUY

/ • /

Max Beerbohm: (1872–1956), Beerbohm was an English writer and critic, but was primarily known for his caricature drawings.
A Passage to India: 1924 novel by English novelist E. M. Forster. It deals with the clash of English and Indian cultures.
Holinshed's Disease: JL's wry self-diagnosis for his faulty memory: "Hole-In-Head's Disease."

85. TL—3

8 February 1993

DEAR MR LAUGHLIN:

Well, if Mr. Bill Rusin thinks little Ivan Rodchenko is "gloomy and sordid," let's hope he doesn't look at the text. I suspect that he doesn't know a masterpiece of Soviet photography from a Grandma Moses. . . .

Norton anthologies. Back when I kept office hours, I used to amuse myself correcting the idiotic footnotes to poems in them. I don't know what wretches are hired to write 'em, but they are entertainingly illiterate. And in Eudora's *Norton Anth of Friendship* they have an author's name misspelled.

Women, as you know, disdain mere language. BJ brought home a recording of French military music today. This means that we're going to France for our vacation.

T. Williams and TSE discussing the calves of ballet dancers is another Beerbohm cartoon.

I must dig out your letter of some months back in which you introduced the ND staff, to see how you characterized D. Spring.

For days I thought he was a girl—what language does Declan come from? Scotland? Ireland? And izzit pronounced DEK-lan? Latin *declans* (from declare) = proclaiming.

Speaking of girls, BJ overheard a sorority nymph saying to another, "Did you go out to see Gertrude Stein signing her books? It was a real thrill to see her in person!" (The signer of books was Gloria Steinem.)

On which note
[unsigned]

Does Norton have veto power over WHAT you publish?

/ • /

Mr. Bill Rusin thinks little Ivan Rodchenko: Rusin, sales manager for Norton publishing, which distributes ND. He considered the photo of a child bathing in a tub which GD had suggested might make a good cover image, and rejected it as "gloomy and sordid." The final decision to reject it, though he talks around it, apparently was JL's. The photo was by Aleksandr Rodchenko (1891–1959), Russian Constructivist painter and photographer. He was an associate of Vladimir Tatlin, about whom GD wrote the title story of his first collection, *Tatlin!*

T. Williams and TSE: An anecdote JL related about going to the Garrick Theatre in London with Tennessee Williams and T. S. Eliot.

86. TLS—3

2/14/93

Dear Guy—

When I tried to wear my Pirates baseball cap while lecturing at Brown the femulist students made me take it off. My chief objection to the Norton anthologies is that in all these years they've never put one of my verses in one of them. I am not liked in academia.

Don't worry. Norton has nothing to say about what we publish, though I suppose if we started a series of pornographic classics they might fuss. It's in writing in the agreement that they have nothing to say about texts. Bill Rusin's judgment on jackets is simply advisory—what he thinks will sell. This only happened once before. We humor him because of his influence on the salesmen.

Will your machine make copies of the lavender print, and the Tate *August Blue* so that Goldilocks could size them up? Or should I ask Declan to hunt? Vanessa (or the Soulful one) would go by the Tate to get a good photo. The Tate's charges, and for the permission, are usually reasonable. We can have color on the jacket—that's in the budget—if desired. . . .

Placatory Verses for Mr. Rusin
Now all must love the Human Form
In Christian, Turk or Jew;
Where Beauty, Love & Mercy dwell
There God is dwelling too.

It has never been alleged that Mr. Rusin reads the *insides* of books. He looks at the jackets, reads the catalog blurbs, and then markets with ZIP.

So be it,
JAS

/ • /

Goldilocks: JL's wife, Gertrude, who designed the cover using Tuke's painting *August Blue.*

87. TLS—3

19 February 1993

DEAR MR LAUGHLIN!

. . . For what it's worth—Ronald Johnson has finished his long poem *Ark* (my title). Jack was going to publish it at North Point. I've pub'd two critical essays on it, and feel it has a vision not elsewhere to be found. Kenner called it a religious poem some years ago. I acted as Ronald's info man while he was writing it. I included the first part in a course once (Olson and Johnson, a joke the students were too young to catch) and students liked it once I'd shown them how to trust the poet and find the hidden figures and outrageous conceits. I've urged Ron to send it to New Directions. It wounds out The Pound Era—RJ coming from Zukofsky and Olson. It's the kind of poem the French would like (or used to like). It's kin to Superville in that it's about creation. 'Sfarz I can understand it, it's about the evolution of the eye (which Darwin thought was nature's masterpiece) so that Nature could see itself.

The mattioli *Lavender* is 2' × 3' and my copier is 12" × 9". And the more I look at *August Blue* (even though it shares a title with the first story) the duller it looks. Enclosed: a very dark repro of *August Blue* and the TE Lawrence (also deplorably dark) that was the beginning of the story.

That Mrs Yak is a Nak was told me here by the fire by Ann Diamond, who had taken off her shoes and socks. You wouldn't doubt a bare-footed 25-year-old UN World Health Organization scout who speaks Nepalese, would you?

I didn't say we were going to France; I said that Bonnie Jean bought a recording of French military music. I'd guessed that I was to take the hint. I can get along with the public French, even in Paris. They have more manners in Bordeaux.

After that Buchanan speech some wag in the sound room played the theme from *La Cage aux Folles*. Not that Buchanan or Bush could have figured out the wit of it.

20 Feb I'm putting this in the mail, so you'll have it, and natter on later. My feeling about the cover is that we have to start all over. The French *Bicyclette de Léonard* and *Tatlin!* have rich details from Renaissance paintings, alluding to nothing in the books. Perhaps Goldilocks can suggest something in that line. . . .

meanwhile,
GUY

/ • /

Ronald Johnson has finished his long poem Ark: Johnson (1935–1998), poet and cookbook author, worked on the poem for over twenty years. Despite GD's advocacy, ND did not publish *Ark*. It was published in 1996 by Living Batch in Albuquerque, New Mexico.
Zukofsky and Olson: Louis Zukofsky (1904–1978), Objectivist poet and author of the epic poem *A*. GD once called him "our greatest living poet." Charles Olson (1910–1970), poet and teacher of Robert Creeley, Robert Duncan, and many more. Best known for his *Maximus Poems*.
Buchanan speech: Pat Buchanan, Republican archconservative. *La Cage aux Folles* was a musical play, then a movie, about a gay couple trying to hide their sexuality.

88. TLS—2

February 24, 1993

Dear Guy:

Courtesy of Hermes the last six days of my miserable life have been abolished. I never want to think of them again. My neck was fighting my head like the battle of Borodino. The pills Dear Doc [gave me] . . . are no better than munching Dentyne gum. Only three hopes: acupuncture or chiopraxy [*sic*] or the doctor in Mexico who cured George Oppen's sister but he doesn't say what he shot into her *[. . .]* and that's a long trip. My sin, my sins, I'm paying for them.

Both Cinderella and I like Tuke's *August Blue*. I've sent the print down to Griselda. If she likes it I hope she can clear it with Rusin. The print is a bit grey but as far as I can see those lads aren't doing anything but skinny-dipping. An idyllic scene, marine pastoral. Vanessa can get a color slide and permission from the Tate. She's done that before for me. Not that you need to make a final decision for a while.

[. . .] Mit dir keine Nacht ist zu lang. On the radio Saturday. *Rosenkavalier.* And the same in the Elegaic Poets. And one night with Angelica I didn't go to sleep at all, just lay beside her watching her breathe. *Was Mann wunscht dass seine Wahrheit ist.* An appropri-

ate apothegm can be found for almost any sentiment, no matter how silly it is. . . .

You say you're astonished if people read your prose. That's easy: your writing is one astonishment after another. . . .

Starting to cough again. I'd better fold. But maybe I can speak of the cover we had on Nika Tucci's stories: a most beautiful saint somebody riding a donkey or something into Renaissance landscape. Nika not exactly saintly. He's the Eyetalian weirdo in *Angelica.*

And so to bed, as the diarists say,
JAS

/ • /

Mit dir keine: "With you no night is too long." From Richard Strauss's 1911 comic opera *Der Rosenkavalier,* with libretto by Hugo von Hofmannsthal.
Was Mann wunscht: "What a man desires is his reality."
Nika [Niccolò]; Tucci's stories: The Rain Came Last.
Enclosed with this letter was the poem "Is Memory" (see *PNS,* 235). JL added in holograph, "First lines are from Woody Allen's film *Another Woman.*" The poem was below a Xerox of an erotic woodcut by Eric Gill. Gill (1882–1940) was a British sculptor, type designer, and author.

89. TLS—3

[March 1, 1993?]

DEAR MR LAUGHLIN!

Well, get the chiropractor AND the acupuncture *virtuosi* in, and see what they can do. I have a friend in Wisconsin who goes to a veterinary chiropractor, and know several people who swear by that art. It may give you a thrill to say you're suffering for your sins, but all those years of sliding down mountains in icy air must have a little something to do with your painful neck. And there's probably as much Calvinism in that comforting remark as in your theological theory.

There are many better Tuke's than *August Blue,* but it would be illogical to use one when this 'un has supplied a title. The one called *Morning Splendour* is the one he's painting in the story. There are two books about Tuke, and neither reports any moral lapses in his Cornish cove. Some London *literatus* reported an urchin on the village street saying that down to Mr. Tuke's you could see John Wesley buck naked and being painted a picture of.

The Tucci cover is splendid: I hope we can come up with something as good. I'm fascinated that you see a saint in the detail. There's a stork, a donkey, and a sheep with their shepherd, but no saint. Did he get off on the way down here?

Eric Gill. I used to work (as printer) to Claire Leighton, who used to pose for him. She said he kept an erection the whole time. He was a pedantic eroticist.

David Jones's biographer tells me that David had *one* sensual encounter—lying and hugging a woman on a couch. I find this moving, and somehow beautiful—it would have interested Kierkegaard, who apparently had no sensual experience at all. Flaubert buggered an Egyptian boy, in case he needed to describe same. Walt Whitman slept with his retarded brother, and God knows what they did in bed.

One of life's oddest moments was back in the 60s, when college kids were doing everything. I was at Haverford, and one day a shy student came to the office and asked me what sex *was.* He didn't know anything, except the vague notion that it's how God uses us to make babies. I'd thought it was all taught in Kindergarten nowadays.

And one of the charmingest: a bunch of seven-year-olds, boys and girls, at Zelda Suplee's nudist place in the Poconos (where I used to play tennis with Karl Marx's great-grand-daughter, aet. 15, in the altogether). The kids had rival theories about sex, and were pretty sophisticated city kids, and surrounded by scads of adults, including their parents. Each was certain of his own knowledge, and I think they didn't trust their parents to know anything so interesting. Anyway, they had everything cockeyed. Innocence is quite real.

Your poem "Is Memory" has lovely rhythms and an admirable simplicity. It's a Yeatsian thought.

My self-invited weekend guests called a while ago to say that they're snowed in in Ohio and have the flu. I like people, but not meeting them. "Old friends the best." And not all of them. I am a monogamist hermit.

2 March Today is Tax Figuring Day, and the accountant is to turn up any minute now. He says I'm a Small Business. I resent having to pay taxes on prizes and my wholly unsolicited MacArthur fellowship. But Ronnie signed the bill that required even Nobel laureates to cough up, while saying out of the other side of his mouth that private Enterprise should support the arts, not government. Well, every time p.e. gives a dollar to a poet or painter, the Feds grab 20¢ of it.

Arbitrariness, I believe, is the hallmark of tyranny.

When I was a knickerbockered and aviator-capped spadger, a Coke cost a nickel, and with 2¢ at the candy counter you could get wonders. Four jelly beans for a penny. The big expense was the movies, 9¢. Uncle Percy owned one of the movie houses, and I could get in free, but I was too proud to do this, and went to the other theatres. I also paid for my buddy Mendel, whose father thought movies sinful.

meanwhile,
Guy

I hope your neck is better.

/ • /

John Wesley: As Wesley, founder of Methodism, lived from 1703 to 1791, GD is probably suggesting another incident like that of the "Gertrude Stein" sighting in the Lexington bookstore.

90. TLS—1

5 March 1993

Dear Mr Laughlin:

So five naked boys bathing in Cornwall have it all over one bathing in a dishpan in a Russian kitchen? OK by me, if it's OK by you. It's your publishing house. And the opening piece is named for the painting. Maybe the Danes will take notice—not a single one of my ravings is in the Copenhagen Public Library. . . .

expeditiously,
Guy

91. TLS—5

3/16/93

Dear Guy—

I like to keep you (and BJ) stocked with useful culinary knowledge. Rita Severi, one of my Italian translators, informs me that the tortellini of Modena, her homeplace, are modeled on the belly-button of Venus.

I've been having some fun correspondence with Anne Carson. I wrote to her because I liked so much her poems about God. *Elle voit des choses que ne voient pas les autres.* A hard girl to fool. Did you see the God poems? They were in *A*[*merican*] *P*[*oetry*] *R*[*eview*]. I can copy some for you if you like. Unfortunately, she'd already promised them to Cummington Press. I like her because she tells me where to get off in a witty way. Re "Sardonicus of Tyre," she said, "If I were your analyst I would tell you it's good you are dealing with your anger this way." Ain't that the truth? I've tried to explain to her that what Sardonicus is angry about is that he's not in the Norton anthologies. She has given me some good leads on where to look for "correlatives" for *Byways*. I think Pausanias has an edifice complex, but a bloke named Athenaeus, an after-dinner speaker, seems promising. I've now obtained her *Eros,* and that should renew my eddie-Cajun. . . . She is a Volcanist; she paints volcanoes that look like the sundaes we used to get at the drugstore counters exploding with chocolate sauce. I shouldn't be irreverent. She's obviously someone to be reckoned with. . . .

Sic ambulat,
JAS

/ • /

Anne Carson: Canadian poet (currently at the University of Michigan in Ann Arbor), author of *Eros the Bittersweet,* and several other volumes of criticism and poetry. ND would publish her collection *Glass, Irony and God,* with GD contributing an introduction, in 1995.

92. TLS—1

30 March 1993
Vincent Willem van Gogh

DEAR MR LAUGHLIN!

Van Gogh came up in a conversation the other day, and my interlocutor said, "He's the one that bit off his ear, wasn't he?" Surely you've made a poem of the Modena tortellini and the BVM's navel. The Greeks said that their standard wine *krater* was molded on the mammary of Pallas. Norman Douglas was complimenting a *calabrese* on her red-bean *zuppa,* and was told it was the Virgin's favorite dish.

In re Anne Carson, I enclose my review of *Eros the Bittersweet.* From *Grand Street.* I missed the God poems. Where is she now? She was at Princeton, but they fired her. She's one of my intellectual pin-ups. . . .

It's a beautiful spring day here. I've had a walk through the park to a second-hand bookshop, and am going to put this in the mail, having been off my stride in answering the mail. More, later.

tardily,
GUY

/ • /

Norman Douglas: (1868–1952), famously hedonistic English novelist.

93. TLS—6

4/4/93

DEAR GUY—

The JL/Schwartz letters have come. I'll send you one when I get more. It's full of magnificent untruths (like about Delmore's "sister" whom I found in a Milwaukee bookstore and carried off to the Drake in Chicago, but was so skeert all she could do was tremble) and complicated witty saws, and, at the end, unbearable sadness.

The thought of poor Vincent biting off his own ear has burned itself into the cortex of my being. The only other person I heard of doing that was Harry Houdini. He did it under water bound with chains, but he had a fake celluloid ear for a prop. V's doing it—and I'm sure he did, or thought he did—is a penetrating metaphor. . . .

Professor Carson is located at Dept. of Classics, McGill University, 855 Sherbourne Street West, Montreal, Canada, 83A 27S. I'd like to be penpals with such a classical doll, but I don't think it's going to work out. When I first wrote her about her God poems (I'll copy those for you) she was brief but civil. Then when I asked her to suggest sub-plots for "Sardonicus of Tyre" she got terse; decided I was a nut. Then she asked if I would publish her version of Soph. *Elektra,* and I had to tell her we had Ezra's on our list. Deep silence.

Anyway I suspect that she wants to be pals with people like Prof Cohen of Berkeley who had a scholarly piece on the Op Ed page of the *Times* recently setting forth that some Greek army recruited loving boys because it made the sojers braver. The Pentagon generals must have loved that.

Thank you for sending *Eros the Bittersweet.* You can come up with more provoking ideas than Brer Rabbit and Possum together. Where do you keep them all? On cards? How can you remember so much? What does your head feel like with so much ideational circulation? Does it give you migraine, pressure of ideas trying to burst out? Or make you feel tipsy? When I smoke a good cigar there can be a feeling like word-grasshoppers jumping around in my head—but nothing at your level.

Your suggestions/explanations should help me to penetrate her. That doesn't sound very nice, does it? But I need help with her, if my erotic life is, even at this age, to reach full development.

I'm in for some revelations. Take the *"phainetai moi kenos . . ."* one of my favorite love poems. I found it in Bill Williams' version in *Paterson.* Bill said that Kenneth Burke had helped him work it up and I just assumed they had it right. He and she sitting face to face. But now, corrected, I look at Campbell in the Loeb. There it very well could be three people, whence could follow jealousy or kicks. Now I go to see what Catullus did with it. (The Cornish translation in the Loeb.) Maybe it could be either: *"qui sedens adversus identidem te / spectat et audit."* That might be two or three?

Am I disgraced? Will I be stripped of my nine Litt Ds? A day in the stocks of the Yard?

But then the learned lady (page 15) speaks of the "rhetorical theory": "the man who listens closely *[. . .]* is not to be thought of as a real person, but as a poetic hypothesis designed to show by contrast how deeply Sappho is affected by the presence of her beloved. As such he is a cliché of erotic poetry. *[. . .]*"

Cat-piss & kitten-piss. This bimbo is too high-falutin for me. What did they fire her from Princeton for? But I won't give in so easily, especially when I have your piece to steer me. It's good for me to stretch my bean, unless it makes the scalp itch, like the young fellow in the TV commercial.

I hear Sandy's car in the driveway, breakfast soon,
JAS

/ • /

JL/Schwartz letters: Delmore Schwartz and James Laughlin: Selected Letters.
Eros the Bittersweet: GD's review of Carson's book was reprinted in *HG,* 135–43.
Kenneth Burke: American writer-critic who practiced a very active criticism, one that was almost re-creation.
I'm in for some revelations: For Carson's discussion of this poem, see *Eros the Bittersweet,* 13–17.

94. TLS—7

4/6/93

DEAR GUY:

. . . Is Anselm Hollo a friend of yours? He has sent me 15 pages of super-zippy translations of Hipponax of Ephesus. I can't believe that any Greek cracked that wise *[. . .]* like Arsenio on the late show. Of course many translators want to recreate their victims in their own images. Like what I do to the *G*[*reek*] *A*[*nthology*] amorists. . . .

Back to your article on *Eros;* it's going to take me many readings to get all the points through, or rather into, my bean. As said before, I'm a turnip head. When you speak of an "imaginary space, the presence of an absence *[. . .]*" I'm pushed back to the confusion I had when I was trying to read the books Merton had quoted in the *Asian Journal,* to get it fixed for the printer. It came to me in notes state, a little tag on his small satchel which read: "In the event of my death this case to be delivered to James Laughlin," and two years I saw in a sea of ignorance trying to figure all those strange ideas out *[. . .]* and specifically "the presence of an absence" takes me back to that night in Trivandrum (did you ever see the poem?) when the fierce old guru—he looked like Oswald Spengler made of black bronze—asked me, "Now you, Mr. America, with your Aristotle, what is in the space between two thoughts?" Vedanta. I hadn't the foggiest, and he wouldn't tell me the answer.

Further on, does it infer that I chase girls because I'm so hungry for knowledge? Similar processes? . . .

[illegible],
JAS

/ • /

Anselm Hollo: Finnish-born poet and translator. JL didn't use these translations. They were later published as *The Poems of Hipponax of Ephesus* by Tropos Press.
Trivandrum: See *Byways*, 255–70.
Vedanta: An orthodox Hindu philosophy concerned with knowledge of Brahma, the Hindu supreme being.

95. TLS—1

Easter 1993 [4/11]

DEAR MR LAUGHLIN:

So you've beguiled La Carson into a witty and bewitching reply. Another virtuous woman on the slide. And Miss Vanessa goes the other way, into domestication. You write me about all these people as if I'd known them for years.

What I want to know about dreams is how I stage them in places I have never been, and which may not exist. It's a kind of travel, I suppose. I once gave so convincing a description of a neighborhood in Little Rock that my friend there went around town looking for it. And there's a country I can't identify, with conifer woods, beautiful wide highways, wrought-iron bridges, old-fashioned globe street lights, and charming parks.

Nope, Anselm Hollo bayn't a friend. I didn't know there were 15 pages of Hipponax, whose only poem I recall is "A man enjoys a woman twice / On his wedding night, and at her funeral." He, Archilochos, and Herondas are the leading Greek Dark Satirists. (Have I ever sent you my Herondas? The classicists stuck their noses up at it, though Grey Fox keeps it in print, and it sells as well as my Diogenes and Herakleitos, which is my all-time best seller.) . . .

My review of *Eros the Bittersweet.* A great deal of it is my paraphrase of the book. I *think* "the presence of an absence" is a sense of loss, or of yearning. Carson makes a big deal of the triangle all art involves—you, Monet, and a painting. In memory, there's what's remembered, you then, and you now remembering. In Sappho's poem we readers must sit in the space where Sappho was, when she observed Jack and Jill gawking at each other. In Velázquez's *Las Meninas,* we must stand in the space occupied by Felipe and his *reina* (reflected in the mirror). The practical use of all this for making cornbread (as Bonnie Jean would say) I don't know. To the guru asking about the space between two thoughts, you should have answered "one millimeter."

Chasing girls is *like* wanting to know something. I don't think there's any cause and effect, though Picasso's amorous life and his creative one were probably interdependent. In the brain there's a little nest of nerves that deal with the sex organs, fingers, and toes. The angel who designed that knew what he was doing.

I'm having an argument at the moment with a young admirer of [Alfred North] Whitehead, who was one of the late (in historical time), tired, syncretric philosophers. I find him all but unreadable. He *was* muddle-headed.

So you're going to Como (the thing you tried to entice me into). My daimon knows the future, and keeps me from getting committed. For instance, on Tuesday I go under the surgeon's knife (hernia) and will crepitate around the house for some weeks. This will be the second operation for a hernia; the first was eleven years ago, caused by repeatedly lifting deadweight a neighbor in a wheelchair onto his front porch. The cause this time is simple fraying of the fascia in the groin, from sin, middle age, and Republicans in Washington. . . .

Your friend Mr. Plimpton has just nixed an interview with me that *The Paris Review* commissioned. The first interviewer was a sensitive young man who was at the disadvantage of not having read my ravings. *I* scrubbed his interview. Then another, wildly ignorant young man came and did the interview over. It was hopeless, but I tried to salvage it by rewriting it. Anyway, Plimpton would have none of it, and I've sworn off interviews for good. They never ask the right questions, and the ones they do ask are usually ones I resent, or don't believe they could be so dumb as to ask. . . .

buon viaggi!
GUY

/ • /

Miss Vanessa goes the other way: Vanessa Jackson had written JL that she was to be married.
My Herondas . . . my Diogenes and Herakleitos: GD's books of translations *The Mimes of Herondas* and *Herakleitos and Diogenes,* both published by Grey Fox Press.
Como: JL was preparing to attend a literary conference in Como, Italy.
Mr. Plimpton: George Plimpton, publisher of the *Paris Review*. GD and the *Paris Review* did finally agree on an interview, conducted by John J. Sullivan. This was published in issue #163 (Fall 2002).

96. TLS—3

15 April 1993
Henry James
Lionardo da Vinci
Robert Walser

DEAR MR LAUGHLIN:

I can sit up and type for a while, at least. The operation went very well indeed. They take the staples out on Tuesday. I crepitate about in jammies and dressing gown. My pain pill is something Coleridge could have done wonders with: six-track dreams going by at 70 mph. A witty nurse says the street price of the pill is $18 the trick.

Right after the operation I managed to get off to Declan a book with Tuke's title painting in it. It turns out that I taught Declan's father Michael at Haverford. Small world. . . .

16 APR My ability to type was not, yesterday, as unlimited as I'd thought.

Spent the evening reading Eckermann. Goethe is a writer I find very difficult to like, but his talk and enthusiasms are beguiling. The translation is Margaret Fuller's, corrected and added to by some Oxford boffin. It all reads like a fairy-tale.

19 April Here I am up at 8 (early for me) wondering how the mail and practically all my work has got into such an unseemly snarl. I will have been in pajamas and dressing gown for a week tomorrow, when the stitiches (they're staples) come out and I can anhelate toward health and mobility. Having gone a whole day without the pain pill, I had to revert to it last night, along with the ice pack, and dreamed through 12 hours of dreams that would have kept Herr Doktor Freud busy for a week. Sex, fire, flood, strange cellars, storms in attics, people long forgotten.

Some astute theorist says that we don't have *a* brain, but a systems of brains, mentalities rather than a mentality, and no one ego. A continuity among these ganglia is sanity and integrity. My best brain is busily interested in things; all my other brains could have been used to make a dog, or a donkey.

I'm spending my evenings with Eckermann, and wonder why North Point calls it *Conversations with Eckermann* by Goethe, when (I've just looked) it is *Conversations with Goethe* by Johann Peter Eckermann? Also why some illiterate has gone so long unchallenged in titling Wallace Stevens's Opus Posthumus *Opus Posthumous.* Which is neither Latin nor English.

And a nonexistent book by Joyce, *Giacomo Joyce*? That's simply a notebook of trial passages and drafts, on which J.J. wrote his name. I'm ashamed of Ellmann for claiming that it's a long lost work of fiction. . . .

and meanwhile,
GUY

/ • /

Coleridge could have done: English Romantic poet and critic Samuel Taylor Coleridge (1772–1834). GD may have been alluding to Coleridge's opium addiction.
Margaret Fuller: (1810–1850), New England transcendentalist and associate of Emerson, author and champion of equal rights for women. Her translation of Eckermann's *Conversations with Goethe* was first published in 1839. She, her husband, and infant son died in a shipwreck off Fire Island.
Ellmann: Richard Ellmann, Joyce scholar and biographer.

97. TLS—2

4/21/93

DEAR GUY—

I feel wretched. There I was feeling sorry for myself because the conference was, mostly, so awful—those longwinded blowhards—and you were UNDER THE KNIFE. (Our black cook for 50 years, Wonza, always said she "would take the needle but not the knife.") Why didn't you tell me this was going to happen? I would have been down on my bony knees talking Latin for you. . . .

I hope you'll be as pleased as I am with the layout for your jacket that Gertrude/Cinderella/Goldilocks did. (There is also Beulah, a good biblical name, but I'm forbidden to use that.) She is so clever. She had found a copy shop down in Torrington that gives good color (the Tuke looks lovely) and they have some nice types which, by pushing a button they can make them print fatter or thinner, taller or shorter. It's magical. They like the design (elegant simplicity) at the office and she'll be sending a print down to you soon.

It sounds as though it hurt a lot. Was the nurse pretty? Now don't go lifting things again.

Best,
JAS

98. TLS—3

4/22/93

DEAR GUY—

I hope you're mending, and that the pain has abated. What's the name of the painkiller, if you remember it, that costs $18? I'd ask my doc what he thought of it for the arthritic pain in neck and head. He's tried half a dozen pills and none of them seem to work for more than about three hours. (Fortunately, the pain usually stops by itself around midnight so I get decent sleep.) . . . Ann would endure the worst pain before she would take an aspirin. That was her character. But not mine. I'm a sissy about pain.

Last evening I had the first happy, comfortable evening since I went off on the Italian misadventure. I was stretched out flat, head flat on the sofa, with my favorite Dvořák playing (the *Serenade for Strings,* do you know it? So mellifluous, so inventive) reading and re-reading the letters from you that came while I was away. Your letters are the best that have ever blessed me. Ezra's were too jumpy, and Rexroth's were too vituperative. Yours have the best style and the way the phrases are assembled is magical. Ovidian. We were forbidden by Fitts to use terms from one art on another. But the way you "modulate" your themes and ideas and quotes is like listening to Ravel or R. Strauss or Martinů. No fooling. Wit and a kind of tenderness for learning and the tradition.

What I'm driving at, what I've wondered about, is what you *do* with your letters? I was horrified when you said that you didn't make copies. Of course, in time the scholars will dig them out wherever the originals are, and selections will be published. But what about now? Why wouldn't others be delighted by them? Not scads of readers, there has to be the cultural background for them. But Ezra used to say he would be content if the right seven (or was it 17) readers read him. And there would be the problem of notes, I guess. Notes could break the rhythm of the flow.

Which brings me to the subject of George and the problem of the right interviewer. Because of his social jitterbugging and his doing TV commercials in his Boston accent George has his detractors. Some call him the male Jackie-O. But I think he's a serious character. When that bunch of boys finished Cambridge and went to Paris to start *Paris Review,* he was the one who really put the magazine together and kept it going. I think he invented the interview format. He takes them very seriously and works hard on them. I saw that when he did the 2-part interview on me. It was done by a jerk and George did a lot of good shaping and rewrite. He maintains standards.

I think you would be hard to interview because your work is what it is, and your mind runs on its own tracks. To get it right you would have to ask the questions as well as answer them. George did let Jimmy Merrill do something like that. . . . Jimmy explained his games with the Ouija board and related matters in, as I recall it, a rather arch tone which was suitable to the subject matter. (I'll leave a space here so I can fill in the issue number of *PR* when I find it: #122, Spring '92.)

Now let me try to put letters and interview together. Let related passages from the letters be the responses. Then you make up the questions that fit the answers. This would not be an attempt to present your work and ways of working in orderly fashion. It would be a mosaic. A presentation of what is in your head.

To categorize the passages from letters would be a computer job. I don't think my son Henry, our computer whiz, is literary enough to do it. But there are others around who could.

I have no idea whether George could be sold on this. I'm sure he would want to see it first. But if he demurred there are other highbrow mags, or it could even be a job for Leslie Miller at Grenfell Press, who is always asking me for projects. I don't think I could get it past Griselda, bless her dear conventional heart.

Am I crazy? You betcha. But if the idea revolts you, forget it.

Best,
JAS

/ • /

2-part interview on me: The JL interview was published in issues #89 and 90 (Fall and Winter 1983).
Jimmy Merrill: James Merrill (1926–1995), American poet, best known for his epic trilogy *The Changing Light at Sandover,* published in 1982. Some of his work, including the trilogy, was written using a Ouija board. In 1977 he won the Pulitzer Prize for poetry.

99. TLS—2

24 April 1993

DEAR MR LAUGHLIN:

Patient is the aptest word in English. I can do such things as toddle from the car to the bank (Bonnie Jean driving), and creep around the house. They've taken the staples out.

Good intentions being as good as the deed, I can appreciate your genuflected Latin without its having happened. I'd suspected a hernia, from the puffy groin, and there was only an interval of three days between diagnosis and repair, as they call it. Out-patient assembly-line surgery is all the rage nowadays, and St. Joseph's has it down pat. Test, questions, pubic shave, and in you go. BJ collected me at 6 (went in at noon).

There was one cute nurse, with freckles and a pert nose. The rest were built on the lines of a refrigerator. The EKG male nurse was probably gay, very gentle and witty. The woman who shaved my pubic symphysis was out of Grant Wood. . . .

Day before yesterday I had a visit all afternoon with Mihai Spariosu, of Yale. He translated *Tristram Shandy* into Roumanian and is altogether a fine fellow. He writes books about ancient Greek games and acting. He's a buddy of Virgil Nemoianu, also a Roumanian exile.

Virgil has been to visit, too, a few years back, and BJ says I hire actors to impersonate Roumanian intellectuals who stage these visits. Last summer the Peruvian Minister of Culture came. It turned out that he hadn't read a word of my scribbles; my name is on some kind of a list.

Our man Turke turns out to be from a long line of Quaker philanthropists and reformers (prisons and insane asylums). I suppose the family fortune had accumulated enough by his time that he could spend his life on the Cornish coast painting the local youths in the altogether. He was, apparently, not gay (that the researchers can pin down, the snoops) though he was fondly avuncular toward his models, educated them, and found them gainful employ after their boyish beauty faded. One of them did "have fits" later on, which his maiden aunt attributed to posing in the nude, but then we all know maiden aunts. . . .

ad interim,
Guy

100. TLS—3

26 April 1993

Dear Mr Laughlin:

The painkiller is Percocet (and I see that Bonnie Jean, always the thrifty shopper, has got me the generic exact copy Roxicet). I really can't speak for it, as the kind of minor surgery I had didn't run to persistent or sharp pain.

Freud, like Ann, would not take painkillers.

Yes, I know the Dvořák *Serenade for Strings.* In the matter of Ez's letters, I used to go over to Catherine Drinker Bowen's, in Bryn Mawr, and decipher them for her. Ez was writing her about Coke and Adams, whose biographer, as you know, she was. Santayana confessed that he couldn't make head nor tail of them. I wonder why Fitts didn't want the terms of one art applied to another? It could be that it had become an overwrought gimmick. Whistler's musical terms; Eliot's; and the poets' use of painterly terms (*portrait d'une femme*).

There's an overlap in all the arts. The poet's images are visual, and his meter is musical, as is his language. My fiction is a kind of drawing.

What do I do with my letters? I send them to people who have written me. Some years ago Jonathan Williams collected up our correspondence, and no publisher would touch it. (I had nothing to do with this, except give my consent.)

As for the interviews, I'm done with them. Never again. I'm willing to talk technicalities (sources, subject rhymes, and so on). Both the interviewers the *PR* sent here were going on the assumption that I have a coherent philosophy, or a set of likes and dislikes, which, if they could only get to, they would know something. The first wanted to explain everything by my being a South Carolinian; and the second kept asking my opinion of one thing after another. It's all rather like a student asking Hugh Kenner after a brilliant lecture, "What do you think of jazz?" . . .

If I follow your plan, passages from my letters would be identified by Somebody as the answers to questions which we would then supply?

I can't begin to envision this, as I forget what I write as soon as I write it. That is, I have a vague notion of comments and anecdotes that go into letters. You're crazy in this, as you admit, but it is the craziness of a fertile brain. One strategic objection is that letters are to specific people, who are part of the equation.

In England Philip Larkin's reputation is being destroyed by letters he wrote to his friends, with whom he was on various inside-joke relationships that no outsider (save God) could understand. (Thinking on paper, this; not a flat rejection.)

Apologies for a scatter-brained letter.

salve!
GUY

/ • /

Catherine Drinker Bowen: (1897–1973), author of a number of historical biographies.
Santayana: George Santayana (1863–1952, American philosopher, poet, and novelist who taught at Harvard at the turn of the twentieth century. After World War I, he lived in Rome.
My fiction is a kind of drawing: See also "Writing Untied and Retied as Drawing," *HG,* 266–74.
Jonathan Williams collected up: In 2004 *A Garden Carried in a Pocket: Letters 1964–1968* (ed. Thomas Meyer; Haverford, Pa.: Green Shade) appeared. This included material GD had specifically told Williams should not be included. This prompted what became the final break between the two longtime friends.
Philip Larkin: (1922–1985), English poet.

101. TLS—6

5/2/93

DEAR GUY—

I hope you are all better now and have just come in from your morning's 3-mile jog. Does Bonnie Jean run with you? I note that Hillary does not run with Smiley. It might do her plump legs some good. I think of BJ as sylphan—a slither of Cos. . . .

Professor Carson is giving me the elbow about my eccentric theories on the *GA* poets. Whatever she says, I insist that there are fillers in the lines. I've done enough filling in mine to spot them. I feel a certain rigidity about this lady. I suspect she is romance-immune. But at least she has a kind word for the "translations," which of course are "adaptations" or "suggested bys." I sent her Cat

32. That should finish her off. She writes that Gordon Lish is "considering" her essays at Knopf. Like WCW, Lish will go after anything that moves. His antics are part of the Hermes section (not finished) in *BYWAYS.* Hermes a real tricky character. Foozles a lot. Poor little Canadian girl. A bite or two and he'll drop her back in the barrel.

Gertrude has just come in with her jacket comp. I think it's B*E*A*U*T*I*F*U*L. . . .

Five days almost like summer and the
Bulbs have been jumping out of the ground,
JAS

/ • /

Professor Carson is giving me the elbow: Anne Carson wrote JL that his idea about "filler" was an indicator of an imperialist attitude toward the formulaic language of unfamiliar poetic traditions, in which all parts reinforced one another.
Cat 32: Catullus, Roman poet of the first century B.C. In this poem Catullus entreats the courtesan Ipsitilla to join him in bed. He promises her nine copulations.

102. TLS—1

5 May 1993

DEAR MR LAUGHLIN:

I have just written Sandra and Harry Reese that all my attempts at making drawings to go with your poems keep adding up to nothing, and that I must admit defeat, much as I'd like to be in on this project. The problem is the vagueness of the job. As I said before, I am the wrongest draughtsman to illustrate your poems, even though illustrations are not what's wanted. And that leaves me in a vacuum. I have tried both images and abstractions, none of which seem to me to be in the least appropriate.

I've never been quite so frustrated by a project.
And admit defeat.

Your new *Byways* episode. The Catullus saves it. As with the one about the Texas girl, I find the narrative technique full of untied shoestrings. Your style, however, is such that I can't see how to tie them and keep your distinctive voice. E. G.—

Me up at the Gargoyle. It
Was the night Dylan sprained
His ankle. We got him to his
Place in a taxi and went on
To hers in Chelsea. I think
Her name was Moira. She
Was . . .

(This excises 14 words without the loss of any information.) But I feel like an unforgiveable smart aleck tampering with your Roman verses. "I have kept my eraser in order."

Thanks for Hollo's Hipponax (in the style of my Archilochos of 1964, but with his own lively spin). Beguiling bugger, Hipponax ("Horse Lord"). And I wonder if that's a girl in the party scene. Seems to be breasted, but with a walking stick? And barefoot? Oops! Walking stick belongs to Beard. Them Greeks!

more later, with apologies,
GUY

/ • /

Sandra and Harry Reese: Owners-printers of Turkey Press, which published JL's *Heart Island.* JL had wanted GD to contribute some new drawings to the project.
Your new Byways episode: See *Byways,* 242–43.

***103.* TLS—2**

7 May 1993
Browning
Brahms

DEAR MR LAUGHLIN!

First of all, solicitude and sympathy for Gertrude's diverticular attack, which can be far more serious than a visit to Winsted Hospital. My friend Bob Butman, the drama man at Haverford and Bryn Mawr in my days there, almost left the world, and looked as if he had. Dr. Yon took me off popcorn and peanuts years ago, but not *Snickers* bars. I have ever since claimed to be under doctor's orders to eat *Snickers* bars.

Secundo, the jacket is indeed of a purity, pure. Howsomever [*sic*], I think that my name should be (a) smaller, and (b) lower case except of course for the cap G and D. As it is, it seems to me to be out of harmony with the other type and with the picture. People normally look at books fairly close in a bookstore. Try it and see. A name all in caps is that of a politician, not an author.

I still feel bad about my backing away from drawings for the Turkey Press book. My imagination went on strike. It had nothing to go on.

I'm healing nicely, but Bonnie is down in her back. From exercise and bike riding. She's smeared with *Baume Bengué* and on a heating pad. She was going to drive to Canada this weekend for a meeting of her Feminist Terrorist group.

The WCW section of *Byways* promises to be more interesting than *The National Enquirer.*

I'm pleased to have, at last, the inside stuff on Ez's release. I worked with Archie on it, getting the petition signed. Frost, I knew, was merely a front, for the newspapers. He never went to St. Liz.

La Carson sounds awfully pedantic in her letter. Who does she think she's writing to, a sophomore at Cal Tech? At least you now know that you are an imperialist. But note that she wants you to sit on her knee. . . .

Lovely as your letter is today, and the jacket design, I was most pleased to have a letter from Avram Davidson, dictated to a hospital orderly, and brief but pithy. Avram on his 70th birthday a month ago collapsed with a diabetic attack and lay on his floor for two days before he was found. I'd tracked him (I believe I said in my last letter) to a Bremerton WA hospital. He sounds brave and chipper. I'd talked last week with his nurse, and told her that Avram was a very distinguished writer, "just a notch or two below Tolstoy," which I'd thought was a practical hyperbole. The nurse got this all mixed up, and thought Avram lived in Bremerton near the Tolstoys, and asked what kind of neighbors they were.

Nonrecognition of the great always causes high comedy. Do you remember the Mafioso who was executed by fellow business partners on his doorsteps in NY (back in WW II)? He had in his pocket a list of names (presumably to buy art books as Xmas presents for a daughter). Anyway, the FBI sent out an all-points alert to bring in Caravaggio, Leonardo da Vinci, Michelangelo, and Duccio di Buoninsegna. Shoot on sight. . . .

A student once raved about a really neat girl he'd met, from Suomi, Finland.

Today has been the first really lovely early summer one, with the azalea (red) in full bloom. Got a kid to cut the grass, which was getting to be knee-high, had a walk—a big return to the normal round of things. Being an invalid is interesting for only so long. . . .

ad interim,
GUY

/ • /

the inside stuff on Ez's release: On May 2, JL had written GD that the prime mover in securing Pound's release from St. Elizabeths was his wife Ann's brother-in-law, Gabe Hauge, a speechwriter for President Dwight D. Eisenhower. JL had mentioned Pound to him over breakfast. GD had worked with Archibald MacLeish trying to achieve the same thing.

La Carson sounds: In Anne Carson's note to JL re his translations from the *Greek Anthology* (a copy of which he had sent to GD), she pointed out that Greek *epi* means "upon" in the physical sense, as in "You sit upon my knee," and not in an intellectual

sense. GD is here gently mocking JL's continued sexualization of his pursuit of a book from Carson.
Avram Davidson: (1923–1993), author of nineteen published novels and collections of short stories and essays. He primarily wrote fantasy.
Suomi, Finland: "Suomi" is the Finnish name for Finland.

104. TLS—3

May 13, 1993

DEAR GUY—

Sorry to be mute for so long. For near a week I've been with Job on his dunghill, my aching neck banging. If I take strong pills I get woozy and can't think, if I ever could, while the milder ones don't last long. God punishes those who have sinned.

Naturally I'm very sorry about your decision on the pictures for the little book of scrapings on the rock, but I certainly wouldn't want you to get into something that wouldn't be joyful. As Klopstock remarked, *"Die Kunst muss immer Freude geben."* Not to mention *Schoenheit.* If the Reeses could supply live models *[. . .]* . . .

I'm deeply touched that you fixed up some lines from the Gargoyle Club girl to show how they could be tightened up, as certainly they need to be. "Untied shoestrings" is an understatement. Joe Parisi said it wasn't a poem, and Marjorie Perloff says it goes flat all the time. Looking back to the Rexroth model I see that he managed to keep the language colorful and tensed up. I don't think I'll try to do that kind of polishing now. It would make me get discouraged. Better, I think, to try to get the whole biz roughed out, and then rewrite. They say Lawrence rewrote every book three or four times. No comparison, just a passing thought. Or I might try to get Carruth to help. He is a great fixer-upper, and he needs the work. . . .

Gertrude and I were sorry that you weren't completely happy about the lettering on the jacket. But I gather you were pleased with the way the Tuke looked. I called Declan to find out if there was time for G. to tinker with the lettering but, unfortunately, he said they had been running behind on the jacket and it had gone on to the next production stage. G had hoped so much to please. I think I had told you earlier that from reading the mss. she had developed a crush on you (is that word still in use?), the first, I think, that she had had on a live writer since James Agee *[. . .]* and now that charmer is to Heaven ge-gone. . . .

Best,
JAS

/ • /

Die Kunst muss immer: "Art must always bring joy." Not to mention "beauty." Friedrich Gottlieb Klopstock (1724–1803) was a German poet and dramatist.

105. TLS—2

13 May 1993
Alphonse Daudet

DEAR MR LAUGHLIN!

One of the things in today's mail was Avram Davidson's *Adventures in Unhistory* (Owlswick), signed. Avram died four days ago, just beyond his 70th birthday. He had a diabetes attack, went into a coma, lay on his floor for 2½ days, but had been dismissed from a hospital and put in a nursing home. I had a scrawled letter from him, which I'm still trying to decipher, and a dictated one. He was reading my *Drummer.* He must have signed my copy of his new book just before the collapse. I wonder if the *Times* did an obit? I would place him beside Perelman as a humorist and close to Mark Twain as a compounder of the fantastic and the absurd.

Speaking of irony, what did I find the other evening but Kierkegaard (our Mr. Churchyard) calling Hegel's empiricism "a changeling troll." I swear I'd never read this passage before. It's in *The Concept of Irony with Constant Reference to Socrates.* One of those books Bonnie Jean looks at with lifted eyebrow, much as Bertie Wooster looked at Jeeves's copy of Spinoza.

The surgeon says I'm three-quarters healed (whatever that means), but am still forbidden to jog, lift heavy things, drive a car (he doesn't know I can't), or dance the Highland Fling. He says I'll be as good as new sometime in July. Damn.

I've been rereading (for the whatevereth time) *Don Juan,* which may be the funniest poem in English—certainly the greatest stylistic *tour de force.* It's proof enough that God doesn't read our books that Byron didn't get to finish it. Juan was to have become a ranting Methodist in Yorkshire. Also our most deliciously naughty poem. . . .

meanwhile,
GUY

/ • /

Perelman as a humorist: S. J. Perelman (1904–1979), author and screenwriter. Perelman claimed that his mostly humorous writings were influenced by James Joyce's stream-of-consciousness style. Among the many films he scripted were two for the Marx Brothers, *Horse Feathers* and *Monkey Business.*
Bertie Wooster looked at Jeeves's: Characters in the series of novels by Anglo-American humorist P. G. Wodehouse (1881–1975). Jeeves was Wooster's butler.

106. TLS—3

17 May 1993

DEAR MR LAUGHLIN!

. . . Convey, please to Gertrude that I'm NOT "unhappy" with the cover. I like it immensely. My feeling was that only Joyce or Ez or Chaucer merits such outsized type in relation to the title and the paper area. But if she did it out of admiration for my crazy prose, I'll withdraw my kvetching. One of my many faults (ask BJ) is a willingness to tinker with anything. In Heaven I'll criticize the style and fit of my wings. I'll find shortcomings in the pearly gates.

You'll soon have a whole shelf of Letters. I'll have to go back and see what's in Schwartz. . . .

18 May I read some Delmore Schwartz last night. He had a great deal of originality as well as a heaping measure of the poets of the time: MacNeice, Auden, Spender, even Frost. It's curious how differences and resemblances stand out only after an epoch is over. The famous patina of "period"—or junk (which can become charmingly Antique). There's no way of getting Aesthetics out of history. Art of the highest order is exempt from aging—Joyce, Proust, EP, Hopkins. And some (Kafka, Picasso) get *more* modern with age. The most interesting trajectories in time are those whose initial shine goes dull in a generation (I'm thinking of Kipling, Booth Tarkington, and O. Henry), lies low, and then emerges bright and fresh.

Both Hemingway's tight style and D.H. Lawrence's sloppy one are now in the attic. Neither had any sense of humor whatsoever; this tells a lot. The Terribly Serious writer is serious in relation to his age, and the eternal verities wear very different clothes from one age to the next.

I've finished Avram's book—*Studies in Unhistory*—that came out while he was dying. It's for people who delight in Burton (Robt, of the *Anatomy*), Pliny the Elder, Montaigne, and Hakluyt. Each essay comes up with an unlikely origin for the mandrake, dragons, mermaids, werewolves, and such. A book for bright teenagers, and old codgers nodding by the fire. . . .

be well!
GUY

[added in holograph:] It sounds as if you wanted *decorations* for the Reeses' book. By *drawing* I thought you meant the elaborate work that takes me an hour a square inch—even if I had ANY idea of what to draw.

/ • /

MacNeice, Auden, Spender: British poets and playwrights Louis MacNeice, W. H. Auden, and Stephen Spender, grouped together as the "New" English poets, for their informal language and socially engaged poems.
For people who delight in Burton: Robert Burton (1577–1640), author of *The Anatomy of Melancholy;* Pliny the Elder (died A.D. 79), foremost Roman authority on science; Michel Montaigne (1533–1592), famous for his *Essays;* and Richard Hakluyt (1552?–1616), English geographer, were all encyclopedic writers and gatherers and compilers of information.

107. TLS—3

27 May 1993

DEAR MR LAUGHLIN:

. . . Proofs for my ravings per ND came yesterday. Declan and I are working on the snafus (they used two systems of quotations dashes), and I think I'm seeing the typos, and the outsmartings. (I have trouble with typesetters who think they know English—my lion who's the pitch for St. Paul says that he's a numble beast, speaking good Elizabethan, and this gets "corrected" to humble.) This is the stage I used, habitually, to withdraw my manuscripts from North Point, in despair and doubt, or cancel half the text. But I've learned, and did all the major surgery on this book before typesetting. If it weren't Memorial Day weekend, I'd send proofs back tomorrow, so's I can't delete great hunks of 'em. At least I can seal them in a package. I found one sentence with no verb in it whatsoever.

My student Erik Reece came by yesterday, bringing to show me a first edition *Quia Pauper Amavi,* excellent condition, which a friend of his had found in a second-hand shop for $4! I only have a 1st of *Personae.*

Your "Engines of Desire" is a touch Superviellesque, though largely purely Laughlin. (In a French book for kids years ago I remember a whimsical drawing of an angel attacking Adam's *queue* with a monkey wrench. And on Danish TV there's a robot with a faucet for a *membrum virile,* which ran water when the children on the show turned it on, with squeals of laughter.) I wonder if the last line is necessary?

Love has pitched his tent
In the place of excrement.

Lovely poem. Your genius is a coiled spring, the tighter the better.

The ear has two functions: hearing and balance. Nose: smelling and breathing. Tongue: taste and speech. The eye: depth perception + other seeing (reading, color information). *Is* there a part of the body with only one function? The brain manages both its automatic neural system (breathing, reflexes) in addition to all its other wonders.

God was very wise to make our sexual organs double-purpose. I wouldn't want to know what religious fanatics would do if penises could be thought of as only a limb of Satan. As witness clitorectomy in Islam.

Mammae. I once saw a film about sculpture by the Dogon. The photographer followed a funerary image from wood to completion. The figure was of an old woman, kneeling, but with firm out-standing breasts. The anthropologist asked why. The sculptor said that, yes, Dagoda had lived to a venerable age, "but there are those of us who remember her when she was young." . . .

ever onward!
GUY

/ • /

My student Erik Reece: Reece was later to write the text for *A Balance of Quinces,* ND's book of GD's drawings and paintings.

"Engines of Desire": See JL's *The Secret Room,* 23. The published version of this poem about reproduction and elimination occurring by way of the same organs doesn't include the lines GD suggests are not needed.

108. TLS—5

5/29/93

Dear Guy—

The three P's: Pain, People and the Post. Life is all cluttered up. An inundation: we have had little Prof Frick (species *musculus barbatus*) from U of Toronto who invited himself for a day to root in the Pound archive and stayed for three nights—I had to charge him 10 cents a pull, he made so many copies; and we had the director of the BU film about Jas, scouting for locations; I offered him the tree-house that Patchen built in the wood near the old office; and the script-writer for the film on Tennessee being made by the *American Playhouse* series. A nice-enough Southern chap, but I told him I would not say on the air that poor, suffering Tenn, when he was going on a, to him, important date, would give himself an enema, but I would read a poem or two. Nobody realizes that Tenn wrote some charming romantic poems. We fought over how to characterize the poetic quality in some of the "high" speeches in the plays. He thinks it's just what the words say, and I claim it's also how they sound. Tenn had a very good ear. Then yesterday came Mr. Minkoff, rare book dealer, a brave little fellow, his legs are putty from polio, and he drives his car with handles. Can't pronounce anything correctly in any language, but he did buy 6000 worth of books (duplicates). If I had foreseen to save 10 copies of first editions of the early ND books, I'd be rich. And the mail. Queries from the office about facts I must look up in the archives for them; and letters from discontented authors who must be soothed. Perhaps you think of me as a soothsayer, but I'm really just a soother. . . .

Once again the village Selectmen have denied my right to march in the Memorial Day parade. I've again showed them the pictures from the *Salt Lake Tribune* of me training paratroops to ski at Alta. They say that was business not sojerin. . . .

I could swear that when I went to bed the pointed end of that

solitary egg in the living room was pointing south. This morning it's pointing north. What gives? What night
sprite's
making fright? . . .

Two more wicked days, sorry. JAS

/ • /

BU film: A reading JL gave at Boston University in December of 1992 was filmed. *Alta:* Since 1941, JL had owned a ski lodge in Alta, Utah. (Several of his authors over the years felt he spent too much time there, rather than devoting himself twenty-four hours a day to ND.)

109. TLS—2

7 June 1993

DEAR MR LAUGHLIN!

Keep your eye on that egg. What a life up there in the wilds of Connecticut. Bearded archivists in the guest room and hogging the Canon copier; film directors in the tree house; script writers in tents on the lawn. Rare-book dealers hauling off the library in wheelbarrows. Discontented authors.

Of Pain, People, and the Post, I'll take the Post any day, as I can deal with it in some fashion. I'm half-lucky with people. I had a nice morning today with the architect who's going to renovate my backyard studio. I *think* he understands what I want. I built the studio myself, years ago, and now it leaks and lets in bugs which have eaten, to date, seven paintings.

And they won't let you march in the Memorial Day parade, and why do you want to? Neckbrace, cane, and keeping in step. The agony would not be worth the glory.

Parades are great things, though. Do you know that the military band is Turkish? The Janissaries invented it. Everybody took it over.

Lord Cornwallis surrendered to music ("The World Turned Upside Down"). Lee crossed the Mason and Dixon Line to "Dixie" (standing in his stirrups). The black regiment that marched into Richmond stepped to "The Year of Jublio" (Henry Clay Work). Custer rode into Little Big Horn to "The Girl I Left Behind Me."

William III crossed the Boyne to "A Mighty Fortress Is Our God."

So your ancestors fought mine in the War of Secession? The United States Navy sank my family's ships, the *Edisto* and the *Ediwan.* Grandpa Sassard (from Bordeaux) went down with the *Edisto,* holding his Bible to his bosom and saluting the Confederate flag. Grandpa Fant exchanged friendship rings with Fitzhugh Lee. . . .

I got a book today on Wyndham Lewis in type so spidery that I can't read it. My God, but Lewis's talent as a painter did not cross the Atlantic with him. I've never seen such deterioration in an artist. Most painters get better and better with age (Goya, Titian), but not Lewis.

8 June Summer's humidity and heat turned on yesterday. I'm waiting for the Architectural Review Board to approve my plans to renovate my backyard studio. Naturally they are late. Bonnie Jean has called them a name that used to be unprintable. . . .

A letter from the HRHRC in Austin asks me to *give* them my papers. I'd like to lighten up the house by disposing of mss and letters but it's scarcely fair to BJ to give them away, especially as the HRHRC "deaccesses" (as they euphemize selling literary papers to other libraries). For years I've been placing letters to me in the South Caroliniana Library (these are gifts, as I don't hold with selling the incoming mail, and they assure me that they will not be available to scholars until after we are all angels). . . .

meanwhile,
GUY

/ • /

The Janissaries: the elite military unit of the Ottoman Empire.

Wyndham Lewis: (1882–1957), British painter, novelist, and critic. He helped found the English abstract art movement called "Vorticism." When World War II broke out, he came to North America, first to New York City, then to Canada, and finally to a small college in Windsor, Onatrio.
HRHRC: The Harry Ransom Humanities Research Center, at the University of Texas at Austin. Not long before he died in 2005, GD sold his papers, library, and paintings to the HRHRC.

110. TLS—2

Summer Solstice 1993 [June 22]

DEAR MR LAUGHLIN:

The Man in the Wall will convince even the most bilious and meanest critic that you are a prince among poets. You are a master of the opening line, and, what's rarer, of the closing line. Good in between, too. As American as a T-model Ford. My hyperbole (poetically true) is false in that no young writer could have such a fund of experience or so ripe a wisdom or irony with so sharp an edge.

Thanks also for Susan Howe whose talent is immense but whose style is, shall we say, eccentric. She has read entirely too much Olson.

I refuse to believe that you thought O. Henry an Irish writer. As the French say, you pull the leg. Penguin asked for a list of distinguished people to send these little books to, so I sent them a list of *friendly* distinguished people. English profs—even those happily retired—are not supposed even to think about O. Henry. We Kentuckians, however, do our own thinking. The Russians call him O. Genry, not being able to say an H. Adolf Gitler. Yernest Gemingvay. They adore Zhemz Phenimor Kyper.

I chose the cover paintings for the O. Henrys. That's Havana passing for Trujillo.

All I want to know about India is in your account of a hundred women mowing a golf course with their fingers.

Declan is only half-guilty in the matter of the indents. Apparently

I sent a printed text for the one story, with indents different from the rest of the manuscript. He is quite charming on the phone. . . .

Gertrude is a charmer on the phone, too; I must think of an excuse to talk with her again. Maybe we can swap a phone call between you and Bonnie Jean for one between Gertrude and me. When Gertrude called lightning was leaping about like devils and venerable trees were crashing across lawns and houses. . . .

My studio out back is to be renovated, plans having been OK'd by the architectural review board, which kept calling it my garage. Fesser Davenport, it was explained, is an amateur painter.

So Erik Reece and I have moved a hundred paintings into the house, and I'm back at work on an 8' by 4' canvas, with which I haven't got a clue what to do. I'm going to try to give it to Denmark.

Nobody will look at my work. The woman from MOMA with whom I did a book on Art of the 40s, Riva Castleman, came down to lecture and was by for a drink. I showed her one painting, at which she smiled politely and looked away.

. . . What if I make up a painter, sign his name to the pictures, and then write a glowing article on him? Will that do it? . . .

ad interim,
GUY

/ • /

Susan Howe: Poet and essayist. ND published *The Nonconformist's Memorial.* "Olson" refers to Charles Olson.

111. TLS—3

17 July 1993

DEAR MR LAUGHLIN!

Put Gertrude in the middle of the floor in the next lightning storm, on a rubber mat, and wearing rubber-soled sneakers.

If you don't have a copy of my *Every Force Evolves a Form,* I'll send you one. In it there's a piece ("Pergolesi's Dog") in which La Borgese and her typist dog figure.

It is so humid that a map thumbtacked to the wall has just sagged and fallen off. . . .

Your beautifully phrased optatives for my studio are appreciated, though there are no pipes. The roof is in a Dempster Dumpster, along with the floor, and inner walls. Next, we jack up one wall, which has bowed out, and pour a concrete base for it to sit on. Then a concrete floor. The roof is to be a coppery green tin. My workers are a professor of architecture at the university and one Richard Hudson, a.k.a. Mr. Fixit. They work like demons, and in this heat. They do not step on the peonies. I help as I can, forbidden to lift anything heavy. The level of conversation is high, as they're readers and seem to know something of art. . . .

I have ridden a horse once. I was with a horsey person who invited me to go for a ride around his property. Two horses were saddled and brought out. I put my foot in the stirrup, swung into the saddle, shook the reins, and started up. We rode all over meadows and through woods. I could have broken my neck. As it was, we had a nice ride.

I've also driven an automobile once. I was out along the Saluda River with my highschool English teacher Frank Rainwater, and his wooden leg came off. Some species of pin fell out of it and we couldn't find it. So I, a nondriver, drove us back. This was during the war; traffic in town was light, and we had the country roads to ourselves. . . .

Declan called this morning to say that he's sending page proofs. I feel so guilty, all this conscientious attention, and the book isn't going to sell over 18 copies. This is my seventh book of fiction, and I know by now that people simply can't read what I've written. And if they can, they can't figure out what I mean. Advertise it as Light Comic Philosophical Fiction, suitable for age 10 (with parental guidance) and Bright Teenagers. . . .

herzlich,
GUY

/ • /

Put Gertrude: JL had written GD that their house had been struck by lightning and Gertrude had been thrown from a window seat to the floor.
beautifully phrased optatives: JL had written a "blessing" of sorts (included in a letter dated July 13) for GD's studio in progress. Various structural members were addressed—the pipes et al.
herzlich: "warmly."

112. TLS—2

28 August 1993

DEAR MR LAUGHLIN!

Knocking you about are they? I had been concerned, worried, apprehensive. In the anthropology of South Carolina illness is a taboo subject, a private and guarded affair. So I'm never certain what boundaries of decorum I'm breaching when I agonize about a friend's ailments. I myself like to know all the gory details, and to tell them. In the army I was the one who could hold the vomiting drunk's head without the least squeamishness.

But you are up to xeroxing (canonizing) cross-eyed whales with Arion and Diana giving it trouble; and up to typing letters; and back to your famed style and lucidity. You could lose half your mind and still be smarter than anybody else in Connecticut. . . .

Indolence would be my advice also. The Victorians recommended rest for everything. I trust Gertrude to discourage you from mowing the hay.

I have been fretting about being elected to the Society of South Carolina Authors. For one thing this society is a buncher club women who have never read a word I've written and imagine I'm an inspirational writer (why else would you write a book?) and would be horrified if they read my stories. The club lady on the phone, a classmate of 45 years back, emphasized that Henry Timrod was an early member, and William Gilmore Sims, and Mary Chesnutt. God knows. I have of course to go to a banquet in Charleston. My suspicion is that it's all genealogical: I'm kin on my mother's side to Ravenels and Sassards. I've been trying to get out of it. My sister (who calls it "the author of the year award") has called Bonnie Jean, to have her "make me" accept it. BJ, in her coldest Ohio voice, said that she didn't make me do anything, nor I, her. . . .

I do hope the small stroke proves to be a temporary disadvantage.

Before I melt,
GUY

/ • /

Knocking you about: Over the course of the summer, JL had been writing GD about his health problems, the drugs he had been taking, his arthritis headaches, dizziness, etc. At times he walked with two canes, and after collapsing had been taken to hospitals by ambulance and by helicopter. On August 23 he wrote that he had had a small stroke.

113. TL—2

9 IX 1993

DEAR
MR
LAUGHLIN

Apollon and his sister Artemis driving away the plague. It would be good news to hear that you are better, some better, even a little bit better.

I hope I have better manners than to burden you with business, but I'll tell you what I'm offering the New York office, namely my translation of Herondas which Grey Fox brought out ten years ago, has depleted the stock of, and is reverting rights to me. Knowing your devotion to The Classix, I thought you ought to have first refusal. Donald Allen (who's not well either) mumbled something about "a small fee," but I believe that by law I have the rights. Herondas is my Ugly Duckling (though it has been much used as a text for a Univ of CA class) in that the reviews by Classicists were sniffy and of course the other kind of reviewers had never heard of Herondas or of classical mime. Herondas (or Herodas) has never been in the canon, as he's scarcely uplifting, and it takes some imaginative cooperation to follow what he's doing.

By Donald Allen I mean Grey Fox Press, SF.

This is for your info. I'll write Declan, as my editor, and he can propose it (or not) to Griselda, or however things are done at New Directions.

I have weaseled out of my election to the Society of South Carolina Authors, and am thoroughly ashamed of myself. . . .

ad interim,
[unsigned]

/ • /

Apollon and his sister: A drawing of two classical figures with bows, photocopied at the top of the letter.
Donald Allen: Writer, anthologist, and editor of Grey Fox Press.

114. ALS—3

9/15/93

Dear Guy—

I wish I could say I was some better, but I ain't, and like the Father of Our Country I can only lie if I'm writing a poem. The dizzies are unremitting and I can only read the headline in the *Times.* . . . Only pleasure is jumping in the lake—colder every day—and cutting out deceased plants from the flower garden. . . .

However, today's letter, Apollon and Artemis, I find something to get interested in. The Herondas, a text I've always found very interesting. Unique. I called Declan to suggest that he *not* approach Griselda on it right away. G. is a pearl beyond price—the one who makes the wheels turn—we are swine before her pearls—but classics are not her dish. She tends sometimes to make quick judgments. I'd like to have Declan [illegible] a bit. She would say that the new super stores that have swept the country in the last years would not buy [illegible], an isolated book. (Do they have a super store in Lexington?) I think the way to get around this would be to insert Herondas in Barbara's "Bibelots" series. Have I shown you any of these? I'll send some down. . . . The pattern is that a super store buys them by the batch. Thus they would take Herondas to get, say, a Henry Miller, or Pound's *Diptych.* I think it would work, and that G. would accept the idea, if only as a marketing experiment. May I try that? The length is just right. . . .

Yrs in Xt, through Mary,
with a smile,
JAS

***115.* TLS—3**

20 IX 1993

DEAR MR LAUGHLIN!

. . . Do I gather from your letter that despite your ailments and debilities you go swimming in an icy lake every morning? And hack at weeds in the garden? You might as well get in your helicopter and come down here, where the renovation of my studio has appended to the work force Abbie (through whose frayed jeans one can see black underpants) and Andrea and even Doris. My remark one day ("Why are there no girl carpenters?") must have got back to the College of Architecture. Previously I'd had Keith, Mike, Ron, and Chris.

Bonnie Jean says the girls can't paint worth a damn, but then BJ is a hard critic to get around. I've put in two full days, sore foot and all. Good fellowship all around, but once the girls joined us, they expected lunch, so I've been doing baloney sandwiches and bean soup and pound cake at the noon hour. The project (begun 13 July) is about half done. The cats assume I'm building them a house. One window has been placed at cat height, for Belinda and Flix to look out of.

Students are refreshing. Andrea said that she is writing a thesis on architecture and music. In the course of the conversation (we were painting side by side) I discovered that she had never heard of Mahler, Stravinsky, or Vivaldi. To name but three, I suppose. There's a whole generation in college now that has heard of nothing.

All my attempts to be nice invariably go nowhere. I thought I'd spare you a decision about the Herondas. From now on, I will do all business with The Founder. I *did* write you and Declan at the same time. . . .

Do we have a super store in Lexington? I suppose Joseph-Beth's would be such an emporium. They would put Herondas under KENTUCKY AUTHORS. But you are, as of now, talking format before you've seen the text (I'm assuming). It would be wonderful to have it as one of the Bibelots. . . .

meanwhile, with hopeful wishes,
GUY

116. TLS—2

23 September 1993
Caesar Augustus

O POET!

. . . But to more practical things. On your Oxford card you say: "Are the other Greek books in print? Need for coagulation?"

'Zmatter of fack, again, the California *Archilochos, Sappho, Alkman: Three Greek Poets of the Late Greek Bronze Age* has also just reverted rights to me, after about 30 years, in one form or another

(*Carmina Archiloci,* U. Calif, back in the 60s; *Sappho,* Michigan, again the 60s; the *Alkman* was in some mag—*Arion,* I think—before he joined the trio in Calif edition).

Herakleitos and Diogenes still in print at Grey Fox.

Your "Secret Language" is beautiful. Touch is, by golly, a language of its own, with many dialects.

The very last Herondas mime—the little boy with a June-bug on a tether disturbing Grandpa's afternoon nap—seems to me the most timeless scene of the lot. There *must* be another scroll somewhere. People dither about the Dead Sea scrolls, which sound like mumbo and jumbo, whereas what we want is more June-bugs and Greek housewives buying shoes at the cobbler's.

The women in the temple looking at the art are my Aunt Mae exactly. In 1939, at the NY World's Fair, she ran her hand over a Rubens, saying "Buzzie (her husband), these are fine old paintings from hundreds of years ago!"—before she was tackled by a guard. Back home, she said, "You have no idea how touchy these New York people are about the things in their museum!" . . .

I know you're feeling crummy, dizzy, and in pain, but as long as you can write two *good* poems at 3 a.m., my sympathy has to be tempered with envy.

onward!
GUY

/ • /

Your "Secret Language": JL's poem "A Secret Language" (see *PNS,* 78).

117. TLS—2

9/28/93

Dear Guy—

. . . Many thanks for dope on the status of your Hellenic traductions. Unless I misread, most of your Greekeries are O.P. and reverted. Should we not raise our sights (sites?) from Herondas in the Bibelot series to a magisterial compendium of all the Greek that can be fetched in—in paperback, of course, to encourage use in the beaneries. "Our Greatest Interpreter of the Classics" booms the jacket.

One little puzzle: you say that the Berkeley (1980) Archie/the Sap/the Boozer has reverted to you. But in *Thasos and Ohio* (North Point, 1986) there are lengthy sections of these folk, no doubt duplicating, though I haven't itemized, and three bits of Herondas at the end. What is the rights situation on these? Did North Point acquire reprint rights from Berkeley? What has happened to *Thasos and Ohio*? Is Jolly Roger distributing it or what? 1986 would ostensibly take demesne over 1980. But big Raj loves money, even small quanitites of it. . . .

"Love of Money is the marketplace for every Evil," you remark in another context. Might not the same apply to Don Allen in respect of *Herakleitos and Diogenes.* (Have I the Grey Fox right? Since the stroke every name bobs about on wavey waters.) I remember him as a pleasant person. He worked for a while at ND long ago; then MacGregor fired him for some reason.

We have had similar situations where a rights holder has accepted a small share of royalty in a supervening volume. Holder keeps basic rights and lessor (lessee? Absolute logonuttery this AM) has nonexclusivity. . . .

This is all pretty hypnogogical at this stage, but let me dream on, which is all I can do in my pitiful condition. . . .

Jas

118. **TLS—1**

8 Nov 1993
Margaret Mitchell
(who lived here on Sayre Avenue before moving to Atlanta)

DEAR MR LAUGHLIN:

What Sappho said was that Eros is a sweetly bitter *sneak.* Or however you want to translate *herpetos* (a quadruped, a snake, the "all creeping things" of the Bible, a stalker, a snake-in-the-grass, a predator). Her word was *orpetos,* as they had no aitches out there in the sticks on Lesvos. Latin *serpens.*

Miss Sapphy was more partial to Eros's sister Peitho (deleted by Athenian prudery).

I like the Roman (and English) use of y for upsilon (the French *u-grecque*): *glykupikros.*

Seems to me that Sappho was the poet of desire. Love implies fulfillment. Her beloveds got married between 13 and 16, and went off to be the wives of Anatolian army officers (as in the ode to Anaktoria). Why hasn't Jesse Helms banned all of Greek poetry? . . .

any
way
GUY

119. **TLS—2**

18 Nov 1993

DEAR MR LAUGHLIN!

A watchdog or two will keep your weathervanes where they belong.

I didn't say Sappho was a serpent; I said she said Eros was. And not a serpent, a critter that creeps up on you. A stalker.

I happily *have* the City Lights *Selected Poems 1935–1985,* inscribed "GD/JL These *tabullae maculatae.*" I even contributed a blurb to it. My favorite is "The Bible Lady."

Foxcroft should have a broadside of "The Foxcroft Girl" for the dorm walls.

A practical ironist might savor Joyce's remark. In the *Wake* it's the invading Danes who halt *The Book of Kells* (it ends with a half-finished page), and here was an Irish Dane from America who publishes rather than destroys books. Joyce fancied himself "a norseman," and like Wittgenstein, was fluent in Danish.

My friend John Greppin the linguist (he's a specialist in Armenian lists of pharmaceutical terms from Turkish and Greek) alludes in a letter to a review of our book in the *Times.* I hope it's good, for New Directions' sake. I quit reading reviews years ago for the simple reason that they stopped my work on the next book in its tracks. . . .

I could fill up several more pages with Bonnie Jean's gadgets ordered from catalogs. I think the fun is in having them arrive, like a present. Christmas every day. My most exciting evenings (or Saturday afternoons) are our visits to *Big Lots* and *Wal-Mart* and *Pace Warehouse*, where everything in the world is on display. The Marxists frown on this, but I think it's what civilization was moving toward all these years. What else was Marco Polo doing in China and Samarkand? He was playing Bonnie Jean in K-Mart.

Imagine Duns Scotus in an American bookstore. He would take it for heaven.

Napoleon at Waterloo had a mobile library, and Montaigne on his travels took along several trunkfuls of books (all of which were sniffed for heresy when he got to Rome). Even Eisenhower had a little shelf of cowboy pulps in WW II. Roosevelt was halfway through a Perry Mason when he popped off.

Virgil Nemoianu says he is reviewing our book on Radio Free Europe, in Roumania. I imagine peasants (and the cow) listening to their Philco in darkest Transylvania.

be well,
GUY

/ • /

keep your weathervanes: Thieves had stolen a valuable antique weathervane from the top of JL's sheep barn.
Joyce's remark: JL's anecdote about James Joyce meeting him for the first time saying, "I think Laughlin that we met for the last time on the battle field of Clontarf."
In the Wake: Finnegans Wake, James Joyce's famously dense last work; *The Book of Kells,* a handwritten, intricately ornamented book created in an Irish monastery in the mid-eighth century. An Irish national treasure.
Duns Scotus: (1266?–1308), Scottish philosopher and theologian, attempted to devise a proof of the existence of God through a combination of intellect and divine revelation.

120. TLS—2

19 November 1993
Allen Tate

DEAR MR LAUGHLIN:

Three friends have so far sent the *Times* review. . . .

I'm happy for you, and pleased within reason, but it *is* a review of the notes (I told you so) and a mishmash of information. He must have gone to Yale. We Harvard people know that Meleager—the only one who could be alluded to in my title—is the compiler of the *Greek Anthology* as well as a fairly naughty poet in his own right (he gets translated into salacious Latin in the Loeb *Anthology*). He misses the point of the Thoreau story. Oh well: reviewers have to read fast. You're right: "Who could hope for anything more?"

We aim to take in *The Age of Innocence.* As for tipping one's hat, *mais oui!* You wouldn't want a gentleman to catch his death of pneumonia by exposing his head to the weather? The French removed the *chapeau* and swept the air with it. The Elizabethan English swept the ground, after three twirls while making a leg.

It is told of a provincial mayor that whilst so saluting Elizabeth I, he broke wind. He was thrown into confusion and slunk away. He later received a gracious note from his sovereign, saying "I have forgot the fart."

My grandfather James Nardin Fant had a black who preceded him in public (such a one is called a "beater") to clear the sidewalk. "Git back! Git back! Hyar come Massa Fant!"

It's awful to be from the South.

Ronald Johnson had to sell his library to be able to move from San Francisco to Kansas. That's how Anacapa (Anaconda) Books got Ron's copy of *Cydonia Florentia* (which is indeed about a girl).

A supper of black-eyed peas, my own tomato sauce, and hot biscuits (never mind the chocolate sauce) has left me blissfully lazy, and so,

thanks for the review,
GUY

121. TLS—2

26 Jan 1994

DEAR MR LAUGHLIN!

I read *9 Ridge Road* last evening by the fire, and had tears in my eyes toward the end. It's one of the loveliest things you've ever written—and the form is an invention: a collage of poems and letters as well as of your own part in it all. I knew practically nothing of the McDowell treachery—hints of it from Hugh Kenner. It was an extraordinarily moving experience to read it. Ez says somewhere that the highest criticism is that of one poet of another (Dante of Arnaut). And the *history:* New Directions in its heroic beginnings, your perception and faith. I'm very grateful for being allowed to see it.

Is it erudite wit that makes you ascribe the flourishing of the green bay tree to Cicero? It is Psalm 37:35.

I have seen the wicked in great power:
And spreading himselfe like a green bay tree.

The last time I visited at 9 Ridge Rd., WCW could talk fluently about a word that he couldn't winkle out of his aphasia. That is, he would get to a word he couldn't say, but could say "damn it! What *is* the word I want!" Floss was reading him a Japanese novel which he kept referring to as Chinese.

What fascinates me at the end of *Paterson* is the conflation of genius and teratology (it runs through the poem—the hydrocephalic who tells Washington that he wasn't *active* in politics). Toulouse-Lautrec: dwarf and painter.

When I opened the front door this morning, there was HENRY the lost tom sitting on the taffrail. He disappeared the night of the Great Snow, about 11 days ago, and we'd pretty much given up hope that he could have survived the awful cold.

But this good news is countered by the death of Bonnie's mother (71) last night in Middleton, Ohio. Heart failure, and a year-long illness and cruel frequency of operations, in and out of the hospital with an awesome regularity. A Virginian, also named Bonnie. Neither of BJ's parents understood having a smart daughter. They'd wanted a son (which they eventually had) who played basketball.

9 Ridge Road must have a good printer and designer.

I'll put this out for the postman—I only wanted to say what a great beautiful strong READABLE good poem *9 Ridge Rd.* is.

in haste,
GUY

/ • /

9 Ridge Road: JL on William Carlos Williams, see *Byways,* 142–211. This was also published separately as *Remembering William Carlos Williams* (ND, 1995).

Floss: WCW's wife.

the McDowell treachery: David McDowell (1918–1985) was from 1948 to 1950 the sales and promotion manager for New Directions. When JL fired him and he moved to Random House, he convinced William Carlos Williams that JL was doing a poor job as his publisher. This prompted an eight-year split, both professional and personal, between Williams and JL. See *Byways,* 173–81.

122. TLS—2

2/12/94

DEAR GUY—

My now memory gets worse and worse. I can't remember when AND WHAT I last wrote you. But old memory is still pretty good. The other day when I needed the name of Des Esseintes of *A Rebours* it was right at the top of the basket.

Ferlinghetti, to whom I had submitted the Williams book for City Lights to publish, rejected it, writing a silly letter that it wasn't poetry and I must redo it as prose. I told him politely to lance [*sic*] his old carcass from the Golden Gate Bridge, that Griselda was keen to do it at ND. Then three days later he called to say he had changed his mind and wanted it despite the typographical eccentricity. . . .

Carruth has done a superb job on it: cutting, polishing, general *oop-befestiging*. He's a whiz. He wrote a new ending, making himself sound like me, which is a great improvement. He takes off from where the New York poets get out of the old taxi, making that symbolate Bill's increasing readership over the ages.

Did I tell you that Angelica told her brother, Roland Pease, that he should be publishing my verses in his handsome Zoland (whah dah?) Books in Cambridge? He wrote me an invitation and I've packed off to him two lbs of gibber, stuff since *Immured Man,* to choose from. I hope he'll do it, as I don't like to dump too much on the ND troops.

An advance copy of the JL/EP correspondence, edited by Dave Gordon, whom maybe you knew in St. Liz days, has arrived from Norton. I'll send you one when they send me more. Except in the letters from Ez in the 30's it's hard to make out what or whom he's talking about, it's so dizzy, and Dave has labored to produce a mouse with his notes. Ezratic is a special language.

Is the hoary sage of Jargon, NC, going off his marbles? The huge book (who pays for these things?) of photos of backy-growing peasants in the hills is superb, as camera work and sociology, but the 40-page compendium of various folkses "Quotes," including your wisdoms, is ridiculous for the most part and of surpassing inutility. Oh well.

I hope you are pondering what you want to change or add for the coagulated Greek poets. No hurry about this, but I hope we can bring it off, Don Allen having been pacified. Did you send him a large box of lollypops?

Now my back has started to pain badly in the lumpbular [*sic*] region, where damage shows on the x-rays, that from my crashing into a tree on Mt. Washington Firetrail in 1935, and they put me into a motionless cast for two months, which was exactly what they shouldn't have done. Now they get you up and make you start walking the first week so the muscles that adhere to the processes of the spine don't deteriorate, as they have done. Oh well.

Carry forward,
JAS

/ • /

Des Esseintes of A Rebours: Des Esseintes, a nobleman bored with life, is the main character of *A rebours,* an 1884 French novel by Joris-Karl Huysmans (1848–1907).
Ferlinghetti: Lawrence Ferlinghetti, poet and editor-publisher of City Lights Books, San Francisco.
oop-befestiging: Comic German, meaning that Hayden Carruth had tightened up the poem.
Immured Man: Reference to JL's 1993 *The Man in the Wall.*
the hoary sage of Jargon, SC: Jonathan Williams, whose Jargon Society press is located in South Carolina.

123. TL—2

5 March 1994

DEAR MR LAUGHLIN!

I got up this morning with the idea that I might revise all of my translations, loading the worktable with Lasserre's text of Archiloque (as he calls him), Liddell & Scott, sharpened pencils, and other tools of the trade. After a half hour of making my way through an elegy for a shipwreck, I compared my efforts with what I'd done back in 1959 or thereabouts and realized that I was setting out at 67 to undo the work of a thirty-year-old who was once capable of accounting for every grammatical construction in Sappho (Greek tutorial, Eliot House) and whose reading of Archilochos went through some ten revisions. Nabokov is reported to have said to Vera (apropos Marianne Moore's severe revisions), "If you catch me rewriting my texts, please shoot me."

No. I think these collected translations should not be fiddled with. They are what they are. They are the best I could do over the years (thirty years of work). There are lines I want to touch up, errors to correct (I misread a number in Herondas) and some of the one-worders to omit. But, all in all, I think it would be a treacherous act to my younger self to rewrite (my original idea when you proposed that we do this gathering of my translations).

What we have is:
ARCHILOCHOS
SAPPHO
ALKMAN
ANAKREON (the real one, not the "Anacreonta," a forgery)
HERAKLEITOS
DIOGENES
HERONDAS
MAXIMS OF THE ANCIENT EGYPTIANS (from Boris's Italian)

There are also some stray one-poem things: Ausonius, Meleager, and whichwhat, some still in my notebooks.

With whom will I be working on this? Declan?

We need a title. (What we have is what the Victorians would have called a miscellany. Aside from their translator, what these things have in common is their age—and in the Poundian sense that caused me to do them, their *firstness*

/ • /

This letter, "finished enough," as GD remarked, without signature or even a closing parenthesis, was tucked in with one written a few days later.

124. TLS—2

6 April 1994

DEAR MR LAUGHLIN!

. . . Nothing's holding up the translations except a revision of two Sapphos that I never got quite right, and some kind of introduction. I'm thinking of short remarks on each poet. Nobody anymore under the age of fifty has any education whatsoever.

256 pp, noted.

Will speed up.

I get so tired of all this idealism in the universities about multiculturalism. As if they thought it up all of a sudden. Back in 1970 I gave a course in Herakleitos and the Dogon, for sophomores and juniors. Nobody on the faculty noticed, of course, and imagine we've never had multicultural studies until now. Back in the 60s I offered a course in G[ertrude] Stein, and not a single student signed up. Today it would be crowded. The professor, however, has retired. (I don't think I taught anybody *anything.*)

Lovely, that *9 Ridge Road* is to be designed by Leslie and that ND will do it. The scholarly—so-called—work on WCW is for the most part appallingly dull. You will correct the balance. . . .

be well,
GUY

/ • /

the Dogon: A people of the African nation of Mali. GD refers in a number of places to aspects of their culture, including their art and their cosmology.

125. TLS—2

4/11/94

Dear Guy—

. . . That will be great if you can squeeze it down to 2 × 128 = 256. Pages. Two even forms; that will help keep the price down for students. I talked with Griselda about Declan Spring. She says he's maturing and should do a good job for you if you handle any Greek lines. Do you have extra books to cut and paste for the typesetters? Canon copies would do just as well.

Tomorrow I'll call Declan to give him the general background. And Peggy about a contract for you, which will doubtless come off the new computer. They are all agoggle down there over the new computer system, which over my dead body *gekauft war,* but it's great for their morale. . . .

Did Anne Carson have *Raritan* send you their recent number that has a twenty-page poem that I find just wonderful. She interweaves different themes: the Bronte sisters; her mother; her lover abandoning her in a whole flood of, I think, wonderful lines and images. I wish I could latch onto her for ND, but she seems to be tied up with Knopf. . . .

Jas

/ • /

gekaulft war: German for "was purchased."
twenty-page poem: See "The Glass Essay" in *Glass, Irony and God* (ND, 1995).

126. TLS—3

18 April 1994

Dear Mr Laughlin!

I've just been on the phone with Declan. We've got as far as seeing that there's no room for the Egyptians and we still don't know if there's room for much of an introduction. We can just squeeze in the seven Greeks. I'll send him texts in a few days.

Piet Mondriaan was indeed some kind of Theosophist. His great passion, however, was for Mae West (whose only straight line was the handle of her parasol). Wittgenstein fancied Barbara Hutton. Great abstract intellects seem to relish sex goddesses. Apparently Einstein's temperature went up in the proximity of the dumplingesque and the Willendorfian. The appetent eye of great minds is a subject of dubious propriety. Dante, Chaucer, and Ruskin were connoisseurs of the pubescent. Santayana liked football players and soldiers. Clarence King, the great geologist, had a secret black wife, as did Jefferson (they say). Fourier worked all this out (desire as the energizer of all else) but few will admit how right he was.

You're the second to scissor out one of my *illuminations.* The poet Erik Reece has made a collage of a cubist Picasso I put on a letter to him, *en aquarelle.* I watercolor one thing or another while listening to the afternoon news on the radio, from 4 to 5, when BJ turns up.

No, I haven't seen the Anne Carson you mention. . . .

be well,
GUY

/ • /

Piet Mondriaan: (1872–1944), Dutch painter whose mature work featured flat colors, fields of primary color, straight lines, and grids. He used no curved lines. Some of GD's own abstract paintings use grids (less hectic than Mondriaan's).

Willendorfian: The Venus of Willendorf is a famous small (4.5-inch) figure, ca. 30,000–25,000 B.C., with very large breasts and hips, and no facial features.

the second to scissor out: GD had included a small painting in a letter to JL dated March 8, 1994, writing that "the chrysanthemum to the right is by Piet Mondriaan." JL cut it out and made it into a bookmark for his friend Angelica, who was enduring a bout of depression.

127. TLS—1

5/17/94

Dear Guy—

My delicious son Henry is a LIVIN' DOLL.

Shortly after his arrival here large drays began to draw up to the door and huge packages were unloaded. They were followed by little men in green suits who were fed beer to improve their humors. Six hours later a huge, magical machine was in place, the parts linked by tangled strands of the Medusa's hair. It gave off a humming sound, punctuated when an error of procedure occurred, by the quacking of a duck. I attended [*sic*] an explosion or combustion, but all was serene.

Here are a few examples of what I've so far done, with Henry at my elbow, he speaking in a dialect which I guessed to be a blending of Swahili and Romansch. Cathy, my sekatary [*sic*] knows some of this language, and may be able to extract me if I become nasconded in a *selva oscura.* And my training in deconstruction should be helpful.

But pray for me,
Jas

Two of the green men, who were suturers of wood, erected a mobile table which rolls over me when I have taken my ease in my reclining chair. This to do away with the pain that comes when I work straightbacked.

/ • /

a huge magical machine: JL's son had brought and installed a computer for his use. JL immediately wrote poems with the word processor, but, as GD noted in a letter of May 21, "You use your old-fashioned typewriter to say that you have a Space Age computer." JL stuck to this pattern.

128. TLS—2

31 May 1994

DEAR MR LAUGHLIN!

Reading your *Collected* right through is quite an experience. I hadn't seen the postwar German poems before. Thanks for my inscribed copy. A new constellation in the firmament.

Yours of the 22nd. My floral decoration may well have been a thistle. I "watercolor the news"; that is, watercolor while listening to *All Things Considered.* I've just about finished my facsimile Kelmscott Chaucer (begun in the 1950s), and various Renaissance herbals (like Parkinson's great *Garden*). I'm eternally grateful to you for suggesting that I get a Xerox home copier. . . .

Fascinating, your account of Nabokov on the ice slope. I read the *Gogol* when it came out. That whole series from ND was an exciting part of my education. I wish I had known Levin better at Harvard (I hear he's ill). I took his seminars in American Lit and in Comedy, and he directed (sort of) my thesis on Ez, but he was not a prof who socialized with students.

I can't read German worth a damn, and have no feeling for it. Kafka, to my mind, is the master of modern German (as a stylist). Followed by Rilke—both Czechs.

Did the review of *A Table* in Roumanian, which I Xeroxed for you, not get there? You haven't mentioned it. You should have no trouble reading the gist of it.

We're having beautiful weather—cool, sunny, breezy. Good for walking and for sleeping.

I forget if I've reported that Ronald Johnson had a successful brain-tumor operation. I hope that it really did go as well as Ronald says it did. He has a poet-in-residency at Berkeley in the fall.

Moyer Bell did a good job: a handsome book. The poems look right on their pages. The range of experience must be wider and more diverse than in anybody else's poems. You never know what you're going to find on the next page. What the critics ought to go for is the clarity with which each poem is shaped. The style fits the matter in a way that we haven't had since Mark Twain, who never missed in turning a phrase. And I defy anybody to find a dull page.

I'd better put this out for the postman, due any minute. More, later.

meanwhile,
GUY

/ • /

Reading your Collected: JL's *Collected Poems, 1938–1992* (Moyer Bell, 1994). JL replied that Gertrude redesigned the book after JL was dissatisfied with their original design. *Nabokov and the ice slope:* See letter #44.

129. TLS—3

6/12/94

DEAR GUY—

I am deeply sad about the death of Harry Levin. I never took a course with him but he was so kind to me, being an advisor on publishing matters. It was he who put me in touch with Nabokov and various others. He let me publish his book on Joyce, which was the first really good one. He did a superb introduction for our reprint of WCW's European novel, *A Voyage to Pagany.* To do it he read all of Williams so it is rich with insights. And when he published his essays, *Memories of the Moderns,* he leads off with 10 pages about the Boy Publisher. . . .

I hope that all is sailing along smoothly with Declan. I haven't queried him because I want him to stand on his own size 11's. I grow fainter and fainter daily. We must build for the future. . . .

Salaam,
JAS

/ • /

Harry Levin: (1912–1994), literary scholar who taught at Harvard for forty years. ND published his book *James Joyce: A Critical Introduction* in 1960.

130. TLS—2

23 July 1994

DEAR MR LAUGHLIN!

. . . I sent Declan all the stuff for *Seven Greeks* at the beginning of the week. He had everything except the intro and notes, which I couldn't do until he had told me how much space I had for them.

I'd suggested one of Picasso's drawings of nekkid lady and cupid for the cover.

There's a strange bloke I'm corresponding with who has done a *logia* of Jesus (Yeshua as he calls him). A Basque Jew who's now a Mormon, educated in Ecuador, fluent in Hebrew, Greek, Spanish, French, Latin, God knows what. Back when I did Herakleitos, I'd thought of doing Jesus (did Diogenes instead), with his sayings treated as fragments. I didn't have the expertise to bring it off, as many of the logia are in Coptic, and there's a whole theological discipline for working with what Rabbi Yeshua did or didn't say.

Anyway, Benjamin Urrutia (Basque name) is planning to make a vast commentary, which will take years (I have no notion what age he is, over 50 I'd guess), but I've urged him to save the theology and publish the *logia* as an elegant little book, with just enough notes (about tares, leavened bread, leather wine bottles, and whichwhat) to explain his reading. I've urged him to be absolutely literal. Jesus was always saying "up in the sky" (translated Heaven traditionally).

The result should be a startlingly fresh look. "Eat what they put before you." I'll have to help him get it pub'd, as he seems to be a babe in diapers about the world outside Salt Lake City. He wrote his high-school senior thesis on Herakleitos, in Ecuador.

Meanwhile, I'm reading books about landscape gardening, to

erase some of my dismal ignorance. Both Wittgenstein and Kafka spent time working as gardeners. Henry Adams' visit to RL Stevenson & wife was when they were working in their garden, and his patrician eye was offended by their bare feet. But my books are about Loudon, English parks, and the importing of oriental trees and veggies to the West (that's 3 separate books).

A Chinese fan of my scribbles says that my prose has *shu juan qi*—"fragrance of books." The mysterious East. I used to have some sense of how the old Wade transliteration was pronounced; the new Pin Yin is a mystery. When Ez was beginning the Cantos he had no way of knowing that Greek and Latin would drop out of a liberal education, or that his Chinese transcriptions would be changed.

χαίρετε!
GUY

/ • /

logia of Jesus: The Logia of Yeshua, translated and edited by Benjamin Urrutia and GD, was ultimately published by Counterpoint in 1996.

131. TLS—2

12 August 1994

DEAR MR LAUGHLIN!

Obviously Declan went on vacation without telling you that we decided on a cover image, namely the Girl with Doves on a stele (Paros) and in the Metropolitan. As per enclosed. Paros is Archilochos's island, and the doves fit Alkman and Sappho.

The Picasso drawings are in the suite of drawings called "The Human Comedy," too large to be xeroxed, and are not nearly as good as the Parian Maiden. . . .

(I've just shut all my windows, in 90-degree weather, as a neighbor has started in with her leaf-blower, and will be at it for a good two hours. The noise is like that of a jet taking off. The violation of other people's space by noise and light is a feature of Yuppydom—they don't give a rat's ass if their mercury-vapor Fear Monger lights shine in your bedroom or if their leaf-blowers terrorize the neighborhood for hours.)

Hot here, too, but after some mild rainy weather. BJ has finished her summerschool teaching (bibliography). I dabble at one thing and another, mainly reading.

The new Library of American Mark Twain (the historical romances) says in its chronology that MT sat for his portrait to Whistler. I've never heard of it. Have you? I think it's misinformation. Perhaps a crayon sketch, but even that would be known, I should think.

In an ideal world we would have had an Eleanor Roosevelt by Grant Wood.

I think the Parian Girl with Doves will do just fine for *Sept Grecques.*

In haste,
GUY

132. TLS—2

30 Aug 1994
Mary W. Shelley

DEAR MR LAUGHLIN!

. . . Kathy is an excellent typist, but obviously slept through Latin in school.

William III, *Stadhouder* of the Netherlands and King of England, Ireland, Wales and Scotland, never mastered English. When he addressed parliament, he wrote his remarks in French, which his secretary turned into Latin. William is my favorite English king. James II, before him, always ended the day with dancing, music, gambling, and Italian boys singing tunes for the Jesuits. William's evenings were listening to a sermon, and the tipple was water.

His queen Mary's bible is on display somewhere. "This bibble was given to His Majesty and I on our crownation," she has written on the title page.

Thanks for asking about the Twain Whistler. I'm certain it doesn't exist. Yuppy scholarship.

My translator of Rabbi Yeshua may be quite mad, or maybe only eccentric. He certainly makes it all sound like something you've never heard before. . . .

1 Sept Birthday of Edgar Rice Burroughs, who used to keep framed on his wall a letter from Rand-McNally: "We are returning your manuscript as we do not feel that the public will be interested in a white man raised by apes."

Two of the Sapphies in *7 Greeks* have been asked for by McGraw-Hill, for a fat textbook. I have referred them to Declan.

It's practically autumnal here. September is usually our hottest and gummiest month.

The painting I'm working on—*Georg Brandes's Telephone*—has reached the Hopeless Stage. When a painting's first begun, it is all hope. If it goes well, all is fair sailing. At some point it begins to go wrong, needing revision, or painting out. I have just enough talent to get to the approximation of a picture.

be well,
GUY

/ • /

Kathy is an excellent: Because of his arthritic neck pains and the difficulties caused by his stroke, JL would at times dictate letters to a secretary, as here. He would do this only when feeling unable to type his own letters, as he preferred the freedom of thought and language he felt when doing his own typing.

Georg Brandes's Telephone: Brandes (1842–1927) was a Danish literary critic and biographer. The painting is reproduced in *A Balance of Quinces.*

133. TLS—2

5 October 1994

Dear Mr Laughlin!

. . . [You've] had a cataract removed. That seems to have gone smoothly. Advanced age is one damned thing after another. I've had a render and sore tooth lowered. I'd imagined all sorts of things wrong, as the gum was as sore as the tooth, but it was only a bad fit to my bite, corrected in three seconds.

Lovely weather here. We've made an excursion to the Louisville zoo with our friend Judy and her 3-year-old Michael, who kept asking to see dinosaurs. And on another fine day, to the Speed museum, which has a charming provincial collection, including the bronze *Mlle. Pogany.*

Crane-Ross has a review in the next *New Criterion* putting down on somebody's Sappho and preferring mine.

Georg Brandes's Telefon is a painting, not a fiction. I must learn how to photograph paintings so that I have an audience larger than the cats and Bonnie Jean. All my attempts with an ordinary camera get the top or bottom, or left side.

You ask: "Should there be a book of drawings and paintings?" Wouldn't it be instantly remaindered? The only person who might have done it, Arnold Skolnick, has just had his series of unpopular painters turned off. He was doing well (Chameleon Books, subdivision of Rizzoli, for which I did my Burchfield—I asked them to send you and Gertrude a copy, but I don't think they did) until the accountants said he wasn't making enough money fast enough.

What's passing for art now is daubs and piles of rocks. Spoiled Brat Yuppy Art.

I've just read a life of Pastor Leenhardt, missionary to New Caledonia and great French ethnologist. Huguenot saint. He made a synthesis of Kanaka beliefs and a kind of Protestant Sunday School morality, with some success. The Kanaka (Melanesian yam growers) were most interested in arithmetic as the truly useful part of Christianity, and sang the multiplication table as a hymn in church.

Five time five be twenty-five!
Five times six be thirty!
Five times seven be thirty-five!
Five times eight be forty!

The French traders had been cheating them for years. Leenhardt translated Matthew into Kanaka, using their own words for spirits and concepts of mercy, forgiveness, and so on. He held the chair in ethnology that Claude Lévi-Strauss took over on his retirement.

If Ez had known about the multiplication-hymn, he would have put it into the Cantos. Perfect example of a useful and transforming cultural exchange.

I have Dave's *JL/EP Letters,* and am learning all manner of things from it.

The Chinese translations of my ravings will be by Da Wen Po. Grandnephew of Edgar Allan Po, if anybody asks. . . .

meanwhile,
GUY

/ • /

a cataract removed: JL had written about a cataract excision on the 15th of September. He continued writing poems longhand on yellow pads, with his wife typing them up. He was typing his own letters by the 24th.

the Speed museum: The J. B. Speed Art Museum, in Louisville. *Mlle. Pogany* is a sculpture by Constantin Brancusi.

my Burchfield: Charles Burchfield's Seasons was published by Pomegranate Artbooks in 1994.

Claude Lévi-Strauss: French structuralist anthropologist. GD reviewed Lévi-Strauss's *The Origin of Table Manners,* reprinted under the title "The Champollion of Table Manners" in *EF.*

134. TLS—3

10/27/94

Dear Guy–

Many thanks for your letters of the 15th and the 20th. My eyes are still not quite perfect though they have improved, so I'm dictating this to my friend, Kathy, who, remarkably in these days, can do shorthand.

I'm puzzled about Anne Carson. She hasn't answered my last few letters in one of which I made her a definite offer for a book. Maybe it wasn't enough money, but we have our rules and schedules. I hope she will answer and if she's still interested, I'll have the things of hers which you haven't seen on which we have copies, copied for you. Whether her poems are poems, or as she often calls them "essays," I don't think it matters. They are certainly different.

I think you are right that Urrutia's *Logia of Yeshua* wouldn't be quite right for New Directions. . . .

I'm glad you are thinking about the book of paintings and drawings. There might be a lot of problems to work out, but it would be fun to try as long as it didn't end up as one of those awful coffee-table books. I think it might well be a slightly over-sized paperback. I never heard of Erik Reece, but that doesn't matter at all if he's good. Let the work speak for itself.

I don't think I've seen any of your paintings. I certainly like your various kinds of drawings very much. You mention that you sent me a painting of Pound and I'll have to search for that. This house is rather like pictures you see on the TV showing the results of a tornado. Gertrude stopped trying to keep my papers in order some years back.

"Abstractions where you float various images in white space" I found very good. *Orpheus Preaching to the Animals* is a great subject but sounds pretty big to reduce.

As to the size of the book, that would, I think, work itself out as Reece, you and I decide it. Not that I know anything about such matters. 64 pages perhaps.

The problem of color plates is a difficult one because good color work is still enormously expensive. I investigated this a few months ago when I was planning the little book *Phantoms* that *Aperture* is bringing out for me. Good color work still requires four separate plates for each item, and it runs very high. *Phantoms,* which is paperback size and runs 64 pages, was quoted in the $11,000 to $12,000 range by American printers. Then, happily, I discovered the Orient. Colorcraft in Hong Kong is going to do it for about one-half the price of the American printers. Low labor costs. All over the world printing scientists are trying to find an inexpensive substitute for separate plates. Firms in Belgium and Israel are close to it but not perfected. There is, of course, in this country color work that comes out of a copy machine. There's one of those down at a place in Torrington. But the color is still very bad, done by some chemical magic. I decided it would not do for *Phantoms* so it would not do for you.

How do your paintings look when they are in black and white, and intermediate grays, of course? Perhaps the thing to do would be to have regular color plates made for the jacket and the frontispiece. Let's keep Hong Kong in the wings until we actually see what sort of job they do on *Phantoms.* The samples of their work that they sent over were illustrations for advertising folders. That sort of thing.

I must go through all of your books that I have here again and be "re-inspired." So many people have admired your visual work.

I wish my eyes were better so that I could read from Lucian out of the Loeb again. I went through quite a bit of him when I was looking for classical recollectives for *Byways.* He really has the touch.

I'm stalled at the moment on *Byways* because trying to make the computer work gives me the flux. Anger and trembling rise together and inspiration flees to the pubs of Winsted. I don't think Henry really understood my delicate nature when he got me that devilish machine. . . .

Your admiring,
JAS

135. TLS—1

11/10/94

DEAR MIKE ANGULAR [GD]—

Wham! Bam! Bulandro! The paintings are TERRIFIC. Gertrude is torn between ravishment and envy. Burning her brushes.

But definitely call for color. But that's not insuperable. Griselda will be timid, but I'll get Leslie into the act. Not her deluxe printing but her design and packaging.

Are there drawings that can go with them? I have most of your older books. Tell me where to look for what you'd like.

I had no idea of your range or technical perfection of the different types. . . .

Forward on all fronts,
JAS

136. TLS—2

26 Nov 1994

DEAR MR LAUGHLIN!

. . . Erik Reece was here last evening, and we looked at canvases and drawings by the fire, and talked until midnight. He has spent the last week reading my *Opera Omnia,* for clues to the paintings. He is one of the brightest students I've ever taught. He is mature for his age, married to a charming lady psychologist whose parents live around the corner. They're up from Charlottesville for Thanksgiving. . . .

We're just back from an *esplore*—a round of errands on foot—to the PO and library and art store. Thanksgiving was also my 67th birthday. I got a pair of galluses, a shirt, a pair of trousers, two CD's, two novels, a new telephone (the old one was losing its ring, and peeped).

(arrival of mail here)—yours saying that the drawings have arruv [*sic*]. A poorer selection than the paintings, as so many drawings are bigger than the Xerox. . . .

27 Nov Erik was here all afternoon photographing about 40 paintings (without even getting to the 100 or so in the attic). Some of them can only be shown in Denmark on The Hydraulix of Sex Day (sponsored by the Queen), if they have such a celebration.

I also found *A Balance of Quinces* (enclosed). Epstein's *Mating Doves*, the bronze Brancusi *Jeune Homme* + phrase from G. Stein + girl + Fibonacci scale to the left. The canvas is 3½' high. . . .

I'll put this in the mail and save the round of ideas Erik and I came up with.

meanwhile, with all good wishes,
GUY

137. TLS—2

11/28/94

DEAR GUY—

THANKS for making up the selection of the drawings. They're impressive. Wonderful techniques. Gertrude is planning to frame the one of the little boy she forgot to have.

I'm pondering the question of whether we keep the type of jackets, etc., or trim those down. I'm inclined to think we should keep the "framing" in those cases, but what do you think, and what does Erik Reece think?

It's clear that having a good selection of drawings is not going to be a problem.

Should they be intermingled with the paintings, or separate sections?

How to handle captions, where needed? Should they be arranged below the drawings (and paintings), or better to (unobtrusively) number the pages and have the captions grouped in the back? The designer will need to know that kind of structure.

I'm hoping Leslie will design, but she seems to be heavily booked up these days. . . .

Best,
JAS

***138.* TLS—3**

1 December 1994
Rex Stout

DEAR MR LAUGHLIN!

These jugs are the kind of thing I do while the rest of the Republic watches TV. A cancelled panel in a grid drawing—the pen work isn't good enough and displays lazy passages. Neolithic Anatolian pottery. . . .

My Burchfield Book was printed in Hong Kong (38 color plates) and the color is excellent. Printer's ink isn't ever going to duplicate an artist's colors, and color film isn't ever going to get them right. A CD is not a symphony orchestra, and the eye has never seen what a camera catches. I've always lived in the something-better-than-nothing compromise.

As I've already written, Erik and I went through paintings and drawings for two days, thinking up titles for captions (which want to be with the cuts—I hate having to consult pages in another part of a book to see what I'm looking at). Our idea is that Erik's text will be inset, page by page, with cuts of both drawings and paintings. If I'm lucky, God will allow a signature of color pages in the middle of the book.

Erik's going to do a grand job, of that I'm certain. He has written about Ian Hamilton Finlay as if he (Erik) were Walter Benjamin, and about Rothko as if he were Foucault, but now he says he has all that out of his system. He's a great reader—I don't think you can be a writer otherwise.

Every drawing should have all the space possible, right up to the margins. The jugs on the first page here are actual size, and the more drawings are reduced, the more the cross-hatching and stippling turns to burnt toast. . . .

I can't afford to get cold feet. I can't let you or Erik down. . . .

Because Brad Morrow wanted something for *Conjunctions* to run with an interview done by Bernard Hœpffner, I've finished a story (134 pp) for him, and while the fiction fit was on me, did a 15-pager also. If I finish more, I'll soon have a book of similar ravings. The 134-pager took 5 years; the shorter one only about a year and a half. I worry about people like Joyce Carol Oates, who writes a story a day. Does she enjoy it? Does the devil make her do it?

Supply of firewood just delivered. Reading Erle Stanley Gardner with an afghan over my knees by the fire keeps me sane.

2 Dec Just back from the day's walk, bringing back 4 canvasses (virgin canvasses to be made love to).

Joan Crane seems to be finishing (after 10 years) her bibliography of my ravings.

Isn't there a bibliography of ND in the works?

I'm not in any wise telling Erik what to write, but I answer his questions about iconography and ideas; e.g. the Randolph Bourne portrait is a kind of essay on him. We had a long talk by the fire about painting and writing. You can't say anything in a painting; you can only show. In writing you can do both, though writing must be completed by the imagination and visual experience of a reader. When I began scribbling fiction at age 40, I had figured out (slow learner!) that "The man got off the bus" is all you can do, and have to trust the reader on out. The fat man, the yellow bus, the day rainy, and so forth, but nothing can help further. Nouns and verbs in grammatical order. With choice of diction. "The slender and dapperly dressed gentleman descended too quickly from the bus and fell against a Puerto Rican mother with an armload of groceries."

Drawing a man getting off a bus takes days. Describing it, three seconds. A sculptor couldn't do it at all.

I'm babbling.

meanwhile,
GUY

Thank Gertrude for liking whichever little boy I sent among the drawings.

/ • /

These jugs: At the top of this letter, GD had photocopied a 3-by-×3½-inch ink drawing he had done of two jugs.
The 134-pager: GD is here referring to "The Cardiff Team," excerpts from which were published in *Conjunctions.*
Erle Stanley Gardner: (1889–1970), detective novelist, creator of Perry Mason. GD was fond of reading detective novels, which he called "tecs."

139. TCS—1

11/30/94

REVERED MASTER [GD]—

I don't want to push, shove or crowd you, but it's not clear to me, though you've said kind things about her pieces, whether you have the steam or burning desire to do a foreword for Anne Carson's book. I do think she needs some explication, and I am mute on her, though lost in wonder. Returning her contract to Declan she opined that the Jaz strikes her "as one of the civilized humans left among us." What does she WANT? I shall FAX her in the morning that I am a Presbyterian lad who does not do improper things, no matter how much provoked by red shoes and fancy laces.

Ka ta loi poi (which I can't spell).
JAS

140. TLS—1

5 XII 1994

Dear Mr Laughlin!

People who send early Xmas cards are world leaders and Presbyterians.

I'm *willing* to write an intro to La Carson, but would be interested to know if (a) she wants an introduction (she's perfectly capable of writing a brilliant one herself) and (b) one by me. The only thing of mine she might know is my review of *Eros the Bittersweet* (I sent you a copy once, it was in *Grand Street*).

By "returning her contract to Declan" do you mean signed or rejected? (Have just called Declan—to learn that AC *has* signed a contract: you made it sound as if she had conspued it.) That is, for all we know, AC may think I'm the wrongest person in the world to introduce her.

Kaì tà loipá. "And all the rest." If you aspire to a high Greek style, you can say *loipémata* instead of *loipà.* Or if you are in a playful mood, *loipadária.* . . .

in haste,
φιλοτατως καὶ τα λοιπαδάρια
Guy

/ • /

conspued: This unusual word means "to spurn contemptuously."
φιλοτατως καὶ τα λοιπαδάρια: *"Philotamos kaì tà loipadária,"* meaning "Friendship and all the rest," using the "playful mood" form *loipadária.*

141. TLS—1

1 Jan 1995

αἳ δε φυχαὶ αὑ τῶν μήχαναι εἰςὶ
ἀλλήλοις ἐπὶ ταὶς διαφθείριαις ἡδοναῖς

Dear Dr Handspring! [JL]

This is the blind leading the blind, for sure, but last night reading Plutarch I came across the word for *dissolute,* and saw that I could get somewhere (about C+) in making a rendering of your sentence. Literally, "their souls instruments are to each other for their dissolute pleasures." (Note that I'm using the Soviet sigmata, as approved by Oxford.) It's probably Greek babu. Also, ghost-writing, to be passed off before nit-picking classicists as *your* Greek. You can say that in a dream you encountered a nice Greek girl with large olive eyes and this is her translation. . . .

A prosperous and Happy New Year!
Ὲςπερέςςα
[unsigned]

/ • /

a rendering of your sentence: JL had sent the manuscript of his poem "The Gods," asking if GD could render the last sentence into Greek. See *SR,* 48 (where ἀλλήλοις is spelled incorrectly).
Ὲςπερέςςα*:* "Evening thoughts," roughly equivalent to "Good evening."

142. TLS—3

14 Jan 1995

Dear Mr Laughlin!

A Danish moon calendar, making a poem of time. The very small print under the moons gives the (abbreviated) days of the week, which are analogous to ours except for Saturday, *lørdag,* which translates "bath day."

I rejoice that your Greek grammar dates back even further than mine, so that you are easily pleased, right down to the calligraphy, where I was merely striving for legibility. All modern Greek hands are based on that of Porson, who dispensed with all the maddening ligatures and shorthand of Byzantine *Handschrift*. . . .

Erik Reece has chosen ten paintings for color plates, and has all but finished his text. (I haven't seen it.) Two of the paintings are problematic. One was eaten by termites before I rebuilt the studio summer before last. I think I can repair it. (It's on canvasboard [*sic*], and the termites ate the backing—I've remounted it on fibre board.) The other (not in your batch of photos) may upset Norton by an anatomical explicitness.

A rough count of my daubs came up with 250 canvasses and lots more drawings.

Technical info: are the paintings to be photo'd as slides or as color prints? There's a woman in town who photographs paintings for local artists. I'll get in touch with her when I know what the printer wants, slides or prints.

Erik is one of those rare people who *like* to write. When he was a student his papers were so much better than anybody else's that I invited him to supper. He told me later that he was scared witless—another professor had told him that I hate students and am an arrogant bastard. What fetched Erik over supper was my account of an evening with Beckett at the *Closerie des Lilas,* and learning that I'd known Ez and WCW and Zukofsky and James Laughlin. He discovered later than I'm an amateur, secret painter. So the next Xmas his wife Mary asked to buy a painting, the family savings in hand. I sold her *Still Life with Apples and Pears* for 10 cents.

meanwhile, at full tilt,
GUY

/ • /

Danish moon calendar: GD had Xeroxed his *MÅNEKALENDAR 1995* onto his letter. The phases of the moon for each month and day are illustrated.
Porson: Richard Porson (1759–1808), British scholar and critic, made important editions of works by Aeschylus and Euripides.
Handschrift: German for "handwriting."

143. TLS—1

21 Feb 1995
WH Auden

DEAR MR LAUGHLIN!

Various items of news;

1. Oxford wants to put several of my Greek renderings in *The Oxford Book of Classical Poetry in Translation.*
I've referred them to Declan.

2. Thomas Meagher, *The Common Reader* books-via-mail man, is going to feature *7 Greeks.* I've given him permission to quote a few lines, and have written him a squib about my theory of translation. You probably get his monthly catalogues.

3. I've just mailed you Erik's monograph. I went over it, as you can see, tidying it up one place or another. You're going to say it's too long, but we'll cross that bridge when we come to it. . . .

venite O primavera!
GUY

144. TLS—2

2/28/95

Dear Guy—

CHRIST AND A BEAR, as my No. 2 father-in-law used to say when startled. 94 pages of text! I had imagined it would be an essay of about 10 pages which would fit nicely into a 64 page book, mostly of drawings and paintings, the color pages done in Hong Kong.

But Wellington didn't flip at Waterloo, he just regrouped his forces. Erik's piece is quite something, and he writes so well. He seems to know your work front and backwards and say very perceptive things about it.

So it looks like 128 pages which is two 64s, if that will accommodate plates of all the pictures he writes about. . . .

I think there is enough of the green in the till to handle this bigger book. Don't worry about that. As Gertrude says, "You can't take it with you." This should be a very impressive book, a credit to all involved, a service to ART, and it's almost like a biography of you, at least of your work. Interlacing what you wrote with the pictures should make it vendable.

Very best,
Jas

That's good news about Oxford, an important collection, good to be in. And also the *Common Reader.* Your cup brims. Mine leaks. Stranger and stranger verses keep appearing. I think there is a Danish elf living inside my typewriter. I've noted odd droppings under it, things that moles eat.

No word from St. Anne about the introduction. . . .

/ • /

No word: GD had submitted an introduction to Anne Carson's *Glass, Irony and God,* but asked that JL forward it to Carson for her comments.

145. TLS—2

10 March 1995

DEAR MR LAUGHLIN!

I seem to be working full time for New Directions Publishing Corporation. Yesterday went to proofing *Seven Greeks* all afternoon and evening, and the morning went to the photographing of works of art, by Mary Rezny, a charming and efficient woman. We converted the living room into a studio, with lights, camera, and easel. We shot 16 canvases in color and about 20 in black and white. A photograph of a drawing she did earlier won't do, and I must have the drawings done by a graphics place.

I will ply my editorial pencil on Erik's text. . . .

meanwhile,
GUY

/ • /

ply my editorial pencil: JL had requested that GD edit Reece's manuscript for length.

146. TLS—2

28 March 1995
Maksim Gorki

DEAR MR LAUGHLIN!

Proggers report (as LBJ used to say)—the drawings are being done, and can be picked up tomorrow.

More black and white repros of paintings are also being done (almost, not quite all the ones Erik mentions).

Erik is down in Virginia revising the text after I went over it, tightening, slicing out, and generally copy-editing. The great advantage of computers is that the text is *in it* and can be infinitely revised. . . .

Jonathan Williams is coming to town next week. I've been summoned to a drinks-before-dinner at Guy Mendes's, where I will scarcely get a chance to talk with him. He requires a royal court—about 30 people are invited to dinner afterwards. Whereas I am a hermit. Bonnie Jean and I consider more than four people in a room to be a replay of the French Revolution. Jonathan used to stay here, but it has been years since he has. He wrecks the house, the beds, and is as demanding as a five-year-old.

Why are people so peculiar?

ad interim
GUY

/ • /

Guy Mendes: Lexington photographer and film producer.

147. TLS—2

24 May 1995

DEAR DANISH PIRATE! [JL]

What a happy convergence of poet, printer and binder, *The Country Road.* I'd not seen the Merton before—worth the price of the book alone, as they say. I've just read—re-read—the whole book and think it's your best (but then I've thought that about all your books, and it's unfair to the competition for you to get *better* with each book). Is it the cigars? An aside: you're also the neatest composer of notes in the business. *Merci beaucoup* for my copy and its inscription. The physical book is about as lovely as books can get, as clean as a Doric column. I love purity of diction and clarity of form, but as a prose-writer I have my eye on subject matter—plot, anecdote, realities. There's enough of the real world in these poems to out-do the most strenuous fiction (as our friends the old Greeks would say, *historia*). Things reported by an eye-witness, "history."

Bonnie was telling me yesterday that a child's Batman cape has a tag on it saying that "this product will not enable the purchaser to fly." Lawyers catching up with Magritte. . . .

25 May I'll have to do the Carson intro over from scratch. Damn.

7 Greeks / [*sic*] when a new book comes out I can't *see* it. Not until so much as one reader has looked at it—and then I try to see what they see. Azza book it looks good.

Bill Forsyth. I think *Gregory's Girl* is the very first. As with all his titles, the hidden (reserved) meaning surfaces in the narrative. He must be the last director to believe in innocence.

"The Old Man with the Beard" is wonderful! God, Father Time, a daimon, an angel.

Something very strange is going on with *castor* and *pollux* that I'd never noticed before. Once their names are in Latin, they mean *clean* and *dirty* (or chaste and polluted). In Greek they're Beaver and Good Natured Fellow—Polydeukes (with a sweet temperament).

I like your progression from beaver (beard) to beaver in the stream to Castor in the stars. . . .

You seem to be publishing a book a week.

ad interim,
GUY

/ • /

The Country Road: JL's 1995 collection from Zoland Books.

the Carson intro: JL wrote that Anne Carson had decided to withdraw a sequence titled "Irony Is Not Enough" and replace it with "TV Men."

Bill Forsyth: At GD's recommendation, JL had been viewing films by this director, including *Gregory's Girl* and, later, *Local Hero.*

"The Old Man with the Beard": JL had mailed GD a poem manuscript about an encounter with an old man while on a walk. It includes the lines:

"The beaver (castor Canadiensis), *" he said,*
"is an interesting fellow, and he has a
good family tree in mythology, he's one of
the Dioscuri; *Castor's up there now in the*
night sky with his twin brother Pollux."

148. TLS—3

2 June 1995
Comte Donatien Alphonse François de Sade
Thomas Hardy

Dear Mr Laughlin!

Just a while ago I mailed you the revised intro to La Carson. A copy to Declan, too. The world is coming all to pieces—my doorbell rang this morning. I was upstairs and it must have taken me 30 seconds to nip downstairs to answer it. What I saw when I opened up the door was the Fed Ex girl getting into her truck. She giggled when I pointed out that she'd given me less than a minute to answer the door. (It was a ms from my Mexican translator, who doesn't trust the *Servicio Postal.*)

Norfolk culture becomes more fascinating every detail you pass on of it. Classical Night at the Country Club!

7 Greeks came out nifty and fetching. Our weather has been so unrelentingly wet, however, that the cover curls like a scroll. The bold-face fragment numbers please me: they have authority.

Leslie Miller (whom you seem to be back to again): she's somebody I could work with—she did a beautiful edition of my *Bowmen of Shu.* She has an eye; her posters for the Metropolitan are the last word in elegance.

La Carson doesn't send me anything, least of all *Raritan.* And she's at McGill, which is in Canada, bayn't it?

All this rain has made Bonnie's flowers and veggies flourish like the green tree of Scripture. Do you have Icelandic poppies? Yellow. The flora of Iceland is a family all to itself. In Copenhagen the *Botanisk Have* (garden) has a lovely patch of Icelandic meadow wildflowers, moss, and grasses. The caretakers have to fuss over it, as keeping arctic vegetation in so sultry a southern climate as Sjælland is tricky.

Have I recounted my adventures with my Danish mathematician? He'd written to ask about the multiplication subset patterns in "The Jules Verne Steam Balloon" (first discovered, it turns out, by one Lagrange, as I didn't know). So I showed him a new discovery I've made about reversed numbers and latent nines, previously discovered by Fermat himself. All this is damned peculiar, as I can scarcely add and subtract. Anyway, I seem to have stumbled independently onto the fact (ask the sheep) that

$$(by + z) - (bz + y) = (b-1)y - (b-1)z = (b-1)\ (y-z)$$

That is, if you reverse any number and subtract it from itself, you get nine (after fusing integers, treating zeros as latent nines).

I didn't do any math in school after the ninth grade. . . .

I tried to order a *Da Vinci's Bicycle* (my second collection of ravings, pub'd by Johns Hopkins) to discover that it is Out of Print. They've kept mum about this. Doesn't a publisher relinquish a book when he lets it go out of print? Or does this mean that they've depleted their stock?

The Register of Rhodes Scholars has required us to send in annual reports of books, lectures, prizes and whichwhat, and I've dutifully done this over the years. Apparently they threw them away as fast as they came, as they're compiling a bibliography of us all, and I've just had to supply them all over again with what was published in the annual reports. When I got it done, I saw that I've published 40 titles—not 40 books as such (*7 Greeks,* for instance, was originally 6 separate books, and several of the stories had small-press appearances).

I thought The Age of Computers was supposed to *store* such info, for quick retrieval?

I think you're fretting absolutely too much about color. The Hong Kong Celestials, or whoever, can't do all that much perjury. With a Klee or O'Keeffe, color is of the essence. *Avec moi et* Mondriaan it's a horse of a different tint.

Meanwhile,
GUY

/ • /

Classical Night: JL had been invited to read at the local country club, and agreed if he could read translations of Greek poetry.
Sjælland: One of the two islands on which Copenhagen is built.
Lagrange / Fermat: Joseph-Louis, Comte de Lagrange (1736–1813), and Pierre de Fermat (1601–1665), French mathematicians.
reversed numbers and latent nines: This mathematical discovery figures in two stories in *The Cardiff Team:* "The River," and "Concert Champêtre in D Minor."

149. TLS—2

Bloomsday 1995 [June 16]

DEAR MR LAUGHLIN!

Lovely splendid excellent news—Leslie. And our printer is in Iceland. Erik is in Colorado looking at the scenery and Mary his wife is out camping with Episcopal Girl Scouts somewhere in the wilds of Kentucky. When I have good news for people they are always off on a toot.

Strabo is in a dozen volumes. I can Xerox you the India part, unless you want to peruse S. on the whole world. Of Ireland he says he can't find out anything except that the Irish all kill their fathers and fuck their mothers and sisters in public. He apologizes for the scantiness of his information.

If you will give me Leslie's address I can swap ideas about design with her. I'm certain her former address is out of date. Our last correspondence was her trying to get me to take up etching. . . .

I'm intrigued by Leslie's Icelandic printers. That is, despite Iceland's prominence in literature (they read more books than any other country), I would not have guessed printing as an industry there. *Island* they call themselves, and enjoy the distinction of being neither in Europe nor America. The name is a typical Viking joke: Greenland is solid glacier, and Iceland is green and pleasant. Leif the Unlucky was lucky, and Harald Bluetooth had snowy white choppers. Ha ha. Prophylactic magic humor.

On which note, I'll put this in the mail *[. . .]*

ad feliciter interim
GUY

/ • /

Bloomsday: James Joyce's *Ulysses* is set on June 16, 1904. Fans celebrate "Bloomsday" every year in its honor.
Leslie: JL had written that Leslie Miller would be the designer for *A Balance of Quinces.*
Strabo: (63? B.C.–A.D. 24?) Greek geographer and historian. GD had mentioned Strabo after reading JL's "In Trivandrum" (see *Byways*).

150. TLS—2

26 June 1995

DEAR MR LAUGHLIN!

You could have written all day on your last letter without mentioning that Leslie has taken $983 worth of reproductions to some fishing lodge in Scotland, twice to go through Customs, twice to endure transatlantic crossings. It is my fate to do everything twice, being luckless. Moreover, nobody should take work on a vacation. Don't mention this to Leslie until *after* she's lost everything and we have to start all over.

Erik the Red was *ræd* (wise) or of good counsel. City Hall in Copenhagen is *Et Red Hus.*

Our Erik, Reece, was by last evening, back from gazing on Willa Cather's house in Nebraska. We talked for five hours, regaling ourselves with chocolate milk and fried-egg sandwiches. He and Mary have bought a house on the James River. . . .

I was dashed last night to learn (from Joan Crane) that when George Steiner wrote his piece on me in *The New Yorker* years ago (astounding the English Department) he had read two stories and faked a general knowledge of my *oeuvre.* He has since, to his dismay, read more, and decided that I'm an awful and evil writer. That's his problem. He should have done his homework in the first place.

"*[. . .]* the leafage at the edge of the lake" (in which you nearly foundered) is a beautiful phrase.

Declan says that *Hepta Hellenikoi* has sold nearly 2000 copies. Some of these will be to Thomas Meagher, of *A Common Reader,* which will carry it in its next catalogue. . . .

A letter *from* Leslie. I feel I now have my feet on the ground with this book. . . .

27 June Looking over this letter I see that it is less than gentlemanly. Leslie will not lose the drawings and ms in the salmon run, and I should be grateful to George Steiner.

meanwhile,
GUY

/ • /

George Steiner wrote: Steiner (1929–) is an eminent scholar, critic, and novelist. His statement that "Davenport is among the very few truly original, truly autonomous voices now audible in American letters" was used in GD publicity materials and on book jackets a number of times, even after GD learned this. JL responded (on July 9, 1995) by noting that he'd met Steiner only once, and that Steiner had said, "You educated us all."

A Common Reader, which will carry it: GD mailed JL a copy of these notes, which were printed in this mail-order book dealer's Summer 1995 catalogue to help publicize *7 Greeks:*

> My sense of translating Greek which has been translated many times over, is to make a rendering that just might be near what the original is doing. Pound said that all translations are a photograph of a statue. My interest is in the anthropology of the ancient Greek mind. We understand a little of this, and in any case must make an end run around the Renaissance and the Enlightenment and German Criticism. Hugh Kenner once observed that the Liddell & Scott Greek-English Lexicon is a great work of fiction. As rich as English is, it does not coincide in crucial words and phrases with ancient Greek, or even with Biblical Greek (did Jesus come to dwell *among us* or *in us*?).
>
> What in the world does Sappho's majestic adjective *poikilothron'* mean? It elides with the next word, *athanat'* (deathless) and has confused people for centuries. *Thronos* is a throne, or more accurately, a chair. *Throna,* a clever scholar has tracked down, is a dress. *Poikilos* was an all-purpose word for anything well

or cunningly made, or embroidered, or decorated. Is Sappho showing us Aphrodita sitting in a beautifully made chair, or in her best dress embroidered with fancy needlework?

In Theokritos's Fifth Idyll a goat is eating something. You look the word up, and Liddell-Scott says "a plant eaten by a goat in Theoc. Idyll V."

And Eros is a *herpes*—a serpent, a creeper, a sneaker-upper, a stalker.

Deciding on an English word to do service for a Greek one is like a conversation in which Dizzy Gillespie is said to have asked, in a car, what made it go?

"Well, man, you have gasoline vapor ignited by the spark-plugs, and an explosion that pushes a piston . . ."

"I know all that, man. What I want to know is what makes it *go*?"

The constant question in translation is what does it *mean*? I have a feeling that we're all too often translating on the level of a sign, intended for English, in a Danish restaurant. EXORBITANT TOMATER SOUPE, it said.

151. TLS—2

7/21/95

DEAR GUY—

HALLELUJAH, it's Christmas in July. The Ts of *The Cardiff Team* arrived this morning. I'm sure we'll like it well. I had a tremor of anxiety when I saw your name in Shoemaker's first catalogue. He has always been a thorn. When he was at Northpoint he was often trying to steal ND authors. He did manage to lift Gary, but I've never blamed Gary for that, there were special pressures in that wigwam. We remain good friends. Did you see Gary on the Bill Moyers show last week? A noble Injun, retake of Sitting Bull no doubt. I'll get into *Cardiff* as pronto as possible. Or perhaps skim it and send it down to Declan for close reading. *Cardiff* need not wait for the pitcher book. That is a special JL project and Leslie may take a time with it. . . .

The Ladies at Gale Research think I'm cute. They warble at me on the phone. They want to put all of *Byways* that is finished in a mammoth anthology of autobiographical writings to sell to libraries. I like this idea if there are no gimmicks in it. They will print 2000 copies and sell them for $122. This should give me a public knowledge of the poem that it would take me years to get trying to place segments in magazines. . . .

Best,
JAS

/ • /

Ts of The Cardiff Team: Typescript of GD's book of stories.
to lift Gary: Gary Snyder. He helped bring Asian philosophy into the American consciousness.

152. TLS—2

27 July 1995

DEAR MR LAUGHLIN!

What faith you have in my ravings! I have no self-judgment, and suspect that I'm apt to see my good stuff (if any) as ho-hum, and my outrageous stuff as the best I can do. You might find the first story amusing (it's about Kafka at a nudist spa in Austria, meeting two characters who turn up in *The Castle*). I seem not to have kept a copy of the Contents page, and have now forgotten the exact order I shuffled them into at the last minute. (They have to be in that order, by the way, as things carry over, and some stories must be read before others.) This is, up to a point, negotiable. . . .

One thing going for *The Cardiff Team* is that the jacket is obvious, Delaunay's *L'Equipe de Cardiff* (there are three versions. We want the one in the Museum of the City of Paris. I'll send Declan a Xerox, if and when it comes to that).

28 July Some dilatory rain has got us down into the 80s, nothing to shout about. I've been painting this morning, before the north light becomes a blast furnace. I need to spruce up several canvasses that Leslie will need if she does eight more.

Also have to sign a batcher bookplates for *7 Greeks* to send to *A Common Reader.*

In "August Blue" (*A Table of Green Fields*) I have Tuke painting TE Lawrence. Paul Cadmus has got around to reading it and writes to say that he *owns* the painting, and sends along a snapshot of it. Also says that EM Forster told him that Lawrence posed for Tuke "in Adam's costume" (as the Danes say). Cadmus wasn't quite certain that the painting was indeed of Col. Lawrence, but takes my story as corroboration. I made the story from the merest clues: a watercolor of Tuke's in which TEL in RAF khakis is unlacing his boot on a beach, and the fact that TEL visited Tuke in 1922.

Oof. I've just signed 200 bookplates to be pasted in *A Common Reader*'s *7 Greeks.* Do you suppose they hope to *sell* 200 copies?

Didn't see Gary Snyder on TV. . . .

χαίρετε!
GUY

/ • /

Paul Cadmus: (1904–1999), deliberately provocative, often homoerotic and satirical artist. GD wrote an introduction to a published selection of Cadmus's drawings, reprinted in *HG,* 275–96.

153. TLS—2

29 July 1995

DEAR MR LAUGHLIN!

Gertrude's question—how do I know all the things I know—is a good one in that it lets several cats out of the bag at once. If she means history and geographical detail, the answer is books, travel, and stealing. If she means psychology and the behavior of people, I make it up. As Erik says in the pitcher book, I describe an alternate reality allowed for by nature but not by Janet Reno.

The formula is: an image or idea to go on with. Walt and Sam were two very sophisticated French boys at the Brasserie Georges V. It was a lovely late afternoon, the brasserie is one of our favorites, and we were having a *picon* and watching what was to be seen on the *Place Alma,* enjoying Paris as I think only Americans can. I remarked, and BJ agreed, that the boys were from Gide—too brainy (they had satchels and books) for de Montherlant, too pure and innocent to be from Proust. They seemed to have a friendship of some intimacy, something private that their dull parents knew nothing of. Then, back home and a year or so later, I made up the rest of it.

You may "borrow" *lacunarity,* or anything else. Izzit a word? My characters sometimes use extradictionary words. I forget the context. Mind swapping is probably disapproved of by psychologists.

Back to Gertrude: one scribbles in notebooks, else things will get away from you, and then in making a story *mines* the notebooks. I have enough stuff on Delaunay's painting left over for another story.

I'm pleased—and vastly relieved—that you say "nifty and yummy." Another publisher might have said, "Now see here, Davenport, this is going too far." Doesn't Ezra say in the last Cantos that if you don't go too far, you'll never know the boundaries?

The Crusoe is there to *locate* the theme of making a home out of anywhere, which is what most of the characters are doing, a place where you can *be* (playing field, *Bois,* a café table, camping tent). Is there a theme also of inscrutable messages (paintings, poems)?

Also teams, congeries of people, miniature communities.

My failing, of course, is that I am not a dramatic writer. I admire Chekov; none of my admiration has ever got me anywhere. Animated genre paintings, my scribbles.

30 July Henry the Tomcat has been in such a dreadful fight that he looks like the Battle of Shiloh. He is being kept in. This is no weather for wounds. Belinda, who grooms him and is devotedly an admiring sister, won't go anywhere near him. I cleaned the wounds with soap and water, the best anti-septic, say nine out of ten vets.

There is a kind of freshness to the air this morning, which will give way in just a bit to the oven heat and saturation humidity of yesterday, a record scorcher.

The 5220 copier went on the fritz after doing *The Cardiff Team*—too many pages at once, I think—but Bonnie has repaired it with her Christian Science touch. (She once fixed the lawn-mower by suggesting that I quit fiddling with it and let it rest overnight, and it ran beautifully next day.) That is, she prescribed a night's rest for it, and now it does its stuff. What's missing in Aristotle is the practical impracticality of the female mind.

Now I have to finish a book for the Univ of Toronto Press (commissioned).

coolly onward!
GUY

/ • /

Janet Reno: At this time, Reno was United States attorney general.
Gide . . . de Montherlant: André Gide (1869–1951) was a French writer whose works primarily dealt with conflicts between personal freedom and society's moral and ethical concepts. Henry M. J. M. de Montherlant (1896–1972) was a French novelist and dramatist, several of whose works combined Christian and pagan ideas.
Mind swapping: A reference to JL's poem "Swapping Minds," *SR*, 62–63.
book for the Univ of Toronto: This was to have been a publication of the lectures he gave on still life. This collection appeared as a Counterpoint publication in 1998.

154. TLS—1

8/2/95

DEAR GUY—

Did I dream the beautiful word "lagunaria" or did I see it in your new book, or have I misspelled it? It's a [token?] word for me and I want to use it in a poem, but it's not in the big Webster or the OED. Not that I don't make up lots of words, and who cares anyway? I use it in my draft to mean lack of punctuality.

GOOD. I just found it: lacunarity. A gap (in time) or missing part. But I am stretching it for the poem. I'll draft a bit and please tell me if I'm off the track. Poem is about Angelica who was never on time.

Yr annoying scribbler,
JAS

155. ALS—2

7 August 1995

DEAR MR LAUGHLIN!

Typewriter has gone crazy. Repairman, like M. Godot, will come tomorrow. Ezra used to say that my handwriting is "beautiful but illegible." LACUNARITY is used, as I remember, by Marc Bordeaux in "The Cardiff Team" to mean gaps in his experience. If we looked in Medieval Latin, we'd probably find *Lacunaritas.* Classical Latin has *Lacuna,* a gap, and *Lacunaria,* a ceiling with regular spaces between the beams.

You justify the word in your poem. Though, without specifying that you mean a gap in civilized regularity, you would run the risk of calling her spacey, loony, bubble-brained. Marilyn Monroe was notoriously late. Louis XIV once had his coachman executed for *almost* being late (he arrived as Louie was coming out of the door). . . .

In your poem, "I never reproached
Her for her lacuna*rities* . . ."

That makes it plural and habitual. A lacunarity would be an event, or state, not an abstract quality.

χαίρετε!
GUY

/ • /

in your poem: JL had enclosed a copy of his poem manuscript "Her Lacunarity."

156. TLS—2

10 August 1995

DEAR MR LAUGHLIN!

This Olivetti has just come back from hozzie (as the Australians say). . . .

Had a good talk with Leslie this afternoon. She really does want 8 more color transparencies, and I've been spiffing up canvasses, strengthening colors, changing designs, and washing the acrylic ones. The photographer Mary Rezny is to call tomorrow to say when she can photograph them.

She's sending me the text, now on a computer disk, Monday, for a final going-over.

Da Vinci's Bicycle is now out of print at Johns Hopkins, and they've reverted rights, as the fiction series it's in keeps a book only so long. Would the firm of New Directions be interested in it? It has been done into French as *La Bicyclette de Léonard.* Lots of learned articles on it, as even educated people had not heard of the Dogon, Fourier, Robert Walser, and other Davenport Alternate World bric-a-brac. Would I be glutting the list? It has been used as a textbook several times, to my knowledge.

Or shall we give the reading public a rest from it?

. . . Being without a typewriter for three days and without a copier for a week, I'm behindhand. Three big projects to get out of the way. I suppose nobody is allowed to work on *one* thing.

Liberalism in its maturest form is Fascism, as witness Clinton tooling up to do away with tobacco and sex.

Now they tell us about the detached leg, in combat boot and camouflage trouser, that they found in the Oklahoma rubble. Sherlock Holmes's eyes would have gleamed.

onward!
GUY

/ • /

detached leg, in combat boot: This reported find, at the site of the April 1995 Oklahoma City Federal Building bombing, fueled speculation that there was a third bomber.

157. TLS—3

22 IX 1995
Michael Faraday

DEAR MR LAUGHLIN!

It is chilly per sudden overnight change. And we too have had some rain after a long drought. The way you lift a moth out of the cat's water or the cream or the possum's bowl of water (out back) is slide a spatula, or knife, under it and put it in the sun to dry. It then flies away, as good as new.

Bonnie Jean is a Jain about everything except fleas. There are moths and spiders everywhere this time of year.

It is technically incredible that Leonardo *did* invent the bicycle. Nobody has challenged the discovery, which came to light when the Biblioteca in Madrid unglued the pages of L da V's that some Renaissance wop had pasted in his scrapbook. La Biblioteca acquired the scrapbook after the wop's demise, and as they have never had a card catalogue, forgot about it. A lucky scholar found it in the stacks.

And when they unglued a page by *il maestro,* on the back was an 11-year-old boy's drawing of a bicycle, his name, a caricature of himself, and two *mentulae cum scrota* on bird's legs and with wings. Also his name: SALAJ. (Years later he would be Leonardo's sole heir.)

Did Leonardo invent it and build one for Salaj? And why does nobody mention it if he did? Was life in Firenze so wild that nobody noticed?

Torcelli, Vespuccio, and Toscanelli reading letters from Cristofero Colombo at the *bettola*, Savonarola preaching down at the Bapistry,

Lorenzo de' Medici and Giuliano discussing Plato with Ambrogiano, Michelangelo explaining the divine proportions of the David to Machiavelli, Botticelli sizing up the girls, Lucrezia Borgia sending out for poison, and nobody noticed a cheeky kid on the world's first bicycle?

Erik and Mary will be up from Virginia tomorrow and I will frown darkly on further changes.

The Harvard *Byways* sounds as if it's going to be spicy.

"Poets on Stilts" is a called-for satire, and are they poets at all? I rejoice before the Lord that I have never been to a "workshop" or on a panel. Well, once, as I couldn't turn down Eudora Welty.

Speaking of the young and their ambitions, I was listening to the radio a while ago, a program about how female Olympic gymnasts (O Nadia Comaneci!) are getting younger and younger. My imagination was being served until one of them was interviewed. God a-mighty! She sounded six, and was less articulate than Belinda the Cat.

With a few more heaves and strains, I will have the summer's long haul at the top of the hill. I finished my revision of Benjamin's translation of Rabbi Yeshua this morning (and may even have a publisher). Now I must do an introduction to it. I'm not certain where Benjamin got some of the sayings—not in the gospels. He's up on all the far out in biblical research. Saint *Quelqu'un* was always writing to Saint Whoozis and quoting gospels we know nothing about.

The really exciting stuff is going on with "the Dead Sea Scrolls"—mss from the Qumran Essene outpost and the Nag Hammadi library. Practically all the translators are suing each other over infringements, friends have parted brass rags, and the whole shebang is 45 years behind schedule. And BJ tells me that they've found some more.

Benjamin has turned Jesus into a Zen poet. All this started with B's reading "August Blue" in *A Table of Green Fields*—my only reader (sfarz I know) who saw that the part about Yeshua is concocted from Jewish and early Xtn sources. . . .

Joan's bibliography. It is in the hands of the printers. At the last minute they wanted 27 drawings to decorate it. I hope to have the stoic control not to look at it.

Relafin. Sounds like a make of racing car. My only medicament is bicarb of soda, for when (as tonight) I've dined on fried okra (as eaten by the gods), corn soufflé, biscuits, and ice cream.

meanwhile, onward!
GUY

/ • /

It is technically incredible: GD likely meant to say *credible.*
Poets on Stilts: See JL's *PNS,* 152.
Relafin: A new medication JL's doctor had prescribed for his terrible arthritis pains.

158. TLS—2

3 October 1995

DEAR MR LAUGHLIN!

What thwarted your consultation of the Sioux-Greek dictionary is Anne Carson's up-to-date use of the archaic sigma, now approved of at Oxford and Cambridge in favor of the sigmata you and I are used to, in its two forms, internal and final. *kata kosmon* means "appropriately," literally "according to good order." *Kata* meant anything a Greek wanted it to—Liddell-Scott's definition rages on for three dense columns. *Kosmos* is almost as chaotic. Its basic meaning is *order* ("the cosmos"), but because the Greeks drooled over beauty, it came to mean beautiful, and got used as a word for *a jewel,* the moon ("night's ornament" is in *The Cantos* in Greek). Hence our cosmetic, cosmology, cosmic, and, I assume, the common modern Greek girl's name *Kuzma.*

The gospels are all *kata* Matthaios, Markos, Lukas, kai Iohannan.

Phone just rang—that mail-order bookstore *A Common Reader.* They've sold the 200 copies they had of *7 Greeks* that I signed paste-in labels for, and they want me to sign 200 more.

Thanks for Leslie's note. I had one something like it. And for La Carson's economic essay on the economies of Simonides and Celan. She *sees.*

Darwin in his early notebooks made lots of entries about the trickiness of memory. Life seems to be symmetrical in that the two extremes resemble each other. Second adolescences, second childhoods. People who have acquired a second language lose it. The elderly Conrad had a thick Polish accent that he did not have as a young sea-captain. I know of an old woman who reverted to her native Welsh in California, and the family had to hire an interpreter. . . .

Haven't seen *Plainwater.* I think we can take it as a working hypothesis that as far as Anne Carson is concerned I don't exist. This is not complaint or pique. She provided a blurb for *7 Greeks* and allowed you to ask me to do an introduction to her poems, both of which were professional courtesies. Classicists usually consider me a poacher and a bootlegger.

My intellectual pin-up is Elinor Shaffer, who writes about Coleridge and Sam Butler.

4 *October* Rain! Cold wet autumn rain, aye golly. I shouldn't have written the above about Anne Carson. *Eros the Bittersweet* is a book nobody else could have written, and she is the real thing as a poet.

Jack Shoemaker has *The Logia of Yeshua* and so far hasn't rejected it. I tend to be mother-hennish about my ugly ducklings. My favorite Aesop is the mother ape who declares her baby to be the prettiest of all the animals.

meanwhile,
DR. KAT A. KOSMON, PH. D.

/ • /

the Sioux-Greek dictionary: On September 30, JL had written that Anne Carson had mailed him a copy of her new book *Plainwater,* with a gift inscription in Greek. JL had trouble translating it, and mentions his "little dictionary, published, I think, for the Indians on the Sioux Reservation."

the economies of Simonides and Celan: Carson later expanded these ideas to book length: *Economy of the Unlost* (Princeton, N.J.: Princeton University Press, 1999).
Elinor Shaffer: See her *Erewhons of the Eye: Samuel Butler as Painter, Photographer & Art Critic* (London: Reaktion Books, 1988).

159. TLS—3

15 Oct 1995
Nietzsche
Wilde
Virgil

DEAR MR LAUGHLIN!

. . . *A Common Reader* has now decided that *7 Greeks* is a Book of the Year (among many others); I'll send the catalogue page to Declan.

Jack has taken *The Logia of Yeshua,* and is asking the Dalai Lama for a blurb. $5000 advance. I thought sure I'd end up having Bill Bamberger, or some such small press, print it, and get stuck with the printing bill. . . .

18 Oct Letters get bumped from the typewriter. Golden autumn days with blue skies. I dreamed last night of having three houses that I lived in, none familiar in *any* detail, all vivid and interesting. This phenomenon of dreams of places you've never seen (like your ongoing road) ought to be looked into. It defies Lockean psychology (the mind as *only* what it has experienced) and Freudian "dream as anxiety drama." It seems to be pure imagination, without worldly origin. Why should I dream that in one of my houses a nice old lady keeps a sweet shop in one of the rooms? Or that 621 Sayre has marble doors? Am I writing fiction in my sleep? My "Haile Selassie's Funeral Train" is the transcription of an elaborate dream, just so.

It is plausible (to me) that the mind at all times, awake or asleep, keeps creating a parallel, or alternate, reality. I don't know of a psychologist who writes about this. Freud was down on day-dreaming (revery) [*sic*] as a drift toward mumpery and mental instability. Yet living multiple lives simultaneously seems to be an enrichment rather than a deflection. Psychologists are indifferent [to] (or afraid of) the imagination because they *can't get at it.* It is wonderfully interior, all one's own, private and inviolable.

The Bible, both Testaments, is full of worry about what's "in the heart," suspecting evil and mischief. All art must come from this interior reality. The "world" of Klee is NOT a "mirror" held up to reality.

Freud *did,* by the way, make up his patients' dreams. He justified this by saying they were "characteristic." And he once admitted that his dog dreamed, when it was "running in its sleep" by the fire—rather effectively knocking his theory on the noggin, as what dog thinks of his father as a rival for his mother's love and couldn't possibly have castration fears. . . .

Cats, who sleep more than any other animals, must lead the large part of their lives in dreams.

meanwhile,
GUY

/ • /

"Haile Selassie's Funeral Train": GD story. See *DVB,* 108–13.
The "world" of Klee: Paul Klee (1879–1940) was a Swiss artist whose primarily abstract works were said to convey the feeling of dream images.

160. TLS—2

28 October 1995

DEAR MR LAUGHLIN!

To wish you a happy birthday, with an extra helping of pumpkin pie and a good cigar. . . .

We're having blue skies alternating with black clouds and blustery rain. Your autumn will be far more advanced. Autumn, at some steady rate known to meteorologists, comes down the map (spring moves *up*). That amazing man Michelet charted all these rhythms of seasons and winds and ocean streams years ago in his exploration of "silent history"—it was he who traced the Line of Fire around the Pacific as one of the geodesic circles inscribed on the circle of the globe, at right angles to the equator. (For years I thought the Parisians had named a street after the equator, until I figured out that it's Ecuador Street, named for the embassy of that exotic republic.)

I've had this thought, and am not certain of the protocol: namely, that we might place some of the stories in *The Cardiff Team* in respectable magazines, as our publication date is a whole year away. The first story, "The Messengers," just might go into *The Hudson Review,* which published my first fictional ravings years ago (and most recently "47 Views of Mount Fuji"). Is this kosher? I don't read contracts, but I believe they standardly say that a publisher becomes the agent for a literary property, so perhaps it falls to Declan to approach Fred Morgan or Paula Deitz. Texts in magazines function as advance advertisement.

You may have heard from Declan that *A Table of Green Fields* has been nominated for The Dublin International Prize, and that Dublin wants to know IF—blithering big *if*—I'm short-listed, will I fly at my own expense to Dublin to see if I win? As I can't imagine *A Table* winning, and as I don't like being coerced into guessing games, I am pragmatically declining. The NY Critics Book Award (or the other one) started this barbarian business (using the Oscar awards as model) of assembling writers to announce a prize at the last minute. Their fulcrum is vanity, of which I try not to have any of [*sic*].

The nominator is mysteriously the Municipal Library in Lyon. Things are getting VERY peculiar when an American book gets nominated for an Irish prize by French librarians.

". . . of which I try not to have any" / "which I try not to have any of"—grammar!

. . . It was Bessie Smith, I think, who said "Age ain't nuthin' but a number!"

Happy Birthday!
GUY

/ • /

That amazing man Michelet: Jules Michelet (1798–1874), French historian and student of geological sciences. He wrote a seventeen-volume history of France, and originated the use of "the Renaissance" as a historical term.

161. TLS—3

Halloween 1995

DEAR MR LAUGHLIN!

You have FOUR Klees! Himmel. (It's just getting dark: the goblins will be along shortly.) . . .

Absolutely I want an offprint of *Byways 1–15.* Those Gale Research volumes cost *più che La Divina Commedia.*

"The Lady or the Tiger?" is not by the great Wilkie Collins but Frank R. Stockton. Wilkie wrote *The Woman in White* (which outsold Dickens in its day). He was a very strange person—the scholars are still counting his wives and mistresses, and he drank back enough tincture of opium per day to kill a horse. I'm one of the few people on Sayre Avenue who has read his *opera omnia,* some of it several times over.

I am, if anything, a Baptist: that is, I was immersed at age 10 or thereabouts. The minister wore a rubber suit. It sprang a leak during the war, and one of Roosevelt's agencies had to be appealed to for vulcanizing, which was denied as having nothing to do with the War Effort. The Southern Baptist Council sent a distressed letter to Washington, and the affair got into the papers. (I was telling this once to the distinguished Czech linguist Vladimir Jelinek, who laughed so hard that he spilled beer all over himself. It was the rubber suit that got him in the ribs.) . . .

1 Nov Scads of wee monsters kept me busy last evening handing out candy. The get of one Yuppy family plunged right into the house and helped themselves from the supply.

Montaigne says we are "dragged into old age facing backwards." And our youth facing forward. He was in his 50s when he wrote this. He doesn't consider that his essays got better and better. . . .

Autumn evenings, reading Strabo. There's a Greek verb for "sailing in and out of the sinuosities of gulfs" (for the kind of sailing in small boats that don't dare lose sight of land). And an adverb for "avoiding most telling a lie." The verbal components fit together like watchworks.

Also learned that they liked to use shortened forms of place names (sounds very modern) e.g. "Lex" for Lexington; "Norfy" for Norfolk, *und so weiter.* Strabo (his name means squint-eye) is always having to explain that Sammy (*Samé*) is both Samothrace and Samos. And the glorious name Thermopylae was normally called *Pylai.*

At Delphi there was an orchestra of lyres and flutes, with singers, that did what sounds like a symphony in seven movements. Nothing is as lost as ancient music.

The Spartans had a marching band of FIFTY silver trumpets.

By Strabo's day (he died when Jesus was 27) the Romans were already carting off all the art they could get their hands on. Strabo always says not "Romans" but "Roman soldiers."

The wonderful old English word for sticks picked up in the woods is *estovers.*

Philologically,
GUY

/ • /

und so weiter: German meaning "and so forth."

162. TLS—2 [Gertrude Laughlin to GD]

11/15/95

DEAR GUY—

. . . First things first—the weather is hideous! Rain and snow and cold and damp. What I have to think of is the two years I lived in Hawaii where every day was followed by *another* perfect day. And you have no idea how boring that can be! SNOW! RAIN! (??) BLOW, YE WINDS! *[. . .]* are you listening?

Second—James! His complaining is magnificent. "My back hurts" "My little finger on my left hand is paralyzed" "I'm sleepy" "I'm a cad, bounder *[. . .]* I'm not working enough" "Do you think I'm fading?" "I don't think it will be long now" "Why do people say I look good? Do you think they see my sad state and are trying to be nice to me?" He IS working *[. . .]* writes poems (I think I'm supposed to say *[. . .]* verse) all the time and now is working on *Byways* again. When he talks about *leaving* I tell him he'd better finish *Byways* before he goes and that usually gets him started. . . .

Love—
G. xxx
(yr. fan!)

163. TLS—2

18 Nov 1995

DEAR MR LAUGHLIN!

Thanks heaps for the Gale *Byways,* so nicely set and wonderfully illustrated. Bonnie Jean says to tell you that you were a real charmer at age 10. I like best the Serious Young Publisher on page 182. You are writing the most pellucid and interesting autobiography since Henry Adams.

And for the news about the Academy's Laughlin prize in Poetry: bless Drue Heinz.

Nary a word from Leslie in months. Her last note said that she was "getting down to the nitty-gritty" of the designing. It has not been "two months" since I sent her all the material; more like six, or better. I'm not fidgeting. The worktable is full of more than I can keep up with. The Sayings of Jesus book keeps me typing. I've just finished the source notes. The collaborator is too poor to own a typewriter. And the *Americans in Paris* book (for which I did an introduction) is about to go to press.

Has there been a review of Gertrude's paintings in the local paper? Most collectors don't know one style from another but they are quick to fall in with a trend.

What classical names, those of your Cambridge nymphs: Eleanora, Theodora, Diana, and Miss Loeb Library. Call her Dorothea, if that isn't too close to Theodora (both meaning "gift from God").

Declan has sent me the Anne Carson: I like her volcano on the cover.

Bonnie Jean got a wheelbarrow for her birthday (among other things). I rolled it home from the hardware store—some 15 blocks—meeting not a living soul, not even a dog. American sidewalks are as deserted as the moon, as if nerve gas had wiped out the population.

Reading *opera omnia.* You would be horrified to know how little I've read. Being a prof was a matter of reading the same things over and over. I'm trying to repair my ignorance. It was Harry Levin's practice to read ALL of any author, an ideal few can live up to, and why should one when there are authors who invite rereading and study? I would much rather have seen all paintings ever done, and all statuary.

Where did I see recently that Charlestonians used to say that if John C. Calhoun wrote a love poem, it would begin "Whereas"? Lawyers, doctors, and bankers have no language for communicating with their customers. Our legal heritage takes its words from Anglo-Saxon, Danish, Scots, and Norman French. Together, of course, with Latin. Phrases like *voir dire* and *oyez!* are used in all courts.

If they're on their toes at the Pulitzers, *Byways* should get this year's for poetry. . . .

Happy Thanksgiving!
GUY

/ • /

the Gale Byways: JL enclosed a copy of this 37-page selection from his long poem, illustrated with photos, as published in the Gale Autobiography Series.
the Academy's Laughlin prize: In 1995 the Academy of American Poets established this prize, to be given annually for a poet's second book. The Drue Heinz Trust endowed it with a $500,000 gift.
The Americans in Paris book: This refers to *Americans in Paris,* by Elizabeth Hutton Turner, published by Counterpoint in 1996. GD contributed an afterword, "Paris the Imaginary City."
Gertrude's paintings: JL's wife had a local exhibit of her watercolors. This was largely ignored.
your Cambridge nymphs: JL had written about and sent samples of the section of *Byways* having to do with his amorous adventures while at Harvard.
the Anne Carson: Glass, Irony and God, with a cover painting by Carson. This is the book for which GD wrote an introduction.
Reading opera omnia: JL had observed that GD must have read the complete works of every interesting author he had come across.
John C. Calhoun: (1782–1850), South Carolina legislator and vice president under Adams and Jackson. He engaged in a historic debate over slavery and states' rights with Daniel Webster in 1833.
Our legal heritage: JL had been working on setting up a trust to keep ND operating after his death, and had grown frustrated with the legal language.

164. TLS—2

11 XII 1995
Aleksandr [*sic*] Solzhenitsyn

Dear Mr Laughlin!

The two richest people I know—Julia Rosenwald and thee—use typewriter ribbons that the most desperate pauper would have thrown away weeks ago. Julia (of the Sears Roebuck Rosenwalds) gets her ribbons at a Korean grocery. She does not, however, set fire to her letters.

Hey! The Common Reader people (the mail-order bookstore) wants me to sign 800 more labels for *7 Greeks.* I've already signed 400. I asked 'em if they intend to *sell* 800 more copies. "Oh yes!" they said. . . .

Jack Shoemaker sent the *Logia of Yeshua* to a Benedictine biblical scholar for vetting. Who says they're OK, having looked up all the references. I hadn't thought of this kind of double-checking while I was working.

I wish we weren't going into Bosnia. Land-mines under snow! The Gulf War was a total disaster. Saddam simply withdrew, after setting fire to the oil wells (which burned for a year). Now Clinton is talking about sending troops to the Golan Heights. The Roman legions were specialists at this kind of maneuver—they went in, defeated BOTH sides, and appropriated the real estate, setting up a provincial governor who collected taxes and crucified dissidents and trouble-makers.

Pantheon is letting *The Geography of the Imagination* go o.p. Another orphan to find a home for. . . .

What about a masseur/masseuse for your legs now that the pond is frozen over?

χαίρετε!
Guy

/ • /

does not . . . set fire: At the bottom of JL's letter of December 7 was a burned spot by which he had written "smoking is BAD!"

165. TLS—2

28 XII 1995
Pío Baroja

DEAR MR LAUGHLIN!

. . . The pitcher book—Erik was up for Xmas (his in-laws live around the corner) and we have placed the Homeless Pix and restored D'Arcy Thompson's Fish-in-a-grid that Leslie forgot. Erik also proofed the text. I will, too, knowing how cavalierly he spells.

You would not know from Erik's text that he and I disagree on practically every topic. Bonnie Jean gives him high marks for not being obsequious while being well-mannered and respectful. He's half Danish (father) and half Kentucky. His wife is as charming as they make 'em. . . .

meanwhile, a Prosperous New Year!
GUY

166. TLS—2

25 January 1996
R. Burns
V. Woolf

DEAR MR LAUGHLIN!

I was 9 when you started New Directions. Aunt Mae had pin-ups of Wallis Simpson all over her house, the Lindbergh kidnapping trial. Amos and Andy on the radio. *Life,* which Daddy bought every week. I wore knickerbockers and an aviator cap. We went to

Charleston and "saw the ocean." It was Uncle Broadus's opinion that there *wasn't* any ocean. "Just a lot of talk."

28 Jan This letter got bumped by business. And then the mail began to backlog, and the Logia at Counterpoint is going to press with my collaborator refusing to have Mantegna's "Deposition" on the jacket—he wants a Rembrandt. Frank Pearl, co-owner (and a merchant banker), personally chose the Mantegna and is miffed that a mere author would balk. I've advised Jack to take Frank aside and explain to him that authors are crazy, eccentric, stubborn, and vain. . . .

We have all the extra images (Lewis, Picasso) for the pitcher book, after agonizing exchanges with museums. Declan helped with the Tate. The Museum of Modern Art was more obstructive than a civilized institution should be. Leslie promises the final design soon. We're racing the stork.

I've sent Leslie Kipling's "An Habitation Enforced"—the best story I know of about having a baby. Kipling toward the end managed to write stories with complex layers of meaning, as rich as Shakespeare's.

Johns Hopkins has asked (without my prompting) to take on *Geography.* Pantheon pretends to bookstores that it isn't its publisher. . . .

meanwhile,
GUY

***167.* TLS—2**
8 Feb 1996

DEAR MR LAUGHLIN!

Leslie called awhile ago to say that the layout has gone off to a copy-editor she uses for a final checking of the texts and captions.

Then it's going off to Iceland to be printed. The stork is to bring little Jack Gugliametti in the middle of March.

My proposal is this: this book is not BY me; it's about my graphix. It's BY Erik Reece. If there's to be a bumping of one book by another, let's let Erik's book go forward (it *is,* technically, in production) and defer *Da Vinci's Bike* or even *The Cardiff Team.*

In any case, it's my understanding that *A Balance of Quinces* is *hors de série* as far as the NY office is concerned—a Grenfell Press/New Directions book.

I, who shouldn't have had anything to do with it (as it's about me), have already spent about $2,000 in having the pictures photographed, and in permissions for Erik's comparative images ($140 to the Tate, $41 to Museum of Modern Art), never mind guiding him through three revisions of the text. I was reluctant to have the book done in the first place, as I don't think my art work is all that good. But once I agreed, I found Erik to write it, as you eventually found Leslie to design it, got the work photographed by a top-notch and very expensive photographer, and have just last week got all the permissions secured (with Declan's help at the Tate).

As for blurbs, I'd like to see this book without any.

Leslie says she's going ahead despite this deferral to next year; and, given the fact of the stork, I think it's only common sense not to stop her in her tracks. . . .

meanwhile,
GUY

/ • /

Laughlin faxed a copy of this letter to Griselda Ohannessian, who had invoked ND's policy of not doing more than one book a year by the same author. She had proposed rescheduling *A Balance of Quinces*. After JL faxed this, *Da Vinci's Bicycle* was postponed and *BQ* proceeded.

I . . . have already spent: GD offered to cover these costs, "out of MacArthur bounty" (the MacArthur grant he had been awarded), but JL asked to be billed, writing on (March 5, 1996), "The MacArthur loot should be reserved for riotous living and balloon trips to Denmark."

168. TLS—4

10 March 1996

Dear Mr Laughlin!

. . . For *Heart Island* bounden gratitude! The design and printing are of a perfection, perfect. Tons of genius went into these newspaper and book illustrations for over two hundred years, with only a few masters among them known and honored—Bewick, Doré, Hablot K. Browne ("Phiz"), the Dalziel brothers, the anonymous engravers for *Harper's* in the 1860s and 70s. The block they engraved on was boxwood. Thirty years ago, when I was Claire Leighton's printer, there was one old man who could make them—small pieces of wood have to be glued together and polished to a mirror surface.

The frontispiece for *The Logia of Yeshua* will be a 13th-century wood-cut that I printed from the original block in 1945 or thereabout. The Chinese were doing woodblock printing when Herakleitos was writing on papyrus with a split reed.

The Danish for "ink" is *blæk.* (Medieval ink was oak-gall and soot.) Black ink may be the oldest literary convention. Part of Blake's genius was that he never used it—his books are in blue, red, brown, and even a startling page of "Jerusalem" (I think) in bright yellow.

And you were going to be a medievalist? Something new, every letter!

I'm hoping nobody will take the *Yeshua* as a sign that I have become pious. We've treated Rabbi Yeshua as if he were a street philosopher like Diogenes. The only theological point Benjamin and I agree on is that Jesus taught that Being has an origin, which he called Our Father, and that all men are brothers. Benjamin says a great many of the sayings are like Zen koans—transcending while galvanizing sense. . . .

Guy

/ • /

Heart Island: JL's collection from Turkey Press. This was the book JL had hoped GD would do drawings for. Instead the book is illustrated with reproductions of old engravings taken from *Le dictionnaire infernal,* an album given to JL by his bookseller, Terry Halladay.

169. TLS—3

25 March 1996

DEAR MR LAUGHLIN!

. . . A copy of our *Logia* went off to you and Gertrude this morning. It is not a threat to faith. In fact, it's a vote of confidence. . . .

It's wood engravings . . . that are done on joined and polished boxwood. Etchings are done on copper. For Claire Leighton I printed prints, not books. I also cut the mattes and mounted the prints. We used Yoshino white, from Japan. Claire was in the art department at Duke just before I came up as a freshman. She was fired by the horrified Methodists for having her students draw from the nude. She had a lovely house out on the Chapel Hill road where I worked three afternoons a week. I learned much from her, about all sorts of things. . . .

Hope Gertrude is improving.

ad feliciter interim
GUY

170. TLS—2

6/6/96

DEAR GUY—

. . . The past week I've been faxing back and forth to Peter Glassgold who is, my good luck, editing and readying *The Secret Room.*

Peter is a pro. He was 20 years at ND, now retired but will take on odd jobs. He's found quite a few of Jas's howlers in the text. He's the one wot translates contemp poets into Anglo-Saxon. Sun and Moon did a book of them. I'll ask if you want it.

To further indebt myself to you, would you by any chance in your scrapbook of old pitchers a wood-blockish print of an old geezer in a Renaissance hat and robes who is bent over his desk in a darkish room writing a poem? Does he look like Erasmus? That's what I want to pass on to Leslie, who will be doing the jacket for *Secret Room.* Flowered framing would be nice but she can concoct that. . . .

Again, *mult grat ag,*
Jas

171. TLS—2

10 June 1996
Gustave Courbet

Dear Mr Laughlin!

Today is not one for finding anything. I've found your Erasmus by Dürer (I would have bet with confidence that it was by Holbein). . . . Still, and even so, and despite all material evidence, I can see in my mind's eye a splendid Holbein (drawing or etching or woodcut) of Geert Geerts (Erasmus's name at home) by Holbein. I despair of finding it.

The morning went to finding the exact info on the pieces in *The Hunter G,* consuming hours of frustrating searches all over the house. Before that, I was faced with proofs of a story for *The Paris Review,* set from scrambled manuscript pages. I untangled it all with scissors, paste and the copier. . . .

meanwhile,
Guy

/ • /

your Erasmus by Dürer: This was used on the cover of JL's *The Secret Room.*
proofs of a story: "Dinner at the Bank of England."

172. TLS—2

24 June 1996
Giacomo Leopardi
Antoine de Saint-Exupéry

Dear Mr Laughlin!

I'm delighted that I guessed right about Erasmus as your alter ego. I've just returned to Leslie proofs of Our Picture Book for the umpteenth time; this sortie was into the cut captions, which her demon copy editor wants just so, and not otherwise. Erik thought up the titles, and with blank squares in the proofs I had to guess what the heck the image might be. Erik has a way of seeing things in pure abstractions, lutes and circus wagons and median strips on roads. . . .

Declan says he's sending proofs for *The Cardiff Team* on the 4th of July, and is already laying plans for *Da Vinci's Bike.* I have eight books at five presses. Doesn't this qualify me as a public nuisance?

That bomb in Manchester got Carcanet, Michael Schmidt's firm (they did my *Thasos & Ohio*). All records islamized.

Tell Gertrude that neither turtles nor snakes can bite in the water.

Last Saturday I bought a batch of books, for a quarter each, at the Baptist Seminary's yard sale. Aside from an Ellen Glasglow, they are all boys' adventure novels of the 1920's. I find the sociology of them interesting, as well as the psychology. When we read anything, we sign a contract with the author, tacitly. We know what to expect on the very first page. In these innocent novels there will be nothing like what we've just seen in Bergman's film *Sunday's Child.* Nobody, for instance, pees. Or says *damn!*

But they're time-bound. Readers in 1929 were apparently not

mystified that 3 healthy boys "have a vigorous wash" out of *a bucket of water.* (This in a cabin by a lake.) They also "eat heartily" three meals a day, but what, and where they get the food, and how it's cooked, is left unexplained.

Joan Crane's bibliography of my ravings is out. I got a copy day before yesterday. I'd promised myself that I wouldn't look at it; curiosity got the better of me. I've read Joan's and Hugh's introductions. Jaffe published it (for $75—$125 signed).

χαίρετε!
GUY

/ • /

proofs for The Cardiff Team: When GD received the proofs, he faxed ND that he wanted to withdraw the book. On July 15, Declan Spring wrote GD a letter conveying his and the ND staff's enthusiasm for the book.

173. TLS—2

27 July 1996

DEAR MR LAUGHLIN!

. . . I hope you didn't learn from the NY office that I withdrew my booker stories, and then revised one of them at Declan's insistence, and we're now back in business. It's reading proof that makes me aware of what a piss-poor writer I am. I deleted about 25 pages. Poor Declan. He's good at cheering up despondent and self-doubting authors. (Or, as Kentuckians say, *arthurs.*) . . .

A French TV producer wants me to fly over and be in a four-hour film about Count Balthazar Klossowski de Rola. To save them the expense of coming over here. I don't think I can make myself board Flight 800 ever again. *Je suis chez moi, et j'y reste.* If that's frog. TV people are not to be trusted anyhow. When some American cultural macaronis did a film on Melville (who, they said, was "searching for the meaning of life") they shot an hour or so of Melville's great-grandson Paul Metcalf, one of the most interesting people in the USA. They used about 8 seconds of Paul.

I've not read Hillary R. Clinton's *It Takes a Village*. The *T*[*imes*] *L*[*iterary*] *S*[*upplement*], however, reviews it at length this week. She wants "the state" in the person of psychotherapists to monitor all families with children, jailing those who aren't bringing up their brats according to politically correct and Neo-puritan principles. Did you know that breast-feeding beyond a specified weaning time is sexual abuse? You should bottle-feed, anyway, to minimize touching the child. Jesus.

I can't see any difference between La Clinton and the worst invasions of privacy by the KGB and the SS. That children should be raised by "state vigilance" was an idea dear to Hitler. . . .

anyway/ and more later
GUY

/ • /

Count Balthazar Klossowski: The painter Balthus's self-bestowed title.
Je suis chez moi: "I am at home, and here I'll stay."
Paul Metcalf: (1917–1999), author of a number of collage narratives, including *Both* and *Patagoni.* Coffee House Press published his complete works and GD wrote an introduction for the series.

174. TLS—2

29 Aug 1996

DEAR MR LAUGHLIN!

. . . I am of course properly horrified and filled with pity and terror at your tumbling downstairs and lying helpless for three hours. I rejoice, however, that you didn't break a hip, or neck, or any other bone. . . .

They now think that Parkinson's is the second stage of diphtheria, sneakily dormant for about 30 years. Ever had diphtheria?

I've just got *The Hunter Gracchus* (dedicated to thee) off to Wesley Tanner, after a week of battling with Jack's editor Carole McCurdy. Carole has spent months checking my every declarative sentence (with, God knows, good reason). And then the *Chicago Manual of Style* has changed every rule for commas, italicization, spelling, capitalization, and whichwhat that I learned as a stripling. Carole also has a time keeping me Politically Correct. And we've argued about typefaces, order of the essays, and various other contentions. . . .

I hope your medical tests aren't too tedious.

meanwhile, with fervent good wishes,
GUY

/ • /

Wesley Tanner: Designer for *HG.*

175. TLS—1

9/24/96

DEAR GUY—

Today was a good day because the *Quinces* came and, as a book designer from ND days, Gertrude was enthralled by the book. She couldn't read the type, but with her magnifying glass she could pore over the pictures.

It's such a beautiful book—page after page of handsomely laid out art—it has a feeling of simplicity, serenity and spaciousness.

I'm sure you were working with Leslie on the layouts and I want to thank you.

It's a month till my 82nd birthday, but I feel that you and Reece and Leslie have given me a wonderful present, my ideal of a book.

I think you did a good deal of editing of Reece's text and that's another thing to thank you for.

Your grateful,
JAS

176. **TLS—2**

26 Sept 1996

DEAR MR LAUGHLIN!

Give Gertrude a hug, as from me.

A Balance of Quinces came today, a distinct success. I hope you're pleased with it; I am. You called this book into being, first by thinking of it, secondly by publishing it. I have no idea what the world's response will be, if any response at all. Erik is wildly happy, as he considers being published by New Directions the same as winning the Kentucky Derby, inheriting a fortune, and being knighted by Charlemagne himself.

The color plates are little miracles of fidelity to the color transparencies. Only one black-and-white abstraction got in upside-down—no matter, as they look pretty much the same as sideways or right-side-up. The photo of EP, Joyce, Quinn & Ford is curiously mirror-image; the doings of the archive people, not Leslie. The book has a good shape and feel. . . .

Over the past two weeks I've read Marjorie Perloff's *Wittgenstein's Ladder*. One smart book. She *says* she got the idea for it from a single sentence of mine in *The Geography of the Imagination* in which I point out that Ludwig's examples of Ordinary Language sound remarkably like Gertrude [Stein]. A remark made 30 years ago—and you have to be Marjorie to take so random an observation and run with it all the way to the goal post. . . .

meanwhile,
and hoping to hear better news about Gertrude,
GUY

/ • /

remarkably like Gertrude: GD's comments are in the essay "Narrative Tone and Form."

177. TLS—2

1 October 1996

Dear Mr Laughlin!

I'm bracing myself for the critics, if any, saying that I can't draw. The art world is as fashion-ridden as the theatre and novel-writing. My guess is that we will be greeted by silence. It's pleasure enough for me that you like the book and make it into a birthday gift. I resolutely refrained from monkeying with Erik's text except in matters of organization and spelling, and in the end he did the severe cutting that was necessary.

The book, remember, was *your* idea. . . .

The postman and his mule has just brought *The Secret Room.*

I sat right down and read it through; rather, re-read it, having seen so many in typescript. It would be your best book except that would be comparing it to the *Collected,* which is hard to compete with. When you get better and better, as you do, book after book, critical observation is disarmed. More splendid examples of a masterful technique. The joy of a perfected style is to watch you open yet more corners and closets of "the secret room" (which turns out to be the whole damned world magicked by your imagination). What's truly wonderful is that it's all a pure poetry of deeply human observation. No cranky theories of history, no transcendental myths or philosophy, no traumatic confessions, no revolutionary idealism. Just good poems. . . .

χαίρετε!
Guy

***178.* TLS—2** [GD to Gertrude Laughlin]

Armistice Day 1996 [November 11]

DEAR GERTRUDE!

. . . I never inflict my books on people, but as *A Balance of Quinces* is Erik Reece's book, I foolishly *bought* a dozen copies and sent them to various people. The responses are what psychologists call Flat Affect. I might as well have sent copies to horses and chickens. A Danish lady's sole response was to ask whether I attended fashion school to learn how to draw men's suits. Jonathan Williams says the paper is wrong. Julia Rosenwald said, "Gee, thanks! Will you sign it for me?"

People are sheep, and don't dare say *baa!* until the sheep in front has said *baa!* They have no gumption of their own to make ANY observation.

James has kept me informed of your eye problems. WET macular degeneration sounds perfectly awful. I shudder to hear that you are driving, but that's your business and maybe part of restoring sight. You're making yourself see. . . .

The Cardiff Team came Saturday, from Declan, as well as a Xerox of the cover design of *Da Vinci's Bicycle.* I still find it hard to believe that I'm published by New Directions. My book of essays at Counterpoint (dedicated to James) should be out any day now. Barry Magid has proved with *50 Drawings* (also just out) that (a) you can't engrave pen-and-ink drawings on plastic—might as well use burnt toast—and (b) that you can't print them on a hand press.

Now that winter's here I sit by the fire of evenings reading.

We were going to vote for Mickey Mouse last week, but decided to behave and vote for Ralph Nader. First time I've not voted Democratic.

Why did the Polish assembly-line workers have to wear deep-sea diving suits?

They were building a submarine.

Love & Best Wishes
GUY

179. TLS—2

12/17/96

Dear Guy—

HOSE & HER! The best writer around has dedicated his book to me. And it looks like a very good one. After reading up on the Gracchi, I turned to your first chapter and learned a lot. All the stuff about Kafka. You have dug well and deep.

My eyes are weak for tight-set prose but I plan to read a section a night in bed. Already my copy margins are scribbled with pencil notes and I'm sure there will be more, including where it says "poem" in the margin.

I'm not offended by the last line on the back flap of the jacket. I've always understood that you have old commitments to Jack, and am just glad that you've sent as much to ND as you have.

. . . Be assured that ND would always take on anything that you wanted done. Declan, I suppose, is sobbing. You're his hero. A serious young man. He has now been given by Griselde a title of Asst. Editor, which should help. And they all got big bonuses for last year & shares in the Profit Sharing Trust.

Bill Corbett, the historian of New Directions, was here yesterday and asked many unanswerable questions about why books sold so well last year. I dunno. I guess because the Norton travelers read them and liked them.

It's a struggle to keep Corbett from writing about me, not the press, which he is supposed to do. Well I have the right to go over his text and cut some of the "boy publisher" swaddle.

Beware of Fridays the thirteenth. I was out in the North Office looking for something, and suddenly the whole high, heavy tier of cabinets toppled over on me, hurling me to the floor. Happily not on Gertrude's computer, of which the table has sharp edges. No bones bust, just a few colorful bruises. . . .

I don't understand my physicality. The other day I typed three pages with no mistakes, but today there's a mistake in almost every line.

So be it,
Jas

/ • /

has dedicated his book to me: GD's book of essays *The Hunter Gracchus,* published by Jack Shoemaker's new press Counterpoint, is dedicated to JL. *HOSE & HER!* is likely a comic version of "Hosanna and Hooray!" The Gracchi were two Roman brothers in the second century B.C. GD refers to them in relation to Kafka in the title essay.
title of Asst. Editor: Declan Spring had been Associate Editor for several years and at this point was made a full editor.
the last line on the back: JL is referring to the name of the rival publisher, Counterpoint.
Bill Corbett: This history was canceled at JL's death. Corbett (1942–) is a poet and critic. His collection *All Prose* (Cambridge, Mass.: Zoland Books, 2001) includes essays about JL.

180. TLS—2

23 XII 1996

Dear Mr Laughlin!

Please tread warily, as upon eggs, and nail the bookcases to the wall. Where was your Hungarian footman when you were flattened by an avalanche of metal shelves?

The twelve stories that Jack is doing are all from published books (two of them published by Jack). I decided to kill the long stories in *Tatlin!, Apples & Pears* and *The Gunner* and to extract from these discarded works the short tales. Jack thought this up, and I jumped at the chance to gather the humbler small pieces that are not as yeasty and philosophical (and unreadable) as the novella. And ND does one book per author per year, and none of us is getting any younger.

I'm delighted that you're finding poems in *The Hunter Gracchus.* The most distinguished thing about the book is its dedication. . . .

You probably have a house full of relatives for the holidays. Give Gertrude a big hug, as from me.

χαίρετε!
Guy

/ • /

The twelve stories: Counterpoint published a GD book of this title.

181. TLS—2

2 Feb 1997
Ulysses anno 75

Dear Mr Laughlin—

The Secret Room looks extremely distinguished in its cover by Al Duerer. . . .

The first repercussion of *A Balance of Quinces* is that Washington University wants to hang *Orpheus Preaching to the Animals* in a show of writers who are also painters. Bonnie has already found out, from museum friends, that a shipping company specializes in packing and moving Great Works of Art, with a thief-proof truck and armed guards. . . .

Located, yesterday, a copy of *Da V's Bike,* at the 5th rare book store I called. It's on its way to Declan. I have *a* copy only. . . .

I hope Gertrude's glasses begin to DO something.

Apologies for such a lapse in writing.

χαίρετε!
Guy

/ • /

Gertrude's glasses: Gertrude Laughlin had a degenerative eye disease, and glasses fitted with prisms and colored lenses had been prescribed. She also had pneumonia at this time and was in the hospital.

182. **TLS—2**

18 April 1997

Dear Mr Laughlin!

Admire my IBM Wheelwriter 1000. My old Olivetti, after 15 years as my faithful steed, was developing waywardnesses beyond further repair. My repairman, Rafe Tapp, had said on three occasions, "Guy, this is the LAST time I can fix this machine." He's a fellow Indian-arrowhead collector, and I squeezed his son through Freshman English, for which he is eternally grateful. I was surprised that typewriters are still manufactured. A nifty and charming salesgirl named Ginger talked me into this one.

Thanks heaps for the *Byways* segment on your father, highly readable. . . .

Were I to memorialize my father, I think I would focus on blackberrying, which he used to give a whole day to, taking me along and several neighborhood kids. Women don't go blackberrying—which is done in swamps, and because of the briars and the bulls in pastures. Blackberry jam was my father's ambrosia—loaded onto hot buttered biscuits. My mother's one secret (that I know of) was that she put *Certo* in jam, to make it gummier (as recommended by the cooking school she used to attend). The Davenports had a mortal horror of all additives to anything, except salt, pepper, and McIlhenny's tabasco. Daddy was more broadminded than his siblings, who conspued aspirin as "drugs," and were convinced that all canned food was poison.

My mother was Charlestonian by way of cooking, so that Daddy learned to love ocean fish, shrimp, crabs, and oysters, which the rest of the Davenports died to look upon. They pitied Daddy his fate in having a wife who did not serve hot biscuits for breakfast (only lunch and supper). He had to learn to have toast at breakfast (made in the oven, with the butter browned into it).

You, as I remember, have blueberry muffins for breakfast, but then you're a Yankee. . . .

meanwhile,
Guy

183. TLS—1

7/14/97

DEAR GUY—

Bad news here has spread depression. When Gertrude went for her final check-up the pictures showed spots on her spleen. Now she has to have shots of other parts of her midriff to seek out what they mean and what else might be affected.

She is terrorized, but trying to hold up. . . .

From the pit of gloom,
JAS

184. TLS—2

29 August 1997

DEAR MR LAUGHLIN!

Love your ice-man poem. My father used to say that he'd never had any cold ice-tea after the invention of the refrigerator. Ice chipped from the block was somehow colder than ice cubes—and he was right, scientifically. Ice melts in inverse ratio to its surface area, as witness the glaciers and Paleolithic ice in Antarctica.

Five doctors in three places sounds like Molière. Especially when no two of them agree.

I was reading the other evening about an 18th-century cure for practically all ills—breathing a cow's breath. Maria Edgeworth's father was some kind of Irish doctor. Getting the cow upstairs to the sick-room was a hassle, with lots of people pulling and pushing. . . .

In Thoreau's journal the other evening I found the strange phrase "the dreaming of the toads"—and was mystified until I tracked down an archaic meaning of *dream* meaning music or "a joyful noise." Perhaps the ancestor of *drone.* Now I'd like to know how so old a meaning survived for Thoreau to know it.

I hope the medicos get their act together and do something for Gertrude rather than worrying her with their conflicting diagnoses. . . . I distrust the *fact* of their having made medicine into a Major Industry underwritten by the government and the insurance sharks. . . .

Hope this finds things better all around up there.

with best wishes,
GUY

/ • /

ice-man poem: In a letter of August 23, 1997, JL enclosed "The Iceman Cometh." This was the last poem JL sent GD.
Five doctors in three places: Gertrude Laughlin's doctors.

185. TLS—2

9 September 1997

DEAR MR LAUGHLIN!

As you probably don't read *National Review,* I enclose proof that learning is not defunct in the Republic. Buckley had printed a note from Jim MacFarland praising Waugh's delightful whimsy in coining a nonsense phrase like *tohu bohu.* Catholics tend not to have read a word of Holy Writ.

You ask what Hippocrates would prescribe. Hippy seems to be grandly vague about things he can't see. His treatments for internal troubles are delicious—running to soft barley cakes and chicken soup made with onion, coriander, cheese, salt, sesame and white raisins.

Chick peas cooked in honey. And LOTS of wine.

Mutton & octopus stewed in red wine, to be eaten with mashed lentils dashed with vinegar. . . .

with anxious best wishes
GUY

/ • /

I enclose proof: GD enclosed a Xerox of the letters page of the May 27, 1997, *National Review* containing GD's letter explaining that this phrase, which novelist Evelyn Waugh had included in a letter to the Archbishop of Westminster, was "Hebrew, at Genesis I:2. *Tohu bohu* (more literately *thohu wa-bhohu*), 'emptiness and desolation,' is translated in the 1611 English Bible as 'without forme, and voyd.' The phrase was current among Victorians, in and out of vicarages, as a learned witticism, and meant something like Oliver Hardy's 'one fine mess.'" GD's was one of seven letters printed on this subject.
what Hippocrates would prescribe: Greek physician Hippocrates (460?–377? B.C.) was one of the first to believe that diseases had causes other than being punishments from the gods.

186. TLS—1

10/6/97

DEAR GUY—

Things go along pretty badly for both of us. The chemo injections for G's cancer give her nausea. She's very brave about it, but it hurts me to watch her suffering.

My arthritic pains in back and neck seem, alas, not to be diminishing. I couldn't do my timid little walks without the steadying arm of Sandor, my Hungarian encourager. He butchers the English language, but is a kind soul.

I haven't committed a poem in two weeks. They just aren't coming.

All in all it's a desolate landscape. But the spring [*sic*] has been handsome. Maples going golden already.

Und so weiter,
JAS

187. TLS—2

23 October 1997

DEAR MR LAUGHLIN!

. . . I see that a German museum director says that the bicycle that the 11-year-old Salai dei Caprotti drew on the back of a sheet of the Codex Atlanticus is a modern forgery. His evidence is that an Italian restorer remembers holding the sheet up to the light before it was removed from its backing and saw "only two circles." And "some wavy lines." How dumb can Germans get? Of course he saw only two circles, as Salai drew the wheels with *il maestro Lionardo*'s compass—graphite—and drew the rest of the bike in sanguine crayon, which would give a weak show-through when held up to the light.

The mystery is *what* Salai was drawing. A real bike built by Leonardo? Copying a drawing by Leonardo? The drawing is so obviously a child's that I don't think the cleverest of forgers could get anywhere near it. And what would the motive be?

Hugh [Kenner] thinks the "bike" may be a four-wheeled carriage, and that the astounding invention is the pedal-and-chain.

I wish I could cheer you and Gertrude up. If wishes were good medicine *[. . .]*

χαίρετε!
GUY

[On November 12, James Laughlin died from complications of a stroke.]

SELECTED BIBLIOGRAPHY

[FIRST EDITIONS ONLY IN THIS LIST]

⋮

Guy Davenport

Carmina Archilochi: The Fragments of Archilochos (translations). Berkeley and Los Angeles: University of California Press, 1964.

Sappho: Poems and Fragments (translations). Ann Arbor: University of Michigan Press, [1965].

Flowers and Leaves. Highlands, N.C.: Nantahala Foundation/Jonathan Williams, Publisher, 1966.

Tatlin! New York: Charles Scribner's Sons, 1974.

Da Vinci's Bicycle. Baltimore and London: Johns Hopkins University Press, 1979.

Eclogues. San Francisco: North Point Press, 1981.

The Geography of the Imagination. San Francisco: North Point Press, 1981.

The Mimes of Herondas (translations). San Francisco: Grey Fox Press, 1981.

The Bowmen of Shu. New York: Grenfell Press, 1983.

Apples and Pears. San Francisco: North Point Press, 1984.

The Jules Verne Steam Balloon. San Francisco: North Point Press, 1987.

Every Force Evolves a Form. San Francisco: North Point Press, 1987.

A Balthus Notebook. New York: Ecco Press, 1989.

The Drummer of the Eleventh North Devonshire Fusiliers. San Francisco: North Point Press, 1990.

Charles Burchfield's Seasons. San Francisco: Pomegranate Artbooks, 1994.

A Table of Green Fields. New York: New Directions, 1993.

7 Greeks (translations). New York: New Directions, 1995.

The Logia of Yeshua (with Benjamin Urrutia). Washington, D.C.: Counterpoint, 1996.

The Cardiff Team. New York: New Directions, 1996.

The Hunter Gracchus. Washington, D.C.: Counterpoint, 1996.

Objects on a Table: Harmonious Disarray in Art and Literature. Washington, D.C.: Counterpoint, 1998.

James Laughlin

Stolen and Contaminated Poems. Isla Vista, Calif.: Turkey Press, 1985.

The House of Light. New York: Grenfell Press, 1986.

Selected Poems, 1935–1985. San Francisco: City Lights Books, 1987.

Pound as Wuz. St. Paul, Minn.: Graywolf Press, 1987.

The Owl of Minerva. Port Townsend, Wash.: Copper Canyon Press, 1987.

The Bird of Endless Time. Port Townsend, Wash.: Copper Canyon Press, 1989.

Random Essays. Mount Kisco, N.Y.: Moyer Bell, 1989.

Random Stories. Mount Kisco, N.Y.: Moyer Bell, 1990.

The Man in the Wall: Poems. New York: New Directions, 1993.

Collected Poems. Mount Kisco, N.Y.: Moyer Bell, 1994.

Heart Island and Other Epigrams. Isla Vista, Calif.: Turkey Press, 1995.

Byways (selections). Contemporary Authors Autobiography Series. Detroit: Gale Research, 1995.

The Secret Room. New York: New Directions, 1997.

Poems: New and Selected. New York: New Directions, 1997.

Byways: A Memoir. New York: New Directions, 2005.

INDEX

EU Authorised Representative:
Easy Access System Europe
Mustamäe tee 50, 10621 Tallinn, Estonia

www.ingramcontent.com/pod-product-compliance
Lightning Source LLC
Chambersburg PA
CBHW030808310726
48980CB00006B/426/J

* 9 7 8 0 3 9 3 0 5 9 5 0 2 *